JANE DOE

The sleeping bag was soaked through with blood.

A petite, young woman lay on top of it, nude except for a T-shirt and a pair of white socks. Her head had swollen to the size of a basketball and parts of her brain strained against the thin membrane visible through a star-shaped crack in her skull—the kind of wound caused by the quick, violent impact of a heavy, blunt object.

Her lower body was bruised and covered in fresh blood streaming from a deep cut in her genital area. Several coins lay underneath her naked hips, as if someone had placed them there.

Too weak to move, all she could do was moan faintly, her ragged breath gurgling through her swollen, bloody lips.

She was barely alive, but not for long.

And the psycho killer who had done this was still at large.

BOOK YOUR PLACE ON OUR WEBSITE AND MAKE THE READING CONNECTION!

We've created a customized website just for our very special readers, where you can get the inside scoop on everything that's going on with Zebra, Pinnacle and Kensington books.

When you come online, you'll have the exciting opportunity to:

- View covers of upcoming books
- Read sample chapters
- Learn about our future publishing schedule (listed by publication month *and author*)
- Find out when your favorite authors will be visiting a city near you
- Search for and order backlist books from our online catalog
- Check out author bios and background information
- Send e-mail to your favorite authors
- Meet the Kensington staff online
- Join us in weekly chats with authors, readers and other guests
- Get writing guidelines
- AND MUCH MORE!

**Visit our website at
http://www.kensingtonbooks.com**

ROUGH
TRADE

Steve Jackson

PINNACLE BOOKS
Kensington Publishing Corp.
http://www.pinnaclebooks.com

PINNACLE BOOKS are published by

Kensington Publishing Corp.
850 Third Avenue
New York, NY 10022

All Kensington Titles, Imprints, and Distributed Lines are available at special quantity discounts for bulk purchases for sales promotion, premiums, fund raising, educational, or institutional use.

Special book excerpts or customized printings can also be created to fit specific needs. For details, write or phone the office of the Kensington special sales manager: Kensington Publishing Corp., 850 Third Avenue, New York, NY 10022, attn: Special Sales Department, Phone: 1-800-221-2647.

Pinnacle and the P logo Reg. U.S. Pat. & TM Off.

First Printing: January, 2001
10 9 8 7 6 5 4 3 2

Printed in the United States of America

ACKNOWLEDGMENTS

I would first like to thank Joanne Cordova for sharing her story with me. It took enormous courage and was offered in the hope that someone might learn from her mistakes. . . . We can't all be angels, but that doesn't make the rest of us devils. I am one of many who is pulling for her to make it. Secondly, I wish to thank Jim Burkhalter, John Lauck, Dennis Goodwin, Dennis Hall, Dana Easter, Dave Thomas, and Pam Russell of the Jefferson County District Attorney's Office for their cooperation and help. . . . Thank God for the dragonslayers. Thirdly, I want to thank Judge Frank Plaut for his insight, and court reporter Lisa Persichitte for her assistance far above the call of duty and friendship. And I wish to acknowledge the work done by defense attorneys Nathan Chambers and Dennis Hartley; they fought the good fight and put the system to the test . . . which is as it should be. My agent, Mike Hamilburg, and his consigliere, Joanie Socola, deserve my thanks for guiding me through the publishing world. And I would be more than remiss without thanking my editor at Kensington, Karen Haas, for hanging in there for me and making my work better—the true mark of a great editor. Thanks also to my number one publicist, Mom, and her assistant, Dad, as well as Marie Torrisi for being a second mom, and Dick Torrisi for his support and "marketing." And, as always, I must thank my wife, Carla, for keeping the ship afloat, the home fires lit, and her love and faith in me so that I can pursue these projects while she does the hard work.

"He who is without sin among you, let him throw a stone at her first."

—John 8:7

One

May 16, 1997

The sun had not yet climbed above the pine trees to warm the deep shadows along Old Hughesville Road when Amy Johnson and her fiancé, Jason Sosebe, left their home in the mountains northwest of Denver, Colorado. Hurrying, they climbed into Jason's big black truck and were soon headed out the driveway.

They were both employed in Golden, the home of Coors beer and the Colorado School of Mines, some twenty miles to the east where the foothills of the Rocky Mountains end and the plains begin. On the way, they would pass through Black Hawk, once one of the richest gold-mining towns in the Old West, which had struck gold again in 1991 when voters approved casino-style gambling. The locals had changed the old saying from "Thar's gold in them thar hills," to "Thar's gold in them thar pockets," alluding to the tourist-gambler dollars that provided employment for the young couple. Twenty-eight-year-old Sosebe was the manager of a charter bus company that delivered customers from Denver to the casinos. Johnson, twenty-four, was a company secretary.

Old Hughesville Road was a narrow, winding gravel lane off Highway 119 about a mile from Black Hawk. In the town's original glory years, it was little more than a rutted wagon track that wound into the hills to service the numerous mines that dotted the area. In 1997, the area was lightly populated; Sosebe and Johnson would drive past only a few homes and an old abandoned miner's cabin before reaching the highway. The highway itself ran north and then east to Boulder, about forty miles beyond, or south and east in a sort of horseshoe through Black Hawk and down Clear Creek Canyon to Golden.

They had just swung around the corner above the old miner's cabin when they saw a dark blue minivan. It was parked facing uphill in the little pull-off in front of the cabin, which was a tin-roofed affair with an old wooden floor. The cabin stood at the beginning of a hiking trail to an area known as Missouri Falls, and it wasn't unusual to see cars parked in the turnoff. However, there was something that made Sosebe and Johnson take particular notice of this van. Although a favorite of locals, this trail wasn't marked with a sign and wasn't well-known to people from beyond the area, and not only did it seem too early in the morning for hikers, but the van had Wyoming license plates.

Then, as they passed the car, Johnson caught a glimpse of something even odder, which made her do a double take. In the early morning light, she thought she saw a man. He appeared to be dragging a red sleeping bag up the Missouri Falls trail.

Something was wrong. Johnson was sure that she'd seen a body on the sleeping bag. The body's legs were bare, which was strange because it was still cold outside. Her first thought was that maybe the person on the sleeping bag was handicapped and hadn't been able to maneuver a wheelchair past the rocks that bordered the parking area to reach the trail. But that didn't make sense, either. It would have hurt to be dragged over those rocks, and the person on the sleeping bag wasn't moving or trying to brace in any way.

"Jason, stop!" she yelled.

Thinking that his girlfriend was warning him about some unseen obstacle, or perhaps a deer about to bound out onto the road, Sosebe applied the brakes. Then Johnson told him what she thought she'd seen. At first, he didn't believe her. But she insisted, so he turned around at the first wide spot in the road, which was almost to the junction with the highway.

It had only been a minute or less since they passed the cabin, but as they drove back up the hill, the blue minivan went roaring by. To reach them in so short a time, the driver would have had to run to the van and whip a U-turn on the narrow road after he saw them go past. "There's no way he could have put someone back in the van that fast," Johnson said.

As the van passed them, followed by a cloud of dust, Johnson tried to get a good look at the driver but saw only a dark figure through the tinted windows. Sosebe concentrated on the license plate and got the first three numbers. He stopped and backed up so that he could see which way the van turned when it reached the highway. It ran the stop sign at the bottom of the hill and went . . . north, toward Boulder.

Apprehensive of what they might find, the young couple proceeded back to the cabin, where Sosebe pulled into the turnoff. Even from there, they could see part of the red sleeping bag poking out from behind a pine tree partway up the trail. Johnson jumped out of the truck and hurried toward the sleeping bag, with Sosebe following more slowly. When she walked around the tree, Johnson stopped short and gasped.

A woman lay facedown on the bag, her head pointed toward a stream and her feet toward the trail. She looked almost bald because her head was swollen to the size of a basketball, causing the skin of her scalp to stretch until her hair looked patchy. She was a small woman and wore a white T-shirt and a pair of white socks but otherwise was nude. Bright red blood shone wetly on the bag around her head and between her legs. She was still alive. Her breath gurgled through the blood that covered her lips.

When he caught up to his girlfriend and saw the young woman, Sosebe tried to call out for help on his cell phone but couldn't get a signal. He ran back to his truck, yelling over his shoulder that he was going to a neighbor's to call the police.

Johnson stayed behind, placing her own jacket over the young woman's exposed lower half. "It's going to be okay," she said. "Help is on the way." The woman's only response was a low moan.

As it happened, Gilpin County sheriff Bruce Hartman lived just fifteen minutes from the old cabin and was the first to respond to Sosebe's call. His first thought was that he was looking at a teenager. Given the amount of blood and the condition of her head, he was amazed that she was alive, but she moaned again and he ran back to his vehicle, where he put out a call for emergency medical assistance. He also called in a BOLO—police parlance for "Be On the Lookout"—for a dark blue minivan with Wyoming license plates and gave the partial number Sosebe recalled.

It looked like they had an attempted murder, maybe a murder if the girl didn't survive. Hartman ran a small, six-deputy department and didn't have the resources or the experienced personnel to handle a whodunit. So he called upon his colleagues in next-door Jefferson County, a larger, more populated county whose sheriff's office had one of the most modern crime-lab facilities in the country and whose district attorney often supplied investigators to Gilpin for cases such as this.

The paramedics arrived and carefully examined the woman. They had no idea who she was; there was no identification on her. She had suffered a head wound back behind her left ear, which had bled profusely but was now drying and clotted. But what troubled the paramedics more was the fact that she was bleeding from her vagina. There was so much blood below her hips that it had completely soaked through the thick sleeping bag and into the ground. And there was something else odd. When they lifted her from the sleeping bag, one paramedic spotted several coins lying in the pool of blood beneath her pelvis. It struck him as more than a little unusual because she had no pants pockets from which the coins could have fallen.

There was no time to drive her to a hospital. The

paramedics called for a Flight for Life medical emergency helicopter and then rushed their patient to a nearby schoolyard that had a playground large enough to accommodate a landing. Within a half hour the helicopter arrived and "Jane Doe" was on her way to St. Anthony's Hospital in Denver, which has one of the finest trauma centers in the Rocky Mountain region.

In the meantime, the search for the man in the blue van nearly ended quickly when Colorado state trooper Frank Cisco crossed paths with the vehicle heading in opposite directions. Cisco had just received the BOLO when he spotted the van and flipped around on the highway to pursue with his overhead lights flashing.

The driver of the van spotted the trooper and stepped on the gas. The chase reached speeds up to seventy miles an hour along the stretch of two-lane highway that twists and turns like a roller coaster through the mountains toward Boulder. The driver of the van recklessly began passing cars around blind curves. Afraid that the other driver would make a mistake that might cost an innocent driver his life, Cisco reluctantly dropped the chase and radioed ahead.

Soon the blue van was lost to view. Cisco hoped that the driver would slow down before he killed somebody.

Two

May 16, 1997

The helicopter bearing Jane Doe arrived at St. Anthony's, where she was brought into the emergency room. A CAT scan—which essentially gives doctors cross-section pictures of internal organs—revealed that she was in deep trouble. The blow to her head was so severe that it had fractured her skull in a line that went almost straight down from the point of impact above and behind her left ear, and then back through the base in an L shape. Massive internal bleeding was putting an enormous amount of pressure on her brain.

Jane Doe was rushed up to surgery, where two top trauma surgeons were on hand to deal with her wounds. Neurosurgeon Stuart Levy and OB-GYN specialist Harvey Cohen stood at opposite ends of the operating table and worked rapidly to save the young woman's life. It was difficult to tell her age. . . . She was only about five feet tall and maybe a hundred pounds. . . . She could have been a teenager.

The first thing Levy noted was a three-inch stellate (or starlike) laceration at the point of impact on the victim's head. A stellate cut has several branches that run out from a central point. It is usually the result of blunt trauma that splits the skin, as opposed to a single straight line that a weapon such as a knife or a sharp ax would cause.

The laceration, which was relatively free of debris, was the least of Jane Doe's problems. Massive bleeding was occurring on the opposite, or right, side of her brain from where she'd received the blow. To relieve the pressure and reduce the hematoma, Levy removed a triangular section of bone from the right side of her skull and cut the dura, the tough elastic membrane that covers the brain. Blood squirted out in a jet and down his gown from the pressure inside. The brain itself quickly swelled out of the hole, protruding like a mushroom several inches above her skull.

Levy knew then that it was probably hopeless but kept working anyway to stop the bleeding and relieve the pressure. The girl's brain had been severely bruised from a tremendous blow. He found that in addition to the injury to the brain directly beneath the laceration, the so-called "coup" injury, there was a "contra-coup" injury on the opposite side of her head. Coup is caused by the blow itself; contra-coup is when the brain rebounds away from the blow and bounces off the skull on the opposite side with enough force to cause injury.

On the other end of the table, Cohen was just as greatly disturbed by what he found, although for different reasons. A three-inch cut had been made in a lateral, or side, wall of the woman's vagina. The cut had gone deep into the muscle and sliced an artery, which accounted for much of her blood loss.

Cohen believed that if left untreated, the woman would have bled to death from the cut. However, the wound was easily repaired because the incision was as straight and clean as if it had been made by a surgeon with a scalpel. Indeed, the surgeon felt that the nature of the wound—not torn raggedly as though from a rape with a blunt instrument or, however improbably, a hard fall—had to have been made deliberately. And by someone who took his time so as not to cause other injuries. But who would do such a thing?

Levy and Cohen were experienced trauma surgeons who had seen thousands of horrible injuries, but they would take away memories of this particular patient that would stay with them long after others had faded away. As they were operating, the mother of a missing girl was brought into the room to look at their patient. But Jane Doe's head was so grotesquely swollen that it took the woman a few moments to realize that the girl on the operating table was not her daughter. She fled in tears. Whose daughter, the surgeons and nurses wondered, would this young woman turn out to be? Where was her family?

What stayed with Cohen even more than the image of the frightened mother's face was the reaction of the nurses. Emergency room nurses are generally as tough as they come; they've seen it all and usually go about their jobs dry-eyed and with little emotion. Yet, as they all worked together to help this tiny young woman, Cohen noticed that the nurses were crying. Their tears, and those he felt himself on the verge of that day, would move him like few other cases ever had. Later, he would write a letter to the chief of nursing complimenting the nurses he worked with that day for their humanity and compassion. But the young woman on the operating table was going to need a lot more than tears. She needed a miracle.

As the doctors and nurses worked, Jim Burkhalter, an investigator with the Jefferson County District Attorney's Office, arrived at the hospital. Burkhalter had received a call from Jefferson County senior deputy district attorney Dennis Hall asking him to go to the hospital and learn what he could.

The victim had already been moved from the emergency room to the operating room when he arrived, so he wasn't able to see her. But he did run into a nervous detective from the town of Black Hawk. There was a possibility that he knew who Jane Doe was, the detective said. "She might be a victim witness in a domestic violence case." His department had given her an alias and put her up in a large Black Hawk hotel, but, he added with embarrassment, they'd misplaced the name they'd given her for an alias and hadn't been able to locate her. Now he was worried that the woman's husband had found her and that she was the woman on the operating table.

Burkhalter rolled his eyes, but he was able to relieve the other officer of his concerns when they compared physical descriptions of the two victims. A friendly, round-faced man with a quick smile and ready laugh, he looked more like a baker than a detective at first glance. But he was a thirty-year veteran of the Denver Police Department, who had retired from the force just a month earlier to take the job with Jefferson County.

Coming out of high school, Burkhalter knew he wanted to follow one of two vocations: the priesthood or police work. The latter was something of a family tradition, having come from a whole line of cops, including his grandfather, several uncles, and a few cousins. Originally the call to the priesthood won out, and he'd attended the seminary for two and a half years. Then he'd decided he wanted a family. The church's loss was the city of Denver's gain as he joined the police department, where he was joined by his older brother. The family tradition grew stronger when a younger brother became a sheriff's deputy in Missouri.

Twenty-five of Burkhalter's years on the force had been spent as a detective. He'd done his time like any rookie detective working property crimes, but as soon as he could, he moved into what are called crimes-against-persons. For seven years he worked in the homicide division, where he'd seen just about every kind of brutality imaginable.

One of the most bizarre was the case of a disabled man who murdered his competition in a love triangle. In December 1976, Burkhalter was on his way to work when the officer in charge of the bomb squad called him to say they had a possible bomb at "The Projects," a large, low-income, crime-ridden apartment complex.

When the officers arrived, they were guided to an object wrapped in a green plastic garbage bag on the front doorstep of the people who called in the report. They had been the target of a pipe bomb previously. Burkhalter's colleague carefully opened the package.

"Ugh," the other officer grunted. The garbage bag didn't contain a bomb, it was a severed human arm.

At that point, it became Burkhalter's case. Inside the bag with the arm was a note written in Spanish, "This is what's going to happen to your children."

Burkhalter wondered what had happened to the rest of the body. Other officers called in began to turn up other packages with more severed body parts, all left on the doorsteps of families with children, all with the same threatening note. Some of the recipients thought they knew who might be responsible.

There was a wheelchair-bound man in the complex who seemed pretty odd. He went about pulling a toy red wagon behind him, the wheels of which were badly in need of oil. More importantly, he seemed to hate the neighborhood children who would spy on him through his apartment windows as he wheeled around in his apartment without a stitch of clothing on. When he saw them, he'd roll to the door and throw it open to rain curses about the children, who would run shrieking and taunting him.

Burkhalter and his colleagues discovered a trail of blood drops from one of the severed pieces to the door of the suspect. They knocked, but there was no answer. The next-door neighbors, however, answered and had plenty to say. During the night, they'd heard the suspect working in his apartment with a power saw. They knew because every time he turned it on, their television screen filled with snow. Then he'd turn off the saw and there'd be a few minutes of quiet before they heard the suspect's screen door creak open and then the *squeak, squeak, squeak* of the suspect's little red wagon. A little later, they'd hear the wagon's approach, again followed by the opening of the screen door, and then the whole process would begin once more.

"I think he was going to go visit his parents for the holidays," the neighbor said.

Burkhalter notified the police in the areas of the bus and train stations as well as the airport. Armed with a search warrant, he and a colleague went into the apartment of the suspect and quickly located the crime scene, a bloodstained bathtub, beside which lay a gore-covered power saw. A quick look in the refrigerator revealed the victim's severed head, which accounted for nearly all the body parts, except the victim's hands.

A little while later, he was told the suspect had been caught trying to board an airplane. The hands were in the suspect's suitcase.

Burkhalter later interviewed the man, who confessed that he'd killed a friend out of jealousy over a woman. The two men also had a sexual relationship with one another. Following an argument over the woman, the killer persuaded his friend to perform oral sex on him. While the friend was engaged in the act, the killer struck him on the head with a hammer. He'd then dismembered his adversary/lover—and distributed the pieces to the neighborhood children who had been teasing him.

The brutality of the crime and the lack of remorse by the killer had stuck with Burkhalter for a long time. Other cases would as well, like that of the three-year-old girl who was abducted, raped, and thrown down a wooden outhouse pit to die covered with feces, except for the chance discovery by two out-of-state tourists. In that instance, the prosecutor had agreed to a plea bargain that allowed the monster who'd done that to a little girl to go free after just six years and, as the prison psychologist reported, "minimal" progress in sex offender treatment.

Justice was not always fair, and the punishment only sometimes matched the crime. For Burkhalter and men like him, it was much worse in those cases where, for one reason or another, someone got away with murder, and so he kept plugging away.

In 1997, he was nearing retirement with the department when he happened upon a notice on a bulletin board in the Jefferson County courthouse. It said that the local district attorney's office was looking for an experienced investigator. Unlike some cops who would rather have teeth pulled, Burkhalter enjoyed testifying in court. It was a challenge he relished to go up against a tough defense attorney and prove that he had done his job correctly. A position with the district attorney's office would put him in courtrooms on major cases, looking forward to battles with defense attorneys. He applied on Thursday and was called the next day and asked to come in to talk to District Attorney Dave Thomas.

Northwest of Denver, Jefferson County is one of the largest in Colorado and includes a wide variety of terrain and population densities. For most of the twentieth century, it remained largely rural, with large tracts of forested mountains. Beginning in the

1970s and picking up steam ever since, the small cities within its boundaries had expanded rapidly, and more and more homes and communities were springing up in the mountains.

With that kind of growth, Thomas thought his department needed someone with more urban experience than the investigators hired in the past, candidates who had the advantage of knowing the mountains better. He was looking for a city-proven detective like Burkhalter, to whom he quickly offered the job. Burkhalter retired from the Denver Police Department on March 3, 1997, and started his new job the following day. The Jane Doe at St. Anthony's was his first major case for the district attorney's office.

The emergency room staff told him that it didn't look good for the girl—which meant it might end up a homicide case—but there wasn't much for him to do at the hospital. He accepted a bag of clothes handed to him by a nurse. There wasn't much, she said, a pair of socks, a T-shirt, pants, and the jacket that had been laid across her by Amy Johnson.

Burkhalter signed for the evidence without looking in the bag. He was in a hurry to head west for Gilpin County to meet up with John Lauck, the investigator appointed to head up the case.

By the time Lauck arrived at the cabin, the Jefferson County sheriff's crime-lab technicians were already at work; in charge was criminalist Vicki Spellman, who walked him through the scene. The initial call received by Lauck was that a woman had

fallen from a moving vehicle. No one knew if she'd
been pushed or it was an accident. Other than the
fact that the woman had suffered a head wound,
Lauck didn't know any specifics about what injuries
she might have. There was a great deal of blood
inside the cabin, particularly in the back room
where pools had soaked into the filthy old plywood
floors. Spellman said they'd found clothing in the
back room—a pair of sweat shorts and a pair of
maroon-colored women's underwear. The shorts
and panties were intertwined, as if they had been
pulled off.

Spellman led him outside, where she'd used
small plastic markers with numbers on them to
mark every bit of blood where the victim had been
dragged over rocks and up the trail. The suspect
had avoided the nearby stream, she noted, but—
apparently at the point where Amy Johnson spotted
him—he had suddenly veered off the trail and attempted to pull the victim behind a large fir tree
near the stream.

Lauck immediately saw that the original report
didn't make sense. Who would pick up someone
who had fallen from a vehicle, then bring her to
the cabin and put her in a back room while she
bled so profusely? And why would he then drag
her back outside and up a trail? The remoteness
of the area . . . the intertwined clothes . . . the
half-nude victim . . . the blood in the cabin—it
smelled like a sexual assault gone bad to Lauck,
a rape that had escalated to the point where the
perpetrator attempted to kill his victim and then
hide her body.

Lauck, a former police detective who'd been with

the district attorney's office since 1978, assisted searching the area for a weapon, but one could not be found. Then came the news that a blue minivan matching the suspect's vehicle had been discovered in Boulder and was being transported to the Gilpin County Sheriff's Office. He was needed there to write up the search warrant so that when it arrived, the crime scene folks could go over it with a fine-tooth comb.

Less than an hour after its driver eluded state trooper Cisco, Boulder County sheriff's deputies had located the blue Chevy Astro minivan with Wyoming plates in a motel parking lot on the outskirts of the university town. The first three letters on the plate matched the partial description given to investigators by Jason Sosebe.

Boulder sheriff's detective Bruce Norton responded to the scene. He looked in the van to see if he could locate any sort of identification of its owner. He moved carefully so as not to disturb potential evidence, even more so when he saw blood in the van. He found a Nebraska driver's license issued to a Robert Davis and an address book, which he removed. He then ordered that the van be sealed, while he went to his office to see if he could track and identify Davis.

The van was transported to Gilpin County, where Lauck, Burkhalter, and the crime scene technician Vicki Spellman and her crew waited. The van only had two front seats, behind which was an open cargo area. Whoever owned the van was prepared to live on his own for extended periods of time: There were sleeping bags, several fishing poles, bins with clothes in them, and a propane stove. Although it appeared that the owner usually stored his equipment in plastic storage bins roped neatly to the sides of the van, now the interior of the van looked as though a tornado had blown through. Perhaps, the investigators reasoned, there had been a struggle.

Of more immediate interest to the investigators was a pool of blood between the two front seats. Except for a little blood on the passenger seat and a few spots on the driver's side, it was the only significant bloodstain in the vehicle. There was no blood in the cargo space . . . a relevant factor, though they did not realize it at the moment.

Meanwhile in Boulder, Norton was connecting the dots. He'd found a number of documents for creating aliases, so he assumed that "Robert Davis" might not be the suspect's real name. He had an address book, but none of the telephone numbers listed had area codes. He tried the Denver area code attached to the telephone number listed beside "Dad," but got only a confused homeowner. However, he'd noted that there had been several papers and documents in the van and in "Robert Davis's" wallet pertaining to Iowa. He decided to try area code 515 for Des Moines.

The telephone rang and an older man answered. The voice was "country" and its owner identified himself as Robert Riggan, Sr. After listening to the detective describe the photograph on "Robert Davis's" license, the man said he believed that he knew who they were looking for. "It sounds like my son, Robert Lee Riggan, Jr.," he said, then out of the blue spat out, "He's a criminal. . . . He likes the criminal lifestyle."

Bingo, Norton thought. The old man obviously didn't think much of his son, but no, he hadn't heard from him in some time.

The detective asked if his son had any identifying marks. The old man responded that there were two tattoos. The numeral "7" on his leg and a multi-colored rose on his right shoulder above the name "Sandy."

Norton got off the telephone hardly believing his luck. If Robert Lee Riggan, Jr. had a criminal history, then there ought to be a photograph he could match to the photograph of "Robert Davis," as well as a record of his fingerprints. The detective called the Des Moines Police Department, which searched their records for a Robert L. Riggan, Jr. and came up with several interesting items. For one, there was a warrant out for him in Iowa on a theft charge. But far more intriguing was that Riggan had apparently served time on a federal firearms violation, which meant the U.S. Marshals Office ought to have a mug shot of him, *and* Riggan had twice been arrested for sexual assault—though apparently nothing much had come of those charges.

Looking at the clock, Norton was disappointed; it was late Friday and probably too late to get a photograph from the U.S. Marshals Office, at least until Monday. Which was why he was surprised and delighted when a few minutes later, an officer with the Iowa Department of Corrections called and offered to fax him a copy of Riggan's mug shot from the time he spent in that system. Soon he was looking at the fax and comparing it to the photograph of "Robert Davis"—they were identical. He called Sheriff Hartman in Gilpin County with his information, which was relayed to the investigators from Jefferson County.

The police now believed that they had the real name of their suspect: Robert Lee Riggan, Jr. The Boulder sheriff's office made "wanted" flyers using the photograph of "Robert Davis," which were distributed to local police agencies, as well as the media . . . just in time for the evening television news. The victim, Jane Doe, was too disfigured to include a photograph of her, but they gave the newspaper and television reporters a verbal physical description of the woman, including the unusual tattoo on her left foot.

It was a very simple design that looked somewhat like the eye of a needle. It was an ankh, the ancient Egyptian symbol for life.

Lauck and Burkhalter, who'd joined his colleague after looking over the crime scene, never saw the television report. They were busy peering over Spellman's shoulder as she meticulously went through the van like an anthropologist excavating an ancient grave site. Every once in a while, she would point out something she thought might be significant—such as the blood pooled between the front seats—and cautioned them about touching anything, including the roof of the van where she had noticed some smudges and thought there might be something there requiring a closer look.

Spellman searched for potential weapons and located a filleting knife with a tiny spot of blood on the outside of the case. Despite finding tools of various sorts and a lot of camping gear, there was nothing like an ax or a hammer in the car that could have been used to hit the victim in the head. The investigators speculated that the suspect had found someplace to dispose of the weapons between the cabin and where the van was found in Boulder.

The investigators also reinterviewed Sosebe and Johnson. The couple were genuinely concerned about the young woman and hung around long after they were told they could go if they wanted.

Lauck and Burkhalter knew it was a stroke of luck they had come down the road just when they did. Otherwise, Johnson probably wouldn't have seen the man pulling the sleeping bag up the trail. And if they hadn't turned around to investigate, Sosebe wouldn't have gotten a look at the license plate, and the police would have had nothing to tie this particular van to the scene at the cabin. Without the couple, the police might eventually have had a victim with no other clues.

It mattered a whole lot more about seven o'clock that evening. All afternoon the nurses in the emergency room had stayed in contact, hoping they would learn Jane Doe's real identity while she remained alive. This time it was the nurses who were calling with news: Jane Doe had died from her injuries.

The examination of the van took until midnight. When the investigators left the Gilpin County Sheriff's Office that night, the stars shone brightly overhead, undimmed by the city lights of Denver to the east. It was a beautiful place, too bad it had been sullied with the death of a young woman. They had real concerns, too, about whether they would be able to find the driver of the blue van. They had a name and a photograph, but it was obvious that this Riggan was a traveling man who knew how to hide and how to assume a new identity. There was a good chance he had already found a way out of the state.

They wondered about Riggan. If this was indeed a sexual assault that had escalated into murder, was Riggan a serial killer who wandered the country picking up hitchhikers or abducting young women off the streets, killing them and dumping their bodies in remote areas? If so, were there more victims?

A pile of women's clothing had been found in the back of the van, as well as a Colorado identification card belonging to a woman named Joanne Cordova. It was quickly obvious that the card did not belong to the victim found at the cabin. The woman pictured on it was taller and older with dark hair. The investigators feared the worst. They feared that this "Robert Davis," or "Robert Riggan," might have harmed Joanne, whoever she was.

Three

Joanne Cordova

Joanne Cordova was not dead, although that was as much by luck as anything else. At thirty-eight, she was a crack-cocaine addict and a prostitute in the Capitol Hill district of Denver, so named because of its proximity to the golden-domed capital building. That evening, she was visiting a friend named Jimmy when the news came on the television. The lead story was about the police searching for a man seen dragging a woman's body near a cabin in the mountains; the suspect was driving a blue Chevy Astro minivan, which had been found in Boulder.

A moment later, the television screen was filled with the face of a man taken from his driver's license. "Oh my God, JIMMY!" Cordova yelled for her friend, who had left the room.

Jimmy hurried in just as the newscaster described the unidentified victim. Joanne pointed at the screen. "That's the guy who didn't pick me back up that day . . . the guy with my clothes. And . . . oh my God . . . ," she groaned as she realized who fit the victim's description. "Poor Anita."

Anita Paley was a twenty-two-year-old crack head, who'd only been a prostitute for a few weeks.

Poor girl, Cordova thought. Anita had always seemed too frail for the life she had fallen into. She just didn't fit in on the streets. She wasn't tough enough.

Paley was just a nice young woman—the mother of two little girls who were living with her in-laws somewhere back East. She'd shown Cordova pictures of her children and swore that someday soon she would clean up and go back to them.

The last time Cordova had seen Paley, the waif-like younger woman was running out of a house to meet Bob Davis, a man Cordova had spent several days with prior to that night. Cordova even asked Paley to recover some items of clothing she'd left in Davis's van. Paley had flashed her a smile and promised to do just that. . . . But now, according to the news, she was dead and Davis was wanted for questioning.

Joanne Cordova had personally experienced how Davis's personality could change in a flash. She recalled that Paley had told a mutual friend, Shane Delray, that Davis had raped her.

Suddenly she felt a chill go down her back. Davis knew that she might be able to link him to Paley. What if he was looking for her?

Frightened, Cordova called her younger sister, Jodie, who also lived in Denver. Jodie was frantic with worry. A detective had called and said they'd found Joanne's identification card in the van of a man wanted for questioning in an attack on another woman. The detective asked if Jodie had heard from her lately—the implication being that Joanne might have been another victim.

"They said that if I heard from you, you should call them right away," Jodie said.

Cordova assured her sister that she was all right and then hung up the telephone. She didn't know what to do. She thought of little Anita Paley, happy to go meet a stranger for the promise of crack cocaine.

She knew how powerful the urge for the drug could be . . . what it could make you do. There wasn't a day that she didn't crave it herself. It was that craving that had brought her to the level of selling her body for another taste.

"I'll owe you forever." That's what she had yelled to Paley when the young woman promised to bring back her clothes.

Now, the police didn't even know Anita Paley's name. There was no one to call Paley's family and tell them what had happened. Cordova didn't want to get involved. There was Davis to worry about. And the other people on the streets wouldn't take kindly to her being "a snitch." Nobody on the streets was supposed to go to the cops about anything regarding someone else from the streets.

"I'll owe you forever." The words haunted her as she pictured Anita's face looking back over her shoulder at her and smiling.

Cordova talked her dilemma over with Jimmy, a local photographer and radio talk-show host, whom she had only recently met but considered a friend—someone she could turn to for a place to stay without any demands for sex. He was smart—he had a master's degree in criminology from the University of California at Berkeley—and they carried on intelligent conversations on topics far re-

moved from the streets. What Jimmy, in his mid-fif-
ties, also had to offer was good, sound advice, not
that she always took it.

Nor did she want to this time when Jimmy urged
her to call the police. First, there was the fear factor. She knew from personal experience that
"snitches end up in ditches" wasn't just a saying.
But her reluctance was more than that . . . there
was also shame and embarrassment. Joanne Cordova, crack-addicted prostitute, had once been a
Denver police officer.

Joanne Marie Cordova was born July 27, 1958,
into a close, loving family. She never saw her parents fight. She was never spanked. There was a hot
breakfast in the morning, hot lunch at school, and
a hot dinner on the table promptly at five-thirty.

The Cordovas were good Catholics and went to
church every Sunday. The kids—Jeannie, Joanne,
Terry, and Jodie—attended parochial schools, got
good grades, and stayed out of the way of the strict
nuns. Only Joanne and her sister Jeannie, who was
ten months older, knew about "the bad thing" that
had come into their lives.

Joanne was about nine years old and in the third
grade when it happened. Every weekend her family
would go to a neighbor's home, where the adults
would play board games while the kids entertained
themselves until it was time for bed. Then the man
of the house would insist on tucking Joanne in.

There, in the dark, he would make her touch
him in ways and places she knew was wrong. Only
her older sister was aware and intuitively the girls

also knew it was not a subject their parents would want to hear about. It would be many years, and a lot of water under the bridge, before the sisters ever told. But from that point on, it seemed that Joanne was always at the mercy of males.

When she was twelve, she was invited over to a neighbor boy's house. Her mother had warned her about having anything to do with the boy or his brothers. But it seemed exciting to disobey her mother. But inside the house, she was forced to perform oral sex on the brothers and several of their friends. The worst part of the ordeal was looking up to see what she thought was her younger brother staring in through a window, but the face was quickly gone and she couldn't be sure.

A short time later, however, Joanne's mother came to the house and demanded to be let in. She found her daughter hiding in a closet of the house as the boys scattered.

Joanne should have said something, but she was more worried about what kind of trouble she would be in for going into the off-limits house, rather than what the boys had done. That barrier had been breached years before by her parents' friend, and so she said nothing.

Joanne's mother marched her down the street to the home of one of the boys she had recognized running away. "What happened?" Joanne's mother demanded of the boy.

"We didn't ball her," the boy blurted out.

Joanne's mother just stood there blinking in the sun, as if the possibility of *that* happening to her daughter was the last thing she had expected. She just turned and went home, never to talk about it again.

On the whole, the subject of sex was taboo in the Cordova household. With no other way to process what had happened to her, only that it was wrong and she was somehow at fault, Joanne learned to hide her emotions as though looking at the world from behind a mask. Or sometimes, she thought of it as hiding inside a bubble, looking at herself, aware of her surroundings, but mentally in some far-off place.

It was a reaction to shame, guilt, and embarrassment that psychologists would later call "depersonalization"—a common reaction to childhood sexual abuse. The important thing was that behind a mask or inside a bubble no one could touch her, no one could hurt her. She would survive.

One way of escaping reality was through reading, especially mystery books. Her childhood heroes were Nancy Drew and the Hardy Boys. She liked how they foiled the evil intentions of adults by using their minds. She knew that she would make a good detective and one day got to prove it when her prize bicycle was stolen. Systematically, she had gone street by street until she had seen her bicycle in an open garage. The thieves had repainted it, but she was able to prove that it was hers, pointing out a section they had failed to cover, and rode home triumphantly.

In the sixth grade, she was runner-up in a regional spelling bee, with her photograph in a Denver newspaper: just a bright little girl with glasses, who worked hard and did well in school.

Of course, the sexual assaults were bound to affect

her. By fourteen, she was the neighborhood rebel in Tulsa, Oklahoma, where her family had moved. She was always testing the boundaries, looking for high drama and not knowing why. Nothing too serious—mostly sneaking out at night to smoke marijuana and get drunk with her friends. She found that the drugs helped hold the mask in place.

Joanne ran away from home at seventeen with her high school sweetheart, James. She returned pregnant with his child, and they were quickly married. He joined the Army to show that he loved her and could support her and their son, Jason, who was born July 20, 1976. She became the perfect enlisted man's wife, and the perfect mother.

James made $400 a month, $150 of which went for rent, the rest of which Joanne stretched for food and diapers and still saved $20 each and every month. She doted on her son.

But such a perfect life was too tame for Joanne. After a couple of years, she grew bored and found a way to get her husband out of the Army on a hardship discharge. Her family was moving back to Denver and she wanted to go, too.

The young couple and their son arrived in Denver in 1978. A year later, they divorced. She told her husband, who would go on to armed robbery and lead police on one of the biggest manhunts in Oklahoma history, to choose any other state to live in. She and their son were going to remain in Colorado.

By 1980, Joanne Cordova was working as a cocktail waitress at a country-music bar. She was twenty-two years old, a beautiful young woman with long dark hair, dark eyes, and a figure that made men watch her every move. She was always looking for excitement, often leaving her son in her mother's care while she went out.

Her best friend was Lisa, a cop's daughter who made a living as a high-priced call girl. Lisa was wild, happy, and taking life to the edge. Her favorite song was the Kenny Loggins hit with the line, "I'm all right, nobody worry 'bout me."

Cordova had gotten her first taste of cocaine from a dentist who'd introduced her to "free base," a smokable form of the drug. It was a nice high, but it elicited no cravings. Now when cocaine was offered to her in a bar or at a party, she'd take a snort or a puff, but she was more inclined to hide her insecurities behind a mask of alcohol.

It was through Lisa that Joanne met Nate Wayne, a big-spender attorney and a fixture at the bars where she and her friends liked to go dancing. Wayne threw money around like confetti. He wined and dined pretty women and was known for the lavish gifts he gave them—expensive jewelry, clothes, and shopping trips to the West Coast.

One night, Lisa told Cordova that Wayne found her attractive and there might be good money in it if she went to bed with him. At first, Cordova just laughed. Wayne was fat, and she wasn't the least bit attracted to him. But he was also persistent, and she was envious of the gifts he'd given other girls.

"How much?" he wanted to know.

Cordova shrugged. How much would an hour of her time be worth? How much to block out the repugnance of his obese body? She named a price she thought would scare him off, but he smiled and agreed.

She thought about it. Other guys bought her dinner and a movie and expected to go to bed with her. It wasn't like any lasting romance had evolved simply because they were more physically attractive than Wayne. Ever since she was nine years old she'd known that men all wanted the same thing . . . and one way or another they felt like they could pay to get it.

Three times she gave in to Wayne's offers and was surprised afterward that she didn't feel cheap. After all, her favors had not come cheaply; he'd given her checks for $500, $400, and $350. She had mostly wanted to get it over with as quickly as possible. She'd learned from childhood to remove herself mentally from any situation where her body might be trapped, and Wayne made sure there was always plenty of cocaine and alcohol around.

Wayne was taken with her. He said he was going to buy her a new Mercedes. She believed him, but then his checks bounced. When she tried to find him, she was told by another of his girlfriends that he'd skipped town because the FBI was after him.

Angry, she called the FBI and asked about the rumor. An agent took her name but wouldn't offer much in the way of information. Realizing she wouldn't be getting her money, Cordova wrote the whole experience off to youth and figured she was through with prostitution.

The door on that era of her life was slammed shut when Lisa's body was found a few months later. She'd been shot in the head. The police ruled it a suicide, Cordova didn't believe it. If Lisa had been unhappy, she would have known about it.

Some of the men they'd hung around with were certainly more dangerous than Nate Wayne, and Lisa knew a lot of secrets. But the case was closed, and there was nothing Joanne Cordova could do about it.

It was two years later before the name Nate Wayne came up again. Now employed by a computer company as a systems analyst (having worked her way up from administrative secretary), Cordova received a telephone call from an attorney. He explained that he worked for two oil companies that suspected Wayne of embezzling millions of dollars. "The FBI gave me your name," he said. He asked her to meet with him.

Cordova caught a taxi to a hotel and met with the attorney and another man, who turned out to be a Denver cop, Sergeant Truman Leuthauser. The attorney explained that Leuthauser had a side business working for corporations to uncover theft, drug abuse, and other criminal activities by employees.

The two men asked her a few questions, but she didn't know much about Wayne's business activities. "I just thought he was a wealthy guy with a lot of money to blow," she said. He owed her money, she said without explaining what it was for. After they were through asking questions, Leuthauser offered to give her a ride home. Out in the parking lot, he walked her to an expensive-looking car. "Know what kind of car this is?" he asked, opening the door for her. She shook her head. "It's a Jaguar," he said, obviously expecting her to be impressed.

Cordova smiled. She thought Leuthauser was a bit on the geeky side. He was dressed in a cheap polyester suit and was trying desperately to cover up encroaching baldness while sucking in his stomach. But he had an air about him, one of confidence and power; he also apparently had a lot of money, so she gave him her telephone number when he asked.

Leuthauser demonstrated his generosity when he dropped her off at her mother's house. Earlier, she'd told him that she had lost a contact lens, so before he left, he placed a $100 bill on the coffee table. "Buy yourself another lens," he said.

A few days later, Leuthauser called, and it wasn't long before the two were romantically involved. Cordova had never been treated so well. They ate at the best restaurants every night. She taught him how to dress—whether it was in good blue jeans or Cassini suits. He bought her furs and jewelry. They went to the dog track nearly every day, and when they won, which was often, he'd take her shopping.

"Pick out an outfit," he'd say. And after she did, he'd tell her to pick out another. It was nothing for him to spend $300 or $400 on her in a single trip. Not even Wayne had been so generous, and if she saw a connection between the two paying for what they wanted, she ignored it. She thought she was in love.

Leuthauser was fifteen years older, but it didn't matter. If anything, his maturity and the way he took charge of her life made her feel safe. It was several months before he admitted to her that he was married and had kids. But by then, she didn't care; he was hers and rarely spent a night away from her. She was willing to fight to keep him.

After a few months, Leuthauser invited her to move into the finished basement of his home. He told his wife that she was just a business associate who needed a place to stay. It became a daily ritual to wait until she heard Leuthauser's wife leave the house and then a few minutes later he would knock on her door. It was not a very well kept secret. Leuthauser's older daughter, a junior high student, began introducing Cordova as "my dad's girl-friend." Leuthauser's wife would even see them off when they left for "business trips," suitcases in hand.

While he made good money as a sergeant on the police force, Leuthauser made even more through his firm. He invited Cordova to work for him as one of his "operatives" that he placed in companies to spy on the employees.

Cordova knew she would be a good detective. Once, she had even tracked down a man who had stolen her former mother-in-law's car. It was just like being in a Nancy Drew or Hardy Boys mystery. Now she listened raptly to Leuthauser's tales of catching bad guys; he'd been with the Denver Police Department since 1967 and knew a lot of stories.

Some of Leuthauser's moonlighting activities, however, seemed questionable. For instance, in 1982, he was directing a seven-month police department investigation into theft and drug use by employees of a wholesale grocers company, reporting to Denver police captain Leo Bernard. But Leuthauser was also receiving "consulting fees" from the company at the same time.

Cordova was one of the undercover operatives Leuthauser planted within the company as a worker. She even filled out an application and went through the hiring procedure so that only a few company executives were aware that she wasn't just another employee. As such, she was able to figure out who was behind widespread thefts, as well as such infractions as drinking and drug use by employees during business hours. As a "concerned citizen" working for the Denver police department under Leuthauser's guidance, she also made a series of heroin buys from employees that resulted in arrests.

In all, more than fifty employees lost their jobs, although only a few were ever prosecuted for criminal activities. As a result of the success of the operation and their growing relationship, Leuthauser made Cordova a partner in his consulting business. He even listed her in the incorporation papers as company vice president and secretary.

Cordova returned his trust in her by throwing her energies into the business, even designing the company logo and letterhead. Together, she and Leuthauser came up with the company slogan: "Minimizing Losses to Maximize Profits." In many ways, Leuthauser was good for her. She had not used drugs since becoming involved with him. She did not need to hide behind a mask while he was in control of her life. It took her a long time to realize that was not all good.

* * *

The grocery wholesaler was so pleased with the results of the investigation that its owners bought Cordova and Leuthauser an all-expenses-paid trip to La Manzanilla, Mexico, for December 2–9, 1982. A week before she was scheduled to leave for Mexico, however, Cordova saw a newspaper advertisement. The Denver Police Department was looking for recruits.

She was intrigued. Cordova had proven that she was a pretty good detective working with Leuthauser. It had given her a measure of self-worth that had been sadly lacking through much of her adolescence and young adulthood. Becoming a police officer, where she could do some good, maybe even become a detective like her lover, would add immensely to her self-respect.

She asked Leuthauser what he thought of her applying. He wanted her to run all the big decisions in her life past him; it was for her own good, he'd say. Sometimes he'd look at her like she was being childish and tell her to forget it, but in this instance, he encouraged her. There was only one problem. The entrance examination was scheduled for December 7, right in the middle of their trip.

Cordova was disappointed, but Leuthauser had an idea. The entrance examinations were general-knowledge tests and not very difficult. A formality, really, he said. If they could get her sister Jeannie, to take the test for her, they could still go on their trip. Cordova thought about it. She knew it would be cheating, but the test would only get her into the police academy. After that, she would be on her own to get through the more difficult courses. So it was arranged. Leuthauser and Cordova went to Mexico, and Jeannie took the test, placing her thumbprint on the application.

Soon after Cordova got back from the trip, she got a letter in the mail notifying her that she had passed the entrance exam. She was to report to the Denver police academy as a cadet.

Four

Joanne Cordova gave her dress shoes one last buffing. Satisfied that she could see herself in the reflection of the shiny black leather, she stood and looked in the mirror. Everything had to be just perfect—the hat, the shoes, the crisply pressed dark blue uniform of a Denver police officer.

It was graduation day. She had passed her final examinations with flying colors. All that was left was the formal inspection by the captain who ran the academy, and then she and her classmates would be off to their first assignments. She gave herself one last apprizing look and joined her classmates as they formed into squads and stood at attention on a grassy hill on the police academy grounds.

From the start she had done well at everything, except the shooting range. There she couldn't hit the proverbial broadside of a barn. She was so bad that there was a good chance she wouldn't qualify to be an officer.

However, one of the sergeants at the range decided to try an experiment. He told Cordova, who was right-handed, to close her right eye and open her left for her next shot. Normally, right-handed shooters keep their right eye open and vice versa for left-handed shooters.

Cordova did as told and, to her surprise, hit the target. The sergeant had correctly guessed that she had contralateral eyesight. Right-handed and left-eyed, she was soon hitting what she was shooting at from fifty yards away with her stainless-steel .38-caliber Smith and Wesson.

The police academy had consisted of twenty-two weeks of vigorous physical and classroom training. Along with obstacle runs and general courses about the law, there were specialized classes in such areas as crime scene preservation and investigation. Cordova had quickly shown that she had a good eye for detail. She had particularly enjoyed the mock court in which the cadets and their instructors acted out the various roles of lawyers, judge, defendant, witnesses, and jurors. Courts were where it all mattered—she could catch all the bad guys in the world, but if she couldn't help to punish them in court, she might as well not have tried.

With that in mind, the cadets were taught how to conduct themselves when called as witnesses at trial. "Listen politely to the attorneys," the instructors said, "but address your answers to the jury. Make good eye-contact . . . juries believe witnesses who can look them in the eye.

"And whatever you do, don't let the defense attorneys get under your skin. They will question your integrity, challenge your memory of the facts . . . exaggerate any mistakes or oversights you might have made. But you can't let them get to you."

Some of the instructors made going to court sound awful. But Joanne Cordova wasn't worried.

She dreamed of being the star prosecution witness . . . maybe at a murder trial where on her word, a killer would be taken off the streets. She imagined the flustered defense attorney. The defeated villain. She would be a hero. Her family and friends—especially Truman Leuthauser—would be so proud.

After the problem at the firing range, the only thing Cordova had a hard time with at the academy was the sexual harassment she put up with from her instructors and even other cadets. She had been big-breasted since junior high, subjected to a lot of teasing and groping by boys without being able to do much about it. At the academy, half the men couldn't seem to keep their eyes off her bosom when they talked to her, or they'd hit on her even after she let them know she wasn't interested. It bothered her—she wanted to be seen as a police officer not a sex object. There wasn't much she could do . . . her supervisors were as guilty as anyone.

Cordova stayed with it. She'd found something that made her feel good about herself. It was something no man, not even Truman Leuthauser, could give her. As the day of her graduation dawned, she was proud of what she had accomplished, proud of who she was.

However, her self-confidence began to fray as the captain made his way along the line of cadets. He was known to be a real stickler for appearance and for a cadet knowing his or her "stuff." As he inspected the cadets, the captain paused to ask each a question dealing with a police topic.

Fearing humiliation above all, Cordova could feel

herself trying to pull into one of the bubbles from her childhood—to depersonalize. She searched desperately for something to focus on, some tiny detail. Her mind suddenly seized on her other service revolver that hung on her belt. A Smith and Wesson, Model 66, .357 Magnum, serial #195k229, she told herself. Smith and Wesson, Model 66, .357 Magnum, serial #195k229. . . . Smith and Wesson, Model 66 . . .

. . . 357 Magnum, serial #195k229. . . . The captain had reached the cadet next to her. He asked the nervous cadet what a Code 10 meant. Joanne thought it was an easy question—it meant respond with lights and sirens on—but the cadet panicked, he couldn't remember. Joanne's heart went out to her classmate, a friend of hers, as he withered beneath the eye and icy tone of the captain, who had to tell him the correct answer.

The next moment, the captain was standing in front of her. He nodded and even noted aloud that she had been an "exceptional" cadet. Then it was the moment of truth. "Cadet Cordova, what is the serial number on your service revolver?" he asked.

It was the sort of thing police officers are supposed to know about the weapons they carry. Still, compared to a Code 10, it was a pretty tough question. Cordova couldn't believe that she had just been thinking of the answer to keep from going into a tailspin like her friend. "195 King 229, sir!" she replied.

The captain stepped back and eyed her with skepticism. He demanded her gun and, after checking to see that she was right, said loud enough for all to hear, including her parents and siblings who had come to the ceremony, "Very good, Cadet Cordova, well done!"

Joanne Cordova was still walking on clouds when her family and Leuthauser came up to congratulate her when the ceremonies were over. Her mother and father beamed at her and told her how proud they were of her . . . how good she looked in her new uniform.

She couldn't remember ever having been happier.

Joanne Cordova dedicated herself to being a good cop. She repeatedly received commendations for initiative and believed she would easily make detective someday. Actually, her dreams were loftier than that. She wanted to make lieutenant, then captain. She looked up to older female officers, especially one whom everyone thought had a good shot at someday becoming Denver's first female chief of police.

If not, Cordova fantasized, maybe she would.

It wasn't easy being a female cop. Not only did she get less respect than her male counterparts from the criminals on the street, there was less from many of the men she worked with. She had several good partners, especially Pat Jones, whom she regarded as the one true friend on the force she could always count on, even in some ways more than Leuthauser. But she thought of many of her other fellow officers as "jelly donut cops," who showed little initiative.

They, on the other hand, didn't appreciate her gung ho nature. She got a reputation among some as being "difficult" to work with, which meant she took her job seriously. She ignored them and tried to go about her work as she believed it should be done. But even she had her priorities.

Cordova wasn't interested in the small-time crimes. For instance, she ignored the women who stood on the corners of East Colfax Avenue, the main avenue in the area where she worked.

Colfax had once been the main street of Denver, Colorado, the principle business thoroughfare for the Queen City of the Plains, upon which horse-drawn wagons had navigated muddy ruts and cowboys had ambled. It pointed east in one direction toward which the immigrants had come and rolled past the golden-domed Capitol Building and down a slight slope into the heart of Denver.

In its modern incarnation, in the Capitol Hill district where Cordova patrolled, Colfax was a four-lane asphalt strip lined with pawnshops, adult-movie theaters, bars, and a few other small businesses and tiny restaurants that tried to hang on. Its wide sidewalks were the territory of pimps and drug dealers, gangs, drunks, addicts, the homeless, and hookers.

So long as no one was getting hurt, Cordova didn't think it was worth her time to harass the poor women who made their living hopping into cars of lonely men for short, frantic assignations. She knew most of these women were drug addicts who lived from one trick to the next just to get enough money to stay high. The women on Colfax led a hard life—beat up by their pimps or customers, treated like scum by the outside world, sometimes even killed by wackos—they didn't need her to make it any worse.

Cordova wanted to catch robbers, burglars, and especially rapists and murderers. Having been sexually assaulted herself, she knew what it was to suffer the humiliation, the fear, the self-doubts, and even the guilt that accompanied such a traumatic event.

In the mid-eighties, Cordova and her partner were involved in the case of one of the most notorious rapists in Denver history. The man had been terrorizing women in the Capitol Hill district off Colfax for months, when Cordova and her partner responded to an apartment complex where a woman had reported a rape. The woman's recollection fit the profile of the Capitol Hill Rapist, as he had come to be known in the local press.

This man has hurt a lot of women, Cordova thought to herself as she interviewed the victim. *If I mess up, he might hurt a lot more. Or maybe kill someone.* She tried to think of questions that might reveal some small but important detail that might make the difference in the case.

For instance, the victim told her that her assailant had closed the blinds. Recalling that statement, Cordova asked, "Which hand did he use to close the blinds?" His left, the victim said, which Cordova dutifully jotted down.

Eventually a suspect was arrested and Cordova was called to testify at his trial. Partway through her testimony about her interview with the victim, the prosecutor asked, "Which hand did he use to close the blinds?" It had already been established that the man was left-handed.

"His left," Cordova said, referring to her notes. "He used his left hand."

Taken individually, the answer to that question

and the others asked of Joanne Cordova didn't make or break the case. However, linked together with other bits and pieces of evidence, it was damning enough for the jury to convict the defendant.

In another rape case, Cordova and her partner met the young woman down at the city hospital, where she was undergoing tests to which rape victims are subjected to find evidence of the crime, such as vaginal and anal swabs for traces of semen.

Cordova noticed that the woman kept trying to clear her throat.

She knew that the victim claimed to have been forced to submit to oral sex, prompting her to ask, "Do you think you might be gagging on a pubic hair?"

The victim nodded yes. "Don't swallow," Cordova urged. "Try to spit up in this cup." The woman did as told and, sure enough, spit up a pubic hair, as well as other material that later tested positive for semen.

The woman also told Cordova that her assailant had been carrying a small box from a local fast-food restaurant. A little later, Cordova went back to the alley, where the woman claimed the rape occurred, and found such a box.

A suspect was later caught and tested positive when the samples from the victim were matched to his pubic hair and blood type. The fast-food container backed up the victim's story. The man was convicted and sentenced to prison, leaving Joanne Cordova proud of her bit of detective work.

Some rapes were worse than others, hitting closer to home. Such was the case when she responded with her partner to a call that a teenaged girl had been raped. The call came from the girls parents, who were living in a seedy little motel on Colfax Avenue.

It looked like the family had been living in the room for some time. All of their earthly possessions were stacked in boxes and suitcases against a wall, or strewn about the cramped space. The fifteen-year-old victim was very thin and in tears. She'd been gone so long, her parents said, they'd been about to report her missing. Then she'd appeared saying she'd been raped.

The girl told the officers that she was picked up by a man on Colfax Avenue. He'd asked her if she wanted to party and naively she'd thought that was all there would be to it. The man took her to an alley, where he tried to take her clothes off. When she resisted, he took her to his home, where he dragged her down into the basement and raped her on a mattress. He'd let her go after that, threatening to hurt her if she told anyone.

Cordova and her partner drove to the address the girl had given them. It had only been a half hour since the girl got back to her parents' motel room, but the suspect was asleep on the mattress in the basement and soon under arrest.

Recalling a police academy instructor's admonishment that the first few minutes can be critical when collecting evidence, Cordova carefully folded the bedsheets so that any evidence on top was collected. For that reason, pubic hair and body fluids gathered in the folds of the sheet proved the girl had been on that bed with the suspect in question.

Cordova hoped the girl realized how stupid she had been and that she had placed herself in harm's way. Who knew? Maybe the girl had consented to sex and then cried rape when she arrived back at the room of her angry and worried parents. But she was obviously underage, and the suspect was much older and knew better. He got a lot of time to think about it in prison.

One thing was certain, being a cop in the Capitol Hill district was never dull and often downright bizarre, such as the day Cordova and her partner responded to the scene of a reported shooting. They arrived to find a man pacing up and down the sidewalk. He had what appeared to be blood on his shirt but otherwise looked okay. "Where's the victim?" Cordova said as she approached the man.

"Huh?" was the reply.

"Where's the victim?" she repeated.

"I am," the man said.

Cordova looked at him quizzically. He didn't look like he'd been shot. Then he opened his mouth like he was at a dentist's office and pointed inside. There was a bullet lodged in the top of the guy's mouth.

Some aspects of the job were almost funny, at least afterward. Like the burglary call she responded to when she was patrolling alone one day and arrived at the scene in time to see two black males running down the alley with a variety of purloined electronics equipment. She hopped out of her car and ordered the men to stop, but they took off running, dropping their loot along the way.

One man went over a fence like a cat being chased by a dog. The other kept running down the alley with Cordova in pursuit. She caught up to him and pulled her gun. "Freeze!" she yelled. To her chagrin, he just turned and ran in a different direction.

She couldn't shoot the man in the back, so she put her gun up and continued the chase. Finally she was able to persuade a citizen to assist her and the suspect was apprehended.

She returned to her police car with her suspect, his hands cuffed behind his back. No other officer had responded to her call for backup, so she decided to pick up the dropped equipment as evidence. She looked up to see her suspect running the other way down the alley with his hands still behind his back.

With a sigh, she got up and ran until she caught up to the man. She lifted his hands and he lost his balance and went face first into the dirt and offered no more resistance after that. . . . Which was good because Cordova didn't think she had the energy to chase him down again.

Joanne Cordova particularly liked the cases in which she got to use her detective skills. In one, she'd been called regarding a stabbing and arrived at the scene to find a man bleeding from his neck. He described his attacker as a black man with a cross tattooed on his forehead.

If the assailant was one of the regular denizens of Colfax Avenue, Cordova figured, that sort of identifying feature had to have been noted before by a police officer. The officers who patrolled Colfax and other high-crime areas of the city frequently stopped suspicious characters to question them and later write contact cards, describing the physical characteristics and whatever personal information that could garner. The information was then transferred to a computer.

Back at the precinct headquarters, Cordova plied through the computerized contacts until she came across one describing a black man with a cross tattooed on his forehead. It gave her the man's name, but finding him on Colfax, many of whose inhabitants distrust and rarely cooperate with the police, was going to be difficult.

A week after she located the card, however, Cordova and her partner were called regarding a complaint about a loud party. They were in the process of telling the occupants to tone it down when she noticed a black man across the room. He was "nodding," the term for someone on heroin due to the appearance that they are nodding off to sleep. He had a cross tattooed on his forehead.

The characters at the party were a rough group, and the suspect had already knifed one man; things could have gotten a little dicey for a female cop and one male partner if they just tried to arrest the man. Cordova said nothing until she and her partner were out the door; then she quickly explained and they called in backup. A few minutes later, they were barging through the door and had the suspect handcuffed before he had a chance to resist.

The suspect gave his name, the same one Cordova had from the contact card. He was later identified by the victim as the assailant in the stabbing and convicted of attempted murder.

Hot as an oven and filthy in the summer, cold and harsh in the winter, Colfax exposed Cordova to the worst humanity had to offer: a woman who had been stabbed more than twenty times by her boyfriend; the teenager who, strung out on drugs, shot herself in the head in her parents' basement; babies abandoned in Dumpsters.

Life was cheap and the ride could be over in the blink of an eye, like the man who sat down in a chair with a shotgun between his bare feet pointed at his head and then pulled the trigger with a toe. The blast removed the top third of his head and splattered it against the wall behind him.

Like any young cop, Joanne Cordova still dreamed of apprehending a killer and testifying at his trial. Finally she got her chance.

It wasn't exactly a whodunit. A man called the dispatcher to say he'd shot his wife in the head. Cordova and her partner were the first to arrive on the scene. The man hadn't lied, his wife lay in a pool of blood in the middle of the living room with a bullet hole in her forehead and her brains spilling out the back.

The case appeared to be pretty open-and-shut. Still, Cordova knew that cases had been thrown out of court or lost during trial because of sloppy police work. She was determined to do this by the book.

"She was yelling at me," the man said as Cordova focused on remembering every word verbatim. "I picked up a beer can and took a drink. Then I picked up a gun and told her, 'I'm going to shoot you if you don't shut up.'" His wife kept yelling, he said. "So I shot her."

She didn't want to write down his confession in front of him, thinking a notebook might make him clam up. However, when she got the opportunity to be out of his presence a few minutes later, she wrote it down word for word.

Several months later, she was called into court where the man was now trying to claim that he'd shot his wife by accident. Cordova testified as she had been taught, listening politely to the attorneys, then looking at the jury to give her answers in a calm, detached manner. "He said he told her, 'I'm going to shoot you if you don't shut up.' Then he said she wouldn't stop yelling, 'so I shot her.' "

The cross-examination wasn't as dramatic as she had envisioned. The defense attorney asked her if she was sure that she had accurately quoted his client. Cordova calmly referred to her notes and affirmed that yes, what she'd just said was exactly what the defendant had told her. Word for word.

The jury took hardly more time than it took to fill out the papers to come back with a guilty verdict. It was the proudest moment of Joanne Cordova's career. A woman had died, but Cordova had stepped forward to see that the victim received justice.

The only thing wrong was that it had been too easy and the defendant wasn't much of a killer. Just an old drunk. She looked forward to when she could lock horns with a really bad man.

Dreams were becoming reality for Joanne Cordova. She was a good cop and continued receiving outstanding performance evaluations. She was also part owner of the consulting company with Leuthauser, which allowed her to buy the nice things in her life, including a Corvette, a four-wheel-drive vehicle, and a home with a $1,000-a-month mortgage.

Meanwhile, she and Leuthauser continued to live the good life—the best restaurants almost every night and frequent trips (even one to Mexico in which Leuthauser's wife and Cordova's younger sister, Jodie, accompanied them).

For two and a half years, Cordova and Truman Leuthauser were lovers and business associates. She was aware that some of his side activities—like taking consulting fees from companies while conducting an official police investigation—while maybe not illegal, would probably be frowned upon if the department knew about them. But he'd been doing it for so long, she figured nobody really cared.

Leuthauser was all about power and control over other people. He had a way of finding out everyone's deepest, darkest secrets and used that sometimes to get his way. He certainly knew everything there was to know about Cordova. She just never thought he would use it against her.

A new police chief, Tom Coogan, came on board in 1983 and declined to grant Leuthauser hundreds of hours of claimed overtime that were, in fact, hours spent as a consultant. Coogan also transferred Leuthauser from the detective bureau into a substation as a patrol supervisor at night. Cordova saw Coogan as the bad guy, not Leuthauser, and they kept right on with their consulting business.

However, in 1985, it all changed. Maybe it was because her job had given her the self-esteem she'd lost as a child, but Cordova grew tired of Leuthauser controlling everything she did in her private life. Especially after she found that he was not only cheating on his wife, he was cheating on her with a third and a fourth woman. She decided to call it quits.

Leuthauser did not take it well. "I made you, I can break you," he told her. And that was exactly what he proceeded to do, though he did it slyly.

On July 27, 1985, Joanne Cordova's twenty-seventh birthday, she got a call from her sergeant saying a *Denver Post* newspaper reporter had called asking for her. With a sense of foreboding, she returned the reporter's call.

The reporter wanted to know if she was aware that criminal charges of second-degree forgery, criminal impersonation, and conspiracy had been filed against herself and her sister. According to the charges, he said, her own department's internal affairs division was claiming that Jeannie had taken Cordova's police entrance exam for her and thus she had been "impersonating" a police officer for the past two-plus years.

Joanne Cordova didn't know how to respond. She panicked and lied. She denied the whole story. She hung up, reeling. Where could the information have come from?

She called her friend Pat Jones and told him she needed to see him. When she got to his house, she told him about the telephone call.

"Did you do it, Joanne?" he asked.

Anybody else and Joanne Cordova would have denied it, but she'd been through a lot with Jones and she trusted him. "Yes," she replied.

"Oh, Joanne," he groaned. "What have you done?"

Her response was to simply cry. She knew then that her life was ruined.

The day after the call, the *Denver Post* ran the story under the headline COP ON BEACH AS SISTER TOOK EXAMINATION. Internal affairs was contending that Captain Leo Bernard, who was retiring shortly, claimed to have overheard the Cordova sisters talking about subterfuge in a bar. It was ridiculous. Bernard had never been around her and her sister. But he was friends with Leuthauser.

Just how good a friend became clearer later when she learned that Bernard had been given a position as chief of security with the wholesale grocer she and Leuthauser had assisted. Although he would later deny it to her face, she believed that Leuthauser had passed the information to Bernard to pass on to internal affairs.

Some of her fellow officers came to her defense. The story quoted a police supervisor, "who asked not to be named but said he knows her well," praising Joanne Cordova as a "fine officer."

Initially, Cordova dared to hope that the incident would blow over. *I didn't commit a crime,* she told herself. *I cheated. I got through the academy on my own. . . . I'm a good cop.*

But neither the newspapers, nor internal affairs, nor the district attorney, who apologized to her but said it was a "precedent-setting case," would let it go.

Joanne Cordova and her sister turned themselves in and were given a tour of the Denver city jail before being released on bond. It was a horrible place—hard walls under harsh lights, filled with angry, sometimes loud, women. The worst part was the stench of unwashed bodies in a tightly enclosed space.

As a city jail, it was practically a second home for crack addicts, many of them prostitutes, who lacking a fix would go into a sort of "crack coma" and lie in their bunks sweating profusely hour after hour. It wasn't a clean sweat but one that smelled of chemicals and poisons oozing from the body. In this state, the women might not shower for three or four days, and they smelled like it.

Leaving the jail that day, running through a gauntlet of newspaper and television photographers, Cordova swore she would do anything never to return. She just wanted the whole thing to go away.

As the headlines continued to hit the newspapers, she began to notice the dirty looks from officers who never liked her because she was a woman or because she was more dedicated. But more than anything, as she began to crawl back behind the mask, inside the protective bubble of her childhood, she didn't want her family to be any more embarrassed than they already were.

Three days after the story broke, Cordova went in to talk to her captain, Ari Zavares. He had always been supportive; her commendations had always come through him. Now she told him she thought that she should resign from the force.

"Are you sure?" he asked. "I'd hate to lose you. . . . You've been a good officer."

Cordova's mind was made up. She couldn't handle the humiliation. "Yes, I think I should." And then it was all over. It was August 1, 1985, the day she would always remember as the worst day of her life.

Devastated, she couldn't eat or sleep. Former

partners and other officers who knew she was a good cop called to check up on her. Jones stopped by frequently, worried that she might do something drastic. But while she didn't want to live anymore, neither could she kill herself.

However, she thought that there was a chance she might die of a broken heart. She'd lost the one thing that mattered most to her, her career, betrayed by a man she had loved.

It was her mother who insisted that she not take the betrayal lying down. "Don't you let that man do that to you," she said. "Fight back."

Cordova thought about what her mother had said. Of all the men who had hurt her—the molester, the boys who raped her, her abusive husband, Nate Wayne—none hurt her like Truman Leuthauser. The more she stewed, the angrier she got—until she finally decided to get even. Leuthauser had cast the first stone, but she wasn't the only one living in a glass house.

She went to internal affairs at the police department and gave a seventy-seven-page deposition that, among other things, identified which of Leuthauser's activities she thought the department would find questionable. And, she told the investigators, it was his idea in the first place to have her sister take the entrance exam. She figured the department would want to know how one of its senior officers had seduced a naive, twenty-four-year-old woman behind his wife's back.

In August, another Denver daily, the *Rocky Mountain News*, broke the story that Leuthauser was under investigation by his own department for improperly using the police laboratory and other facilities for his own private projects. He was also being questioned about accepting consulting fees while conducting police business.

The article mentioned Joanne Cordova only in passing—to note that she was still facing charges. It did quote former Captain Bernard as saying he'd had no knowledge of Leuthauser accepting fees while on the job as a detective. However, the wholesale company's officials told the newspaper that Leuthauser had worked for them on a daily basis for seven months and was paid $20 to $30 an hour.

Under fire, Leuthauser resigned from the police department. He kept his consulting business, but Cordova's name was removed from the official paperwork.

The Cordova sisters received deferred sentences. If they stayed out of trouble, the blemish would be removed from their records.

Of the two, only Jeannie Cordova stayed out of trouble.

"Watch it, bitch!" The large black woman hissed, her eyes practically popping from her head she was so angry.

It was only Joanne Cordova's second day in prison and already it looked like it might be her last. The other woman was immense and, apparently, looking for a fight.

Cordova had been helping clean the prison kitchen area—the job she had been assigned—by sweeping the floor. It was 3:00 A.M.; she was exhausted and accidentally swept across the other woman's feet.

Inmates were a superstitious lot. For instance, if one got the heel from the loaf of bread served at a meal, it meant she was going home soon; but if someone swept your feet with a broom, it meant you were going to return to prison soon after you got out.

The huge woman acted as though Cordova had put a curse on her. "I'm gonna kick your ass," the woman said, balling up her fists.

Although frightened, Cordova scoffed. She couldn't believe what she was hearing. Incredulous, and shaking her head, she told the other woman, "If you truly think that me accidentally sweeping your feet is what is going to get you back in here . . . you've really got serious problems."

Cordova's response seemed to catch the other inmate off guard. She looked like she didn't know quite what to do as this dark-haired Hispanic woman not only wasn't backing down, but looked ready to fight her if she had to. But there was a certain unavoidable truth to what the woman with the broom had said. Scowling and muttering curses to "be more careful, bitch," the woman turned and shuffled away.

Letting out an enormous sigh of relief, Cordova looked around the prison kitchen and asked herself, *How did I ever end up here?*

For ten years following her resignation from the Denver Police Department, Cordova had been heading for a fall. Her life hadn't been all downhill, nor had she resigned from the force and woken up the next day in the Colorado Women's Penitentiary.

It was more like a roller-coaster ride with some

ups and downs, except each dip went lower and climbing each subsequent hill on the other side just got harder. Each time she hit a new low, she saw that newspaper headline—COP ON BEACH AS SISTER TOOK EXAMINATION—and was reminded that she had only herself to blame.

The plunge began when she lost her job, but it began to pick up speed with her first hit of crack. In 1986, she was living in a condominium complex when a new couple moved into the apartment below hers. The other woman was sitting on the front lawn one day playing with her little girl when Cordova stopped and introduced herself.

The woman was a pretty black woman and, as Cordova soon discovered, intelligent. She had been a college student when she got pregnant and had to drop out. They quickly became friends.

Ever since resigning, Cordova had been something of a recluse. Every day she bought a six-pack of beer and went to a city park near her apartment and sat beside the stream there drinking one after the other. It was the only way she could think of to get through her days. She had no ambition, no plans. Her life had lost its shiny brass-ring appeal, so it was nice to have met a new friend.

Then the woman called out to her one day from her apartment. "Joanne, come here," the woman said, inviting her in. "You gotta try something." A group of people were in the kitchen, intent on a glass vial that a man—her friend's husband—was holding.

Cordova studied the others in the room: her friend, her friend's husband, her friend's sister, and that woman's boyfriend. They'd all looked up briefly and smiled when she first walked up, but now they were all watching the vial as if expecting a magic trick. Sure enough, soon a white ball formed in the vial.

The "cook" dumped the "rock" and broke it up into several smaller pieces. He then placed one in a glass pipe, which he stuck in his mouth and brought a lighter to the bowl end. Like the sudden appearance of a ghost through a keyhole, white smoke shot into the man's mouth. A tiny wisp of smoke escaped from the bowl, and Cordova noted the smell of chemicals.

She figured they were smoking freebase cocaine. The process used to free the pure cocaine from the "base" of toxins that are a by-product of its creation, as well as subsequent additives used to "cut" the product so it can be smoked, was a bit different. Otherwise, she was familiar with the drug from her days as a cocktail waitress.

She accepted the pipe when it was passed to her with a new white crumb in the bowl. She flicked the lighter and inhaled deeply. Almost immediately she was reminded of smoking freebase with the dentist a few years back and partying with Lisa. Poor, sweet Lisa.

Yet not even the thought of Lisa's death could detract from the euphoria that filled her head like a calming, numbing fog. For the first time in months, she felt good about herself. She knew she had problems, but she couldn't quite recall what they were anymore. Whatever else this new version of coke was, it was wonderful, and Joanne Cordova stayed around until it was all gone. Her life was never the same after that.

She only smoked at first on the weekends, telling herself that she wasn't an addict so long as she could refrain during her workweek. And indeed, for years she was able to pull off being a top salesperson for a large national mechanics' supply company in Denver and then Albuquerque in the late 1980s.

However, crack was altering her life, though at first she didn't blame the drug. In Albuquerque, she had a friend who was a crack addict, smoking every day despite the fact that she was pregnant. Cordova knew her friend wasn't eating well, so she'd made a stew and taken it over to her house. She left the house a short time later; it was a weekday and she didn't want to be tempted into smoking crack. As she walked down the sidewalk toward her car, two young black men were walking up it. She nodded as they passed but continued on her way.

The men apparently didn't have much business with her friend because she had barely unlocked her car when they approached and asked for a ride. She assumed that the men were friends of her friend, so she agreed.

One of the men asked her to drive them to a convenience store. The store was in the wrong direction from where she was going, so the man changed his mind and asked if she would drive them to his sister's house. He gave a street name, which she knew lay in the direction she was traveling.

She began to grow uneasy when they drove through the area where the man's sister was supposed to be living, but he couldn't seem to locate the right house. Her suspicions grew when the talkative one told her to slow down as they passed a jogger. A few yards down the road, he ordered her to stop the car as his compatriot pulled a gun and got out of the vehicle. She was stunned when the gun came out, but that changed to horror when she looked in her rearview mirror and saw that the man with the gun was robbing the jogger.

As she watched, the man who remained with her reached across the driver's seat to turn off the car's lights. He said he didn't want the jogger to be able to see her license plate number. Cordova turned the lights back on and struggled with her companion as he tried to get the lights back off. They were still wrestling when the other man came running back to the car and jumped in.

"Go! Go!" the robber began screaming at her. He pointed the gun and she complied. She balked when the first man instructed her to turn the wrong way down a one-way street. His companion kept threatening to shoot her if she didn't do as she was told.

Cordova was finally able to convince the two men that they should go forward and find another street to turn down. She'd barely made the turn when she noticed the unmarked police car swing around to follow them. "The cops are behind us, you know," she told the others.

"Don't pull over, don't pull over," the first man yelled as his friend pointed the gun at her.

"Bullshit!" Cordova replied. "I'm pulling over." And she did just that, obeying the police officers' "felony stop" demands by throwing the keys out the window and showing both hands as she exited the car. She and her companions then had to walk backward toward the waiting officers, who then ordered them onto their stomachs with their hands behind their heads.

Cordova was taken to jail, where she contended she was innocent. A detective took her to an interview room and told her she had a few minutes to "think up a story."

"Bring me a fucking magazine," Cordova responded, "because when you're telling the truth, you don't have to make up a story."

Cordova spent eleven days in the jail, until the real robbers confessed that she'd been duped into being their getaway driver. They were crack addicts and desperate for money.

Following her arrest, Cordova quit her sales job and went to Mexico to work for a vitamin company. She began dating one of the company owners, who apparently made a lot of money, because they were often jet-setting to parties with rich and famous people. She lived like one of them, too, staying in what passed for a mansion in Guadalajara, Mexico, with its own private swimming pool and two maids to do the work.

It was a good life, but she messed that up with cocaine, too, and a short time later found herself back in Albuquerque with a full-fledged drug habit. Even being robbed at gunpoint and held hostage for three days, all for a cheap diamond ring she'd bought using her parents' credit card, wasn't enough to control the craving.

Not that she didn't occasionally try. She moved back to Denver and in with her parents, getting a good job with a car rental company by telling her prospective boss that if he didn't hire her, she'd go work for the competition. "And you don't want to be competing against me." For periods of time, she'd revert back to smoking only on weekends.

Cordova was discovering a lot about crack. Some of what she learned was by going to the Denver Public Library and looking up whatever she could find about cocaine. But she didn't need a book to tell her crack was different than freebase. Unlike freebase, crack was highly addictive and left its users "jones-ing" for more; that is, suffering physical withdrawal symptoms. Snorters and freebase cocaine users always *wanted* more coke; crack addicts *had to have it.* They craved the feeling it gave them, the power it had over their problems, and they would do almost anything to get it.

She noticed that it did not seem to affect men and women the same way. On crack, men seemed to get more aggressive and more sexually aroused; women she talked to, on the other hand, felt themselves wanting to withdraw to the point of not wanting to be touched, much less have sex.

About the only good thing that had happened to her during this time was the birth of her daughter. She hardly knew the girl's father; he was a one-night stand that neither one of them cared to repeat. She'd made a lot of mistakes with her son, who had spent more time with her parents and occasionally a sister than he had with his mother. He'd been with her when she was on the police force, but otherwise, she'd left his parenting to her parents or occasionally a sister.

She was determined to do a better job with her daughter, but in the end, there was only one thing that really mattered to her and that was smoking crack. It got so that she would spend all of her free time in her bedroom, getting high, while her children stayed with her parents.

There were a couple of attempts at drug rehabilitation, but nothing worked for long. By 1989, she'd screwed up a good job she had with a credit card company. Even though she was making good money, she had stolen almost $13,000 from the company to feed her habit, and knew it was only a matter of time before she got caught.

However, the credit card company wasn't on to her yet when her own drug-induced paranoia did her in. She was smoking a lot, worrying about how to cover her theft, when she became convinced that vehicles going past her apartment building were unmarked police cars. She loaded everything she owned—which by this time wasn't much, as it had all been sold for crack—including a large amount of the drug, and then headed up Interstate 25 for Wyoming, one hundred miles to the north.

Cordova reached Cheyenne when she decided that she'd been followed and turned around to go back to Colorado. She was driving more than one hundred miles an hour, which finally did attract the attention of the Wyoming State Patrol. Her Wyoming pursuers had to stop at the border, but waiting on the other side were officers from several Colorado agencies. She blew right past those cops who were soon on her tail.

A little ways ahead, she saw a police car off the side of the road and what looked like a dark line across the road. She knew from her police training that the dark line was probably a tack strip laid across the highway to puncture her tires. She veered off onto the shoulder of the road toward the police car, sending the officer standing there scrambling, and went around the tack strip.

She was about to drive through another roadblock and in her drug-addled state thought she might escape, when there were several loud bangs on the side of her car, as though someone were running alongside hitting her car with baseball bats. There were a couple more loud bangs when she realized it wasn't a baseball bat. . . . *They're shooting at me.*

Somehow she got through the barrage. As she drove, she tossed items out of her car, including what remained of her crack, which nearly made her more miserable than the thought of someone shooting at her.

Up ahead she saw another tack strip across the road and swerved to go around it, only to discover that more of the strip had been laid on the shoulders. The strip punctured the tires and Cordova's seventy-seven-mile chase crumpled to a stop. The next thing she knew, she was looking at a police officer, who was looking down his gun sight at her.

Cordova was charged with eluding and felony menacing (the officer said he'd had to scramble out of her way) and was offered a deal—plead guilty to one, and the other would be dropped. Her lawyer told her she would probably get probation in either case, but if she pleaded guilty to eluding, she would also lose her license. She chose to plead guilty to felony menacing.

The theft of the money from her company was discovered and she was charged with another felony. Her lawyer again assured her that he had every reason to believe that the judge would sentence her to probation.

The lawyer was so convincing that Cordova showed up in court with her daughter. The next thing she knew, the judge was sentencing her to four years in prison. A social worker stepped forward to take her daughter.

At that moment, Joanne Cordova was grateful that she'd thought that if something did go wrong, she should have a friend in the courtroom. For some reason, she'd called Truman Leuthauser and asked him to come. Despite all that had passed between them, she still loved him and was thankful when he showed up. She hugged her daughter and handed her to Leuthauser, asking him for one last favor. "Make sure she gets to my mother," she cried.

As she was led away in handcuffs, Cordova could hear her daughter's pitiful wails. She figured she had sunk about as low as she could go.

She'd wound up in prison, sharing a tiny room with a steel toilet. It was a whole new world, a whole new language, and a whole new way of life to adjust to—learning such unwritten rules as not to bend over in front of someone else, which was considered a sign of disrespect, unless she was willing to get her ass kicked.

Even in a women's prison, she learned that the tough rule the roost and the rest got picked on. It was a system based on the potential for violence. Saying "If you're froggy, jump" was a way of accepting a challenge to fight. If a friend came up and suddenly started braiding her hair, she knew that someone had threatened to jump her; braiding her hair was to make it harder to be yanked in a fight.

As Cordova discovered her second day when she swept the feet of the other inmate, prisons were filled with superstitions. If a woman didn't finish a book before she was released, then she was doomed to return to prison to read it. "Well, there'll be a lot of these women coming back," Cordova joked with friends. "They all start, but none of them finish reading the Bible."

One of her chief worries was that someone would find out she had once been a police officer. Former cops don't fare well in a prison; she might even run into someone she helped put away. But even that might have been better than the day she looked up and saw her former captain, Ari Zavares.

Zavares had been appointed superintendent of Colorado's correctional facilities and he was on a tour of the women's facility. "My God, Cordova, what happened to you?" he said, staring in disbelief at her inmate uniform.

Cordova didn't know what to say. There'd been many nights she lay awake in her jail cell asking herself that very question. She didn't know, either . . . she could have blamed it on the cocaine, or losing the only job she ever wanted. But those were explanations, not excuses for why she had let her life go to hell. As soon as she could, she slunk away to be by herself.

The only good thing about prison was that she couldn't get any more crack and her head cleared enough for her to realize how if she didn't stop it would destroy her life. *Or kill me,* she thought.

Joanne Cordova allowed herself a good cry once

a month. But that was all. She had to be tough to survive and crying wouldn't help.

Still, it seemed she was doomed to suffer one blow after the other. One of the worst had been when her daughter's father demanded custody of the child, which the court, looking at Cordova's record, quickly granted. The heartache was nearly unbearable. Still, she knew that the girl was better off with her father, a successful businessman who had married and already had another child.

In the days that followed, she often wondered how her life might have been different if she'd fought to stay on the police force instead of resigning. After all, there were cops still there who'd done much worse than she had—beating their wives, drunk driving—and nobody had forced them to resign.

Several of her academy classmates had already made lieutenant. She had been as dedicated as any of them. When she thought about what might have been, she was sick to her stomach.

Out of prison in January 1995, but on parole, Joanne Cordova stayed clean for ten months, working two jobs, saving her money, living with her son and his girlfriend. She was determined to get her life back on track. She couldn't be a police officer, but she told herself that she could be something worth holding her head up about again. Then she made another mistake.

Shortly after she completed her probation period, and the random drug testing that included, she ran into a former inmate friend, who invited her over for dinner. It was a nice meal, but dessert was provided by her friend's boyfriend . . . a dessert of cocaine.

A little over a year later, all of her best intentions had fallen by the wayside. In May 1997, as she was crossing Colfax Avenue, a man in a blue minivan honked to get her attention. "Hi," he called out through the window. "Can I ask you something?"

Cordova stopped and peered in the window of the van. She didn't know the man—a white guy with a sort of waxy complexion and strange pale-blue eyes. "I'm Bob Davis," he said. He smiled and nodded toward the woman in the passenger seat. "This is my wife, Debbie Davis. . . . She wants some coke . . . you wouldn't know where to find any?"

Five

Robert Riggan, Jr.

Bob Davis was not the man's real name. It was Robert Riggan, Jr., and he was a thirty-seven-year-old drifter on the run from Iowa and, perhaps, other dark secrets from his past. For if monsters and madmen are in some part the product of their environments, then Riggan got an early start.

His parents, Robert, Sr. and Vernice, married in 1955. Vernice already had two children, both of them the products of incestual rape: a son, George, who was fathered by her brother Bill, and a daughter, Henrietta, who was also fathered by one of her brothers, though things being what they were, no one was quite sure which one.

Robert and Vernice had four children together, only two of whom lived. The first was Rosie, born October 1956. Then there were two stillborn infants. On March 22, 1960, Robert, Jr., entered the world—already a tragedy waiting to happen—with his umbilical cord wrapped around his neck.

Living conditions at the Riggan household were filthy and crowded, especially after Henrietta and her four eldest children came to live with them. Nine people were crammed into a two-bedroom house. It was so crowded the front porch was converted into a bedroom for Robert, Jr. and one of Henrietta's boys, unheated even in the winter months.

The family was poor. To clothe her children, one of the few efforts she seemed to make on their behalf, Vernice would go to a thrift store on "sack day," where for fifty cents she could stuff a sack full of hand-me-downs.

An obese, bitter woman, Vernice never did a lick of housework, and usually sat in a chair all day complaining about various ailments. When the children were young, the house was cluttered with trash, unwashed dishes, and rotting leftovers. Even if the laundry got done, it would sit piled up on the couch and chairs in the living room until there was no place for anyone to sit. Except Vernice, who had her own chair that only she was allowed to sit in.

When Rosie and Robert, Jr. were both still very young, a neighbor reported their mother to the Iowa Department of Human Services for the filthy living conditions. That resulted in an order that the house be kept cleaned and compliance would be monitored with inspections. However, the social worker conducting the inspections would always call first, which would spur a flurry of cleaning. Vernice would also run out and buy new crayons and coloring books for Rosie and Robert and instruct them that when the worker came to the house, they were to remain seated on the floor around a coffee table, coloring.

Vernice was often ill and once had to go to the hospital with a kidney stone when Rosie was eight and her brother about four. The children were sent to stay with a local minister and his wife for approximately a week. The minister made Rosie uncomfortable by remaining in the room and staring when his wife would strip her down and wash her in the kitchen. But that paled when compared to what her brother told their mother after they returned home.

According to what Vernice later said to her daughter, Robert, Jr. said the minister had tied him up with ropes and sexually assaulted him. The boy had a habit of lying and no one had believed him then . . . at least not until a few years later when the minister was charged with sexually assaulting a young girl.

Of course, it wasn't as if sexual abuse were a stranger in the Riggan household. As Rosie got older, a friend of their father's would come over to the house and give her such appraising looks that even her mother complained. Her father's response, however, was to tell his wife that their daughter was "asking for it," and "that's what she wants, isn't it?"

Even that was not the worst of it. Vernice's oldest boy, George, was a drifter who occasionally dropped in on the Riggan household. Beginning when they were prepubescent, he sexually assaulted his niece, Theresa, and his half sister, Rosie.

The girls had nowhere to turn for help. Robert, Sr. had his own deviant activities. One, his wife discovered, was that he had drilled a hole in the ceiling of the bathroom so he could go up into the attic and watch Henrietta and Theresa bathe.

The sexual improprieties at the Riggan house were not a secret. Clem W. Keyes, a different pastor than the one the kids had been sent to live with for a time, befriended the Riggan children. They seemed starved for love and sought out his wife on Sunday mornings, as she would pay a lot of attention to them. In particular, Keyes found young Robert to be an angry kid, who thought the world was set against him.

However, there was something far more disturbing about the Riggan household than a lack of attention. Keyes dropped by one day to talk to Vernice about a disturbing rumor. He'd been told that teenaged Theresa was being sexually assaulted by her step-grandfather, Robert, Sr. However, when he brought this matter to the attention of Vernice, she asked him to "keep a lid on it. . . . The trouble's with Theresa, not my husband."

The relationship between Robert and his wife Vernice was a rough one. He was a drinker, who would get mean when he was sauced. But Vernice was his match, once breaking his ribs with a thrown water pitcher. She often accused him, with some justification, of flirting with women in the neighborhood, and once even got into a fight with one of the women. Vernice punched the other woman and pulled her hair. The fight ended out in the street with Vernice repeatedly slamming her opponent's head into the pavement.

About the time Rosie turned thirteen, she was acting the part of both mother and maid for the household. She watched over the other children and did all the cooking and cleaning. Once a week, Rosie did all the laundry in an old ring-washer.

Fed up, she ran away. When caught by the authorities, she refused to return home and was placed in the Mitchellville School for Girls. It was like going to heaven. Neither she nor her brother had been allowed to have friends while they were growing up, but now she could socialize with other girls. She had to do chores at the school, but not like she had to at home.

Rosie stayed two years at the school. During that time, there were attempts at reconciliation, but whenever she went home for the weekend, she was just supposed to clean and cook for the others.

She returned home briefly when she was fifteen. Rosie soon ran away again, this time with her boyfriend, and purposely got pregnant, believing her parents would agree to let her get married.

Her boyfriend was afraid to ask her father, but when he did finally work up the nerve, Robert Sr.'s response was, "Good, there'll be one less mouth to feed around here."

The marriage would not be a good one. Her husband sexually molested their daughter and was sent to prison. When he got out, Rosie's parents welcomed him back into the family fold with open arms. Apparently, nothing was that bad that it couldn't be forgiven.

Rosie only had one regret when she left her family home, and that was leaving her little brother, Robert, who was twelve, to fend for himself. From the time he was born with his umbilical cord wrapped around his neck, life hadn't got any easier. When Robert was a one-year-old, he was diagnosed by a doctor as having a sore on the tip of his penis that could have been from a sexually transmitted disease.

In the second grade, young Robert suffered horrible burns to his face when his father tossed a plastic jug of burning gasoline over his shoulder, accidentally striking the boy. His father had been trying to get the family car to start by pouring gasoline into the carburetor. When the fuel suddenly caught fire, the man panicked. The boy was hospitalized with severe burns over his face.

Up to that point, Robert Jr. had enjoyed going to school despite some teasing because of his tattered clothing and family's social status. Like Rosie, he wasn't allowed to make friends, but at least at school there was some interaction with other kids. After he was burned and released from the hospital, however, he was tormented unmercifully by his classmates over his scarred face.

Growing up, Robert only had one real friend in the world, a mongrel dog he'd named Goofy after the Disney character. They were constant companions, the only creature besides his sister who was absolutely loyal and showed him any affection.

His mother certainly didn't. He was barely tolerated. If there was any attention shown, it was usually in regard to something he'd done wrong, for which he'd be whipped with belts or a stick. He was so desperate at times to avoid punishment that he'd hide the belts in a futile attempt to avoid being struck.

Small wonder that young Robert's history with mental health institutions began in June 1972 when he was diagnosed at the Des Moines Child Guidance Center as being depressed. He'd been brought there by his parents, because he seemed unable to control his bowel movements and doctors had been unable to find a physical reason for this.

Robert was suffering from encopresis—or soiling himself in inappropriate situations—and had been, according to his parents, for three years. This is sometimes diagnosed as a psychological condition considered to be a function of a child's self-esteem and most often seen in children who have been ostracized by their peers and caregivers and frequently victims of sexual abuse. Robert's parents had dealt with his frequent soiling of his underwear by refusing to buy him any more.

The psychologist at the child center noted in her report that the boy "cries in quiet, hopeless misery" over his problem, "and does not know why he cannot stop." Robert felt himself to be in physical danger.

"His dependency needs have not been satisfied," the psychologist wrote. "His interpersonal relationships are disturbed and that in some ways people seem unreal to him and he expends considerable energy to make them that way. This seems to provide him some safety from being either absorbed or killed."

The counseling sessions continued intermittently throughout the summer and fall. In September, a psychologist noted, "In some ways, Bob is wanting a strong, benign, somewhat protective adult to oversee him and be involved with him."

In October, the same psychologist reported that the boy complained that his parents didn't want to bring him to the sessions and that his mother often threatened to leave, which frightened him. "Robert probably gets very little that is not negatively based. . . . This couple impresses me as classically emotionally and culturally deprived. Robert is going to need to develop some acceptance of their lack of emotional availability. He must be continuously frustrated in his efforts to get it.

"Bob definitely needs the support of his parents if he is to continue in treatment. He needs not only verbal support from them, but also needs them to support his treatment financially, as well as continuing to come in regularly for their sessions."

There was little to indicate the Riggans were interested in helping their son. According to the psychologist's November report, "Bob was late to group and was feeling that his mother had not wanted him to come to the group at all today. He evidently had to call to tell his mother to come and get him since she was not there, and he was feeling like he had to take all the initiative and responsibility for his coming. Bob was feeling very unsupported and put upon by his family."

Later that same month, the counselor noted that Robert was "uncomfortable" when he was praised for a suggestion he made to another member of his therapy group. The counseling was terminated shortly afterward, according to the counselor's report, "because there was no commitment to change made by his parents."

Two years later, however, Robert, Jr., now fourteen, was again back at the Des Moines Child Guidance Center. A small, angry boy, he was getting into fights a lot at school to prove himself. He was still unable to control his bowel movements, though the encopresis occurred more often at home than at school, an indication of where he felt the most stressed. But in March 1974, his main concern that he expressed to the psychologist was that his mother wouldn't wait for him while he underwent diagnostic testing.

Nevertheless, he was tested and was found to be disturbed enough that the psychologist recommended he receive "residential treatment" at the facility and "intensive psychotherapy. . . . There is substantial evidence to indicate that Robert views the world as a rather threatening place in which to live." This suggestion was ignored by his parents.

In May 1974, Robert was in trouble for stealing. He called his probation officer one day and said he was going to run away from home. His mother got on the telephone and said that was fine with her. This resulted in the boy being referred to the Iowa Mental Health Institute in Independence, Iowa, where he was admitted on June 3.

The counselors found him to be "a likeable boy who wants to get help," though he seemed "very anxious and showing marked signs of sadness." The boy found it difficult to openly express his feelings and was "somewhat paralyzed at times by his overwhelming anxiety." He was also preoccupied with a sense of "failure, anxiety, insecurity and basic immaturity."

"He is a very lonely boy who has few friends," the counselors reported. "When he did things to attempt to gain friends, he only got into trouble. . . . He said he had been sad for a long time, that he had difficulties at home for a long time."

According to reports from the mental health center, Robert Riggan, Sr. made passes at his granddaughters. Nothing was done. Young Robert also reported being sexually abused by the minister when he was a child. Again, nothing was done.

The boy cried easily during therapy sessions. "He is almost crippled by overwhelming anxiety and by his very low self-concept."

Six months later, this crippled boy—abused, lonely, unloved, and very, very angry—was released to his parents. The final diagnostic conclusion of his therapists was that he was merely suffering from an "overanxious reaction to adolescence." He was prescribed daily doses of meloril, a powerful antianxiety drug.

Although afraid of his mother, as he got older Robert occasionally lashed out by hitting her. She wasn't the only woman to suffer as the boy became a teenager. What he lacked in looks, Robert made up for in being able to schmooze girls, particularly those who, like him, lacked self-esteem. He could be a lot of fun—intelligent, always ready for some wild adventure—but his moods could swing without warning and his girlfriends learned that pushing some buttons was likely to get them cuffed as well.

In 1976, he dropped out of Saydel High School in Des Moines during his tenth-grade year. His grades were below average and he'd had thirty-two unexcused absences just in his last term. The day he turned seventeen, he left home and enlisted in the U.S. Navy. Robert Lee Riggan, Jr. was now a traveling man.

Six

"I'm Bob Davis," the man in the blue minivan said. He smiled and nodded toward the woman in the passenger seat. "This is my wife, Debbie Davis. . . . She wants some coke. . . . You wouldn't know where to find any?"

That Joanne Cordova looked like someone who knew where to find crack was a good indication of how far she had fallen. After smoking crack with her former prison friend, the old cravings had returned and soon her money had literally gone up in smoke. She was evicted from her apartment and her life plunged swiftly downhill again.

Crack gave her a mask from behind which she could see the world without it seeing her. But it took everything she had to keep it in place, including what was left of her self-respect.

Cordova went from man to man. Whoever would help her get more crack got her. One boyfriend was the jealous sort. He'd get high and start accusing her of sleeping around. "You're nothing but a coke whore," he'd sneer. "You'd screw anybody who'd give you some."

She heard herself referred to as a coke whore so many times by him that one day she just decided to see what he'd say if she really was one. She got up from their bed and went into the bathroom where she curled her hair and put on makeup. She pulled out her sexiest outfit and began to walk out the door.

"Where you going?" her boyfriend said with a scowl.

"You keep calling me a whore," she retorted, "so I'm going to see if anybody will pay for this body."

With that, she sauntered out of the house, which was just off East Colfax Avenue where the real prostitutes hustled their wares. "Anybody wanna pay me for this body?" she yelled at startled motorists and men walking down the sidewalk. "Who'd pay me to have this body?"

Cars began honking. Men smiled and said they'd be happy to pay. That day she returned to her boyfriend's apartment having made her point. She had no intention of selling herself for a drug—she still didn't know how deep her need for crack ran.

She found out when her boyfriend was arrested and sent to jail in January 1997. Suddenly she found herself out on the cold gray streets with nowhere to go and a drug habit. The next time a man offered money for sex, she accepted.

Now she knew that at last she had truly hit rock bottom. She was a coke whore in every sense.

Joanne Cordova wasn't comfortable peddling her body on Colfax street corners to anybody who drove up with enough cash. As she met a new trick, she "cultivated" him to become a repeat customer. She wanted to establish a clientele of men she referred to as her "ten boyfriends," whom she could call when she wanted to exchange her "time" for money.

Still, she didn't kid herself about what she had become. Call girl. Hooker. Whore. And just because she preferred to visit her ten friends, it didn't mean that when she needed a fix, she was above finding herself in the backseat of a car with her face in some guy's crotch.

Her family knew she did drugs, but she kept the prostitution from them. Fortunately, her parents had moved to another part of the state, so the subterfuge wasn't difficult.

She was also fortunate that not every man who wanted to spend time with her was looking for sex. She had her friend Jimmy, who had a master's degree in criminology from the University of California at Berkley. She enjoyed talking with him about social and legal issues, as well as her days as a police officer. It took her back to better days, and he treated her with respect. But sooner or later, her body and mind would crave more crack and she'd be out on the streets. There was also Shane Delray, a small black man whom most people thought was a pimp, though he denied it. To Cordova, he was a friend who would let her and some of the other girls crash at his apartment when they needed a place to stay.

Prostitution was a nasty, dangerous way to make a living. Movie versions like *Pretty Woman*, where the millionaire who looks like Richard Gere falls in love with the hooker and takes her away from it all, were fairy tales.

Sometimes there were nice men who treated her kindly, such as the Muslim man who was captivated with Cordova but because of his religion couldn't have sex outside of marriage. He solved that problem by convincing her to marry him for three days, in a ceremony complete with a Muslim cleric. The marriage was then annulled and they both went their separate ways.

Most of the men she saw were harmless, just lonely or looking to fulfill fantasies that their wives or girlfriends wouldn't allow. There was the man who had dozens of women's shoes at his home and dictated what shoe she would wear while having sex with him. Or the businessman who told her not only how he wanted her to dress, but what he wanted her to do every step along the way, down to whether she should leave on only one shoe or have just one arm out of her shirtsleeve during sex.

Some were just plain strange, like the man who would get turned on by smelling her armpits. She steered away from any second encounters with those kind, not because she was afraid, but because they were too weird. But she didn't avoid all the strange ones, like the doctor who enjoyed sexual asphyxiation and wanted to be choked during the act. That made Cordova a little queasy, so she began taking another woman, whom she paid a small percentage of what the doctor gave her, to do the "dirty work" while she directed the action and made sure the doctor was content with the outcome.

Then there were guys who wanted to "rescue" prostitutes, Bible-thumpers who'd try to convince the women of the errors of their ways . . . though that often wasn't until after they got what they'd paid the women for. Some of them could be pretty

scary, caught as they were between sin and their
own moral vacillation.

Cordova never had any trouble with a trick that
she couldn't handle; then again, the way she ran
her business, she didn't meet hundreds of men like
some of the girls. She knew that prostitutes disappeared all the time, or were found dead in alleys
or stuffed into trash bins with all the rest of the
community's garbage. Sometimes you never heard
if it was a drug dealer who'd killed them, or some
sick trick who figured nobody'd mind if a prostitute
died.

Cordova heard plenty of stories about tricks who
turned mean and hurt one of the other women.
But like most of the more experienced prostitutes,
she felt she had a good sense for avoiding danger.
About the closest she'd come to being frightened
by one of her tricks was a wealthy businessman who
liked to act out rape fantasies when his wife and
daughter were out of town. He'd carefully choreo-
graph these fantasies, explaining what he wanted
her to wear, from the kind of earrings to the color
of lipstick, sometimes asking her to wear something
owned by his wife. Then he'd run through the scenario—such as her playing the part of a woman
just getting home from a fancy-dress party only to
be accosted by a "stranger" in dark clothing and
a ski mask.

The customer always had some type of facsimile
weapon—a plastic knife or toy gun—with which
he'd threaten to kill her if she resisted. Sometimes
she was supposed to resist and the struggle could
turn violent. Sometimes she was supposed to pretend to be knocked out and then come to as she

was being raped. However, if he got carried away and hurt her, all she had to do was address him by his real name and he would stop. Most of these fantasies ended with the trick killing her. It wasn't until later that she wondered what it took to push some men from fantasy into reality.

However, at the time, Cordova didn't see her clients as representing the real danger in her profession. Forget AIDS. She always insisted on condoms, and didn't inject her drugs like the hookers who preferred heroin. There were lots faster ways to die than diseases.

The real danger was from the drug dealers and gang members and other criminals who inhabited the same streets. She'd been beaten up and robbed. A gang member had pointed a shotgun in her face, and a dealer had threatened to "kill [her] and jack off over [her] dead body." All over coke deals.

Joanne Cordova managed to talk or fight her way out of the worst jams, though she knew a day might come when she, too, would end up down at the city morgue with a toe tag. Although it might sound strange from the perspective of prostitutes, rape was a common enough occurrence. Sometimes she'd be at some man's apartment getting high, when the man would suddenly demand sex whether she wanted to or not. There was no sense resisting; that might only make it worse, more dangerous. It was simply the way things were, the way the game was played.

The true measure of the insanity of crack addiction was that the necessity for the drug outweighed the necessity of living. Cordova and women like her risked their lives every day, let men use their bodies in ways that made her sick to think about, were raped and beaten, just for one more hit of crack.

And the craziest part of all? Some john might turn ugly and beat a woman into a hospital stay, or a drug dealer might pull a knife and slash a woman's face, but if they survived the moment, these women would be right back on the streets as soon as they were able to risk it all again.

Like most crack addicts, Cordova would go on binges, staying high and awake for three or four days without sleeping. Then, when the crack ran out and she was too exhausted to do what it took to get more, she'd drink alcohol to take the edge off and sleep for twenty-four hours or more. Then she'd wake up craving crack and the cycle would begin again.

Needing money, she'd call one of her ten friends or, if none were in need of her services, she would be on a corner trying to attract motorists until she had enough money to afford another high. About the only thing that would interrupt the cycle was being arrested for drugs or prostitution, and then only long enough to make bail or do the time.

When she wasn't working or in jail for soliciting or a drug charge, or getting high, all she wanted to do was sleep. Only when she slept could she forget.

This was Joanne Cordova's life in May 1997, when the guy in the blue van pulled over and asked if she knew where to find crack cocaine.

Thinking she'd score as the middleman, Cordova got into the van and directed Bob Davis where to go. She recognized the woman introduced as "Mrs. Davis"; she was just another hooker from Colfax. Didn't bother her . . . lots of the guys who picked up prostitutes had their quirks, and if Bob Davis wanted to pretend he was married to a prostitute, who was she to say he couldn't?

The first stop was not a good one. The dealer, a large black man, tried to short them on the quantity of the crack. When Cordova complained, he grabbed her by the hair and snarled, "I'm going to drag you out of this van and beat your fuckin' head in, bitch."

As she cried out in pain, Bob Davis looked on as if the two were having a polite conversation. *Well, we know Bob's no gentleman,* Cordova thought after she'd persuaded the dealer not to hurt her.

They eventually located more crack for Davis to give to his "wife" with some for Cordova, who left the couple and went on about her business. She never expected to see "the guy in the blue van," as she thought of him, again.

However, the next day she was walking across Colfax when someone started honking at her. She kept moving, ignoring the honks. She didn't want any cops to see her approach the honker and arrest her for soliciting.

Cordova was depressed. She hadn't had any crack since the day before with Bob and Debbie, and all she wanted was to reach Delray's house where she hoped she could sleep for a few hours. But the honker was persistent and at last she looked up. It was the guy in the blue van. It was Bob Davis.

"I've been looking for you," he said and smiled. "I bought you some clothes."

Although she didn't believe a word, Joanne Cordova allowed herself to be flattered by his come-on. She needed an ego boost, and here this guy was saying he'd been looking all over for her . . . and had brought her gifts. Just like Truman used to, she thought. So she got in the van.

"Debbie Davis" was apparently out of the picture, but Cordova didn't ask what had happened to Davis's wife. Prostitutes weren't exactly known for sticking around; she could have been in Kansas for all Cordova knew.

Even as Joanne Cordova got into the van, Debbie Johnson counted herself lucky to still be alive. She'd met Bob Davis in a seedy Capitol Hill bar. After a few drinks, and a promise to help her find some crack, he asked her to pretend she was "Mrs. Bob Davis." For a day or two, anyway.

What the hell, Johnson thought, she'd been asked to do worse than that. He wasn't very good-looking, but he seemed nice enough, and anything for a little crack. Johnson accompanied him to several pawnshops where he sold items he confided that he'd shoplifted from a department store. Then they cruised Colfax Avenue until they spotted Cordova.

Later that day, after Johnson got high, Davis took her to a department store to shop for clothes. He was more generous than he had to be, and insisted that she pick out pretty underwear, including a lacy red pair. He talked afterward about wanting to take her to some favorite place he had in the mountains. She said she didn't care as long as the crack held out.

They were leaving town when he pulled into an alley and stopped. "I forgot to get something out of the back," he said. She didn't think much of it. She'd noticed that he seemed to have a lot of camping equipment in the back and figured he needed something for their excursion.

Suddenly her benefactor reached around from behind and was pressing a knife against her throat. "Do what I say and you won't get hurt," he said, pulling her with the knife still on her skin into the back where he had a sleeping bag laid out.

Afraid, Johnson wondered what this was all about. She was a prostitute; if he wanted sex all he had to do was ask. It was as if he needed to be violent and angry. He ripped off her shirt and underwear, all the while waving a long, thin knife in her face and threatening to hurt her. She pleaded with him not to hurt her, but he then consummated his violence by raping her anally.

When he was finished, he acted as if nothing had happened. "It's okay," he told her over and over as she dried her tears. He promised to buy her more new clothes to replace those he'd torn. "I like it when the woman resists," was his only explanation for what had happened.

Debbie Johnson nodded. Then he frightened her even more by telling her, "I was going to kill you. . . . I don't know why I didn't."

The woman held her hands up. "I don't need to know," she said. She'd never had a customer turn on her like that—it was like he was two different people. All she wanted to do was keep him calm until she found a way to escape. She pretended it was all in a day's work.

Davis took her to a convenience store where she said she wanted to get a cup of coffee. Once inside, she walked quickly through the aisles and out the back door. She wanted nothing more to do with him. . . . There was not going to be any second chances to find out what he might do with that knife.

Robert Riggan drove around looking for Debbie Johnson. He spotted Joanne Cordova for a second time and asked if she wanted to go with him. She got into the van and they drove to a pawnshop, where he sold a stereo. With that money, he purchased beer and a bottle of schnapps; then they drove to a park on the outskirts of Denver, where he parked.

As they talked, Cordova decided she kind of liked Bob Davis. For one thing, he hadn't asked her for sex. She figured it was coming, but at least it wasn't the first thing that had popped out of his mouth— like it was with most tricks. For the moment, he seemed content to just chat like they were some old couple there to watch the sunset.

She was impressed by his intelligence. He seemed to have moved around quite a bit and knew something of the world. His van was as tidy as an accountant's ledgers; everything was stowed away in plastic containers that were strapped neatly in place. He had all sorts of camping gear and appeared ready for anything. As a survivor herself, she could respect that trait in someone else.

Davis told her he'd like to take her up in the mountains to his "favorite place in the whole world." Maybe, he said, they'd get some things together and go up there tomorrow for a picnic.

"That'd be nice," Cordova murmured as she sipped a beer. She began feeling drowsy in the warmth of the late afternoon sun that poured in through the windows. "You're a nice guy, Bob Davis," she said and meant it as she drifted off to sleep.

She woke up in the dark to the sound of someone talking through a loudspeaker. It was two police officers in a cruiser telling them that the park was closing, and they would have to leave.

Davis waved at the cops and started the van. He had his hair combed over to one side, sort of funny, and was wearing nerdy-looking glasses. "It's my Poindexter look. See," he said, pointing to the police car as it drove off, "they think I'm just a normal guy."

It seemed like an odd comment. As far as Cordova knew, Bob Davis *was* just a normal guy. A little lonely, maybe, a little anal about keeping his car shipshape. Why wouldn't the police think he was just a normal guy?

Usually, a statement like that would have sent up a red flag for Joanne Cordova. However, she was lulled into a pleasant sense of security by memories of spending time in quiet places like the park with Truman Leuthauser. It seemed like such a long time ago she had been with her old lover. He'd shown up in her hour of need at her sentencing and made sure her daughter was delivered to her family, but she'd been too ashamed of what she'd become after that to contact him again.

For some reason, Bob Davis had stirred up the

old memories. Now she just felt tired and let his "normal guy" comment slide.

They spent the night in the van, parked on a street in a quiet neighborhood. Davis had neatly laid out a sleeping bag for each of them. She was pleasantly surprised when he made no attempt to initiate sex.

After Joanne Cordova woke up the next morning, they went to a cafe for breakfast. They were served by a young blond waitress. She was just a girl, friendly and polite, but when she took their order and left, Davis leaned toward Cordova and sneered, "She looks like a whore."

It was the first time she had seen another side of Davis around women. Instead of alarming her, she just thought that it was rude. Who did he think he was sitting with, the Virgin Mary? She knew what she was; he didn't need to be so insensitive.

The incident was quickly forgotten, however, when he took her shopping. He seemed to have a lot of money and urged her to pick out whatever she wanted. She chose several new pairs of 501 jeans, Reebok running shoes, underwear, and two watches.

It was like Christmas. No one had spent that kind of money on her since Leuthauser. She got caught up in the excitement and thought it was a good gag when he introduced her to various people in the stores as his wife. The day got even better when he took her to buy crack. She was soon high, and, with her mask firmly in place, willing to go anywhere.

Davis said he wanted to go on that picnic. It sounded like fun to her. She hadn't been in the mountains for what seemed like ages.

They were soon driving up Highway 119 through a narrow canyon and past the gambling town of Black Hawk. About a mile beyond the last casino, Davis turned off the highway and onto a gravel road. A little ways up the road, he pulled into a turnoff in front of an old cabin with a tin roof on the other side of the road. He parked facing the wrong direction for traffic coming down the hill, but he seemed to have been there before, so Cordova didn't worry about it.

They got out of the van. Cordova stretched as he opened the side door and carefully selected a few items for their picnic, including a little cooler with several beers and a sleeping bag to sit on.

A small but energetic stream ran alongside the path they took past the shack. They walked for a few minutes before they reached a clearing, where Davis spread the sleeping bag. Cordova sat down and took a sip from the beer he handed her. He repeated how much he loved this place as the mid-afternoon air grew warmer and the stream burbled pleasantly nearby. The next thing Cordova knew, she was waking up on the sleeping bag. Davis was gone, and she could tell by the position of the sun that she had been out for a while. Frightened, she stood up.

"Bob?" she called out. There was no answer. "Bob!" she shouted, but only the stream and the insects answered.

Cordova realized she had no real idea where she was. She hadn't paid much attention during the drive. With her fear rising in her throat, she walked quickly back down the path to the cabin. It was with a mixture of relief and anger that she saw the van. She walked back up the path to the clearing. Partway there, she stopped short. Later on, she would not know whether to describe it as a vision or a waking dream, but suddenly she saw herself lying facedown in the stream . . . dead. Her heart was pounding when she walked back into the clearing. Davis was still nowhere to be seen, but she had the distinct impression that he was watching her. Or, if not him, then something evil lurked out there in the woods, something that wanted her.

Fear had almost overwhelmed her when Davis suddenly appeared high up the trail, climbing down a steep rock face with the aid of a rope. A minute later, he walked back into the clearing. "Where have you been?" she yelled, close to tears. "I was scared."

Instead of apologizing, Davis got angry. His face flushed and he shouted back. "Don't you EVER ask me where I go. If we come up here and you want to take some time to yourself, I won't ask you a bunch of questions. The same goes for me."

Cordova was taken aback by the anger in his voice and face. Normally, she would have told a rude customer "screw you," and continued to let him have it for leaving her asleep and alone. Because of what she had felt just moments before he appeared, and the vision of her body in the creek, she stopped herself.

Instead, she cautiously sat on the sleeping bag and patted the ground next to her. "Come on, sit down," she said, smiling. "I'm sorry. I told you when we met that I'm an addict, and I'm just really, really hurting."

There, she thought, *let him "rescue" me in my time of need.* She wanted crack all right, more than ever after this escapade. Something told her she first had to be careful not to push this guy's buttons.

The strategy worked. Davis's angry countenance immediately softened. He had just one request before they left. He wanted sex now.

The demand caught Cordova off guard. She knew what the price was going to be for the clothes and cocaine. But a moment before, he had been practically screaming at her, and now he was talking about wanting to do it "doggie-style" on the sleeping bag.

Cordova shook her head. She was a prostitute, but a modest one. "Not here," she said.

When Davis protested, and began to get angry again, she suggested, "How about in the van?" He agreed.

Back in the van, he dropped his pants and again said he wanted it "doggie-style." She said she didn't enjoy that, but he insisted, starting to grow angry again, and she decided she'd better let him have his way.

The sex that followed was violent. He pulled her hair until she cried out, and thrust himself into her hard, seeming to grow more excited as she complained about the pain. "You fuckin' whore," he swore. "Bitch." He kept thrusting as she tried to tell him that he was hurting her, but that only seemed to make him thrust harder.

When he finished, he went almost immediately back to being good old Bob Davis. He explained that he had only been up the trail looking around an old mine shaft he'd seen on a previous trip when she woke up. He hadn't meant to alarm her.

They drove back to Denver and he took her out to dinner. They again spent the night in his van. The next day, he took her to buy more crack, which made her all but forget about her fear the day before.

After the purchase, Joanne Cordova returned to the van and smoked the drug. This time, however, Davis wanted to be repaid immediately.

"You got your rocks, now I want to get my rocks off," he said crudely. He suggested they have sex right there in the parking lot across the street from the dealer's house.

"Not here," she said. "Let's find some place more private."

Davis threw the van into gear. As he drove, he kept pointing to different spots and asking, "How about here? How about here?"

It was still too public for Cordova, but he was getting angrier by the minute. Desperate, she remembered the previous day; at least it had been out of the way. "The mountains," she said. "How about we go back to your favorite place?"

Davis nodded and they were soon on the highway headed west. They got past Black Hawk but never made it to the turnoff for the cabin. Davis spotted a construction site off the road, empty because it was Sunday, and veered into it and stopped the van. He ordered Cordova into the back of the van, where again the "doggie-style" sex was angry and punishing, as he swore at her and pulled her hair.

When he was through, he got back in the driver's seat and headed back to Denver. Then the car ran out of gas. He blamed her: If she'd just agreed to have sex in the parking lot across from the dealer's house, they wouldn't have been in this fix. He cursed her and grabbed a gas can, intending to walk to the nearest filling station.

"While I'm gone, fix us some sandwiches," he ordered. He handed her a knife and a can of tuna fish.

Cordova did as ordered, though it was difficult. The knife he'd given her had a long, thin blade of the sort used to fillet fish. It was so narrow, she could hardly get any mayonnaise to stay on so she could spread it over the bread.

There were any number of things Joanne Cordova would forget about that day . . . part of the effect of crack cocaine. But she would remember that knife, especially its thin, razor-sharp blade.

When the pair arrived back in Denver, he took her shopping again, as if to make up for his crude behavior. He was again talkative, telling her that he was from Iowa, where his dear mother still lived in a big white mansion. He also told her he'd been making a living as a petty thief for the past eight years, mostly as a "booster," a shoplifter. He was enamored by his own cleverness, bragging about the twenty different identification cards he carried and how he could change his looks like a chameleon to "throw off" the cops.

They spent the night in his van. The next morning, Monday, May 12, Joanne Cordova told him that she needed to be dropped off for another "appointment." She really wanted to go see her friend Jimmy and get away from Bob Davis for a while.

She agreed to meet up with him again later. It was the crack talking—neither fear of his temper, nor his violent sexual outbursts, could muffle that craving. As a token that she meant what she said, she left the black bag containing her new clothes and one of her new watches in the van. "See you in a couple of hours," she said.

When she returned at the appointed time, he wasn't there. He had still not shown an hour and a half later. Cursing herself for having left her bag in the van, Cordova called her friend Jimmy for a ride. He picked her up and they drove around looking for the blue van. At last, Jimmy had other things to do and dropped his friend back on Colfax Avenue.

A few hours later, Cordova was arrested for soliciting an undercover police officer. She complained that he'd entrapped her, but he hauled her off to jail anyway. It may well have been the luckiest arrest of her life.

Seven

Anita Paley

After dropping Joanne Cordova off, Robert Riggan didn't waste much time hooking up with another Capitol Hill prostitute. This one was named Char Fitch. Like the other women, he took her to buy crack. Apparently, Fitch, who told him to call her "Brandy," wasn't as modest as Cordova. She paid for her drugs with sex on demand in a parking lot.

Like the others, Riggan invited her to go "camping" with him. He said he wanted to take her to a cabin he knew of in the mountains. He was prepared for any eventuality, he said, noting the camping equipment in the back of the van. When Fitch's eyes rested on an ax, he noticed and laughed. "Don't worry, I'm not an ax murderer."

Fitch smiled back, despite feeling a chill when she looked in his pale eyes. She wanted no part of a camping trip with "Bob Davis." The first chance she got, she exited the van and walked away.

The next day, Fitch was back at Shane Delray's house when Riggan arrived. She didn't need the crack at the moment, having just gotten high, so she suggested to one of the younger girls that she might want to meet "the guy in the blue van." The girl was Anita Paley.

Anita Paley stood a little over five feet tall and weighed 105 pounds, which made her seem younger than her twenty-two years. Born August 8, 1974, in Portsmouth, New Hampshire, Anita was about a year old when her father left the family. After that, she, her mother, and older sister moved around quite a bit, living for a time in Virginia and then the tiny burg of Eliot, Maine, where her mother's family lived.

During her seventh-grade year, the family moved to Amesbury, Massachusetts, where her mother married Paul Bibaud. He was a good man, who treated Anita as his own daughter, adopting her and giving her his name.

Anita was a happy child, outgoing and able to make friends easily. She got good grades, went to church, loved animals, and talked about becoming not just a doctor someday, but a medical examiner. A natural athlete, she water-skied and was a star in school gymnastics programs.

But Amesbury, a suburb of Boston, was a lot larger than Eliot. There were more things for a kid to do, including more ways to get into trouble. Anita began hanging out with what her mother and stepfather considered a bad crowd.

Only fourteen, she began dating the twenty-one-year-old uncle of a classmate. His name was Aaron Paley. The Bibauds tried to discourage the relationship, but Anita refused to stop seeing Paley, who lived near her school. She was pregnant by the time her seventeenth birthday rolled around, soon dropped out of school, and had her baby on October 31, Halloween. Estranged from her mother, Anita and her infant moved into a home for unwed mothers. Aaron eventually let her and his child into his apartment and the two married the next May.

If she had been a little on the wild side before her pregnancy, the birth of her child seemed to change Anita. She was determined to be a good mother. She got her high school equivalency degree and began working at a nursing home; at the same time, she started taking courses at the local community college. She wanted to be a nurse, in particular a nurse who worked in geriatrics, having found a calling through her job in the nursing home.

Anita Paley had a second child in 1993. She told her mother that she wanted her children to have each other as they grew up. Despite her schedule, she always seemed to make time for Amelia and Abigail, reading to them, taking them on frequent excursions to the park. They were always clean, well fed, and happy. But Anita Paley was not that pulled together. Her husband rarely worked or provided much support. She'd ride her bicycle back and forth to work or school, and come home only to find that the children had not been fed or bathed. She was spreading herself too thin, and then one day, she checked herself into a local hospital to be treated for depression.

When she got out, Anita Paley went back to her family, but not for long. She soon separated from Aaron, taking the kids and moving in with her mother and stepfather. She had her certified nursing assistant's license and was working toward becoming a registered nurse, when she just quit and walked away.

Another man had come into her life in 1995. His name was Edward Neal, a traveling salesman. He convinced her to leave her children—one with her former husband and one with her former mother-in-law—while she traveled around the country with him.

Neal also introduced her to crack cocaine. He often stranded her when they had arguments, forcing her to call her parents for bus tickets to go home. Each time, though, she took him back.

In June 1996, Neal and Paley arrived in Denver, where he left her again. By this time, she was an addict with a habit to support, which she did at first by working in strip bars. But her wages and tips weren't enough to cover her craving, and in the spring of 1997, she turned to prostitution.

In April, she met Shane Delray, whose current girlfriend was in jail, so she filled the void until "Gigi" came back. Paley wanted Delray to herself, but Gigi wasn't giving him up. It was all he could do to keep them apart. Paley grew more depressed. One day, Delray found her in the bathroom cutting her wrists. She wasn't doing a very good job of it and he took her to the emergency room to get bandaged. He believed she had done it more for attention than as a serious attempt to take her life.

In April, Anita Paley met a friend of Delray's named Paul Milroy. The two men had met at a bar where Delray was a member of the band; they were an odd couple of friends. Delray was a black musician, who told police contacts that he saw himself as a sort of "street savior," trying to get hookers into another lifestyle; Milroy was a thin white carpenter.

Milroy offered Paley a room in a house he was remodeling. She could work it off, he said, by helping him paint. There was only one rule, no crack while she lived under his roof.

A kinder fate would have left them alone together. Milroy was an avid gardener and Paley loved flowers. He was in love with her and never even asked her to go to bed with him, though she once offered to pay him back for his generosity. He treated her with respect and kindness, wanting to redeem her from the streets. Instead of sex, she helped paint several rooms in the house and seemed to be regaining some of her old self back— the one with dreams, the good mother.

Milroy was even thinking about asking her to marry him when Easter weekend rolled around. However, Paley was a little down. She talked about how she was missing another Easter morning with her girls and wanted to call them and let them know that she would be home soon. Milroy told her to use his telephone and not worry about the bill.

Paley told him she had something to do first. She left the house with the flowers and the new paint job, saying she would be back soon and call her children. Then they'd have Easter dinner together. Anita Paley never came back.

Instead, Anita Paley returned to the streets. Whatever she might have felt for Milroy, or however

much she dreamed of going home to her girls, her
craving for crack proved to be stronger. She moved
back in with Delray, whom she told she had once
been diagnosed as schizophrenic. She had found a
book on that subject and was reading it on the day
when Fitch introduced her to Bob Davis.

Paley readily agreed to go out with him. She was
new to prostitution and rarely had enough money
to buy more than the smallest quantity of crack.

When she met him, she thought Davis was ugly,
but he seemed nice, especially after he bought her
crack without even asking for sex. He also invited
her to pick from a pile of new women's clothing
he had in the back of his van. Most were too big
for her tiny frame, but she did put on a pair of
lacy red underwear, as she had none of her own.

He took her shopping, where, he said, they could
exchange the other clothes for something that fit.
He told her he'd appreciate it if she'd pretend to
be his wife. She went along with the idea—why not,
she was high and happy—and seemed to enjoy
playacting for people in the store as "Mrs. Bob
Davis." She wanted to do a little pretending herself.
"I like to be called 'Buffy,' " she said. So from then
on, that's how he referred to her.

After shopping, Davis said he had something he
wanted to show her: "My favorite place in the
whole world."

Paley didn't care, a trip to the mountains
sounded fun . . . a break from her miserable existence down on Colfax Avenue. When she returned
to Delray's house in the early morning hours of
Thursday, May 15, she was distraught. Delray asked
her what was wrong.

"The guy in the blue van raped me," she said, and burst into tears. It wasn't that she hadn't expected a demand for sex, but he'd turned violent and sexually assaulted her, forcing her to submit to anal intercourse. Afterward, she said, he had settled down again and promised to buy her more crack if she would meet him later.

"What are you going to do?" asked Delray.

Paley shrugged. She could already feel the need for more crack. He really didn't hurt her and, after all, she was a prostitute. What did she expect . . . Prince Charming? She said she was going to meet him again. In the meantime, she'd just have to get over being raped.

That was easier said than done. Paley spent the rest of the morning reading the Bible on the couch, then got up and went out for a walk. While she was gone, Joanne Cordova showed up at the house.

"Hey, Jo-jo, I need to talk to you," Delray said. He guided her to a back room, where he could speak to her in privacy. "I need to ask you something and I want you to be honest with me."

"I've always been honest with you, Shane," Cordova replied. "What's up?"

"The guy in the blue van, what's he like?" Delray asked. Whatever his other shortcomings, he genuinely liked Anita. He wasn't a pimp like everyone thought, though his girlfriend often acted as a madam, taking calls, and a percentage, for the other women. He knew that prostitution was a dangerous enough business without Paley having to deal with some sick guy who got off by hurting hookers. He wanted to protect her if he could.

Cordova shrugged. She didn't really know what to think of Bob Davis—a nice guy one moment, bizarre and scary the next. "Why?" she asked.

"Anita says he raped her."

Cordova's first inclination was to wonder if Paley was just trying to get more attention from Delray, but she knew the not-so-nice side of Bob Davis and said that it was a possibility. She, too, liked Anita Paley and, though she had known her only a short while, considered her a friend. The younger woman tried to act tough, like she'd been on the streets her whole life, but Cordova thought it was all a bluff. To her, Paley seemed frail and naive . . . innocent in a world where there was no such thing anymore. She would have been surprised if Paley really knew how to get money out of a customer, or would fight for it if the customer balked after services were rendered. The girl rarely had enough money to buy enough drugs to keep her from going through withdrawals.

Paley didn't own much more than the clothes she wore. About the only items she had left of her former life were photographs of her daughters; anything else she owned she'd left at Milroy's. The children were something she had in common with Cordova, who had told the younger woman about her two children, and her own guilt about having failed as a mother. But Paley didn't want to talk much about her girls; she said it would only make her cry.

Joanne Cordova was still at the house when Anita Paley returned that afternoon to get ready for her date. She talked to her young friend, who told her about the rape.

"What?" Cordova said when she heard that Paley was planning to see Bob Davis again. She'd been looking for him ever since getting out of jail on Wednesday. "You're going to see him again? He has my clothes. Please, Anita, when you see him, grab my stuff for me." Paley said she would.

The rape was apparently already forgotten when Davis drove up and honked, because when Paley headed out the door, Cordova thought she looked happy. *He must be buying her a lot of crack,* Cordova thought, not without a touch of envy. She called after the younger woman, "Get my stuff, Anita, and I'll owe you forever."

The little blonde turned and smiled. "Okay," she shouted back. "I promise." Then she was gone.

Eight

May 18, 1997

"She's been cut . . . real deep."

Investigator Burkhalter caught the edge in pathologist Ben Galloway's voice. The doctor was nationally recognized as one of the best in his field—a veteran of more than nine thousand autopsies. It was unusual for him to show any emotion while performing this duty.

Burkhalter and the deputy district attorney Laura Reidel, who had never attended one, had asked to attend the autopsy of Jane Doe. The investigator wanted any pertinent information that might help with the investigation without having to wait for the autopsy report, which could take several days. By the sound of the doctor's voice, Galloway was talking about just such information.

It wasn't the head injury that bothered him. Detached and professional, Galloway had noted that the stellate laceration on the left side of the woman's head had "marginal abrasions" on the sides and bottom of the tear in the scalp. He also reported an oblong bruise behind her left ear. However, there were no scrapes on the ear. Nor were there scrapes on her nose, despite small abrasions above her left eyebrow, on her left cheek and chin.

The pathologist had gone on to note the various abrasions and bruises on the petite body of Jane Doe. Nothing particularly stunning there. Burkhalter was unaware of any other major injuries other than the head, and so he was surprised a little later when Galloway remarked that the woman had a cut in her vagina. A deep cut. One that obviously troubled him.

The detective paid closer attention. Galloway had been the chief Denver medical examiner back when he first started as a detective, and he had attended many such autopsies with the quiet, unassuming pathologist. He knew that what the doctor said now might be vital to the case.

First, Galloway said, speaking into a tape recorder, there were several tiny puncture wounds at the opening of the vagina, as if she had been poked by someone trying to insert a sharp point. Second, there was an inch-long laceration just inside the opening. But it was the third wound—a deep cut four inches inside the woman—that had caused the doctor to pause and remark before regaining his composure and continuing on.

The wound wasn't a jagged tear, as Galloway sometimes saw in rape victims. No, he felt that a blade had been used to inflict this wound, a very sharp blade that had pierced deep into the muscle, slicing a more than three-inch gash, and severed an artery. He had no doubt that the wound had been inflicted purposely.

Burkhalter was also stunned by the revelation. *Shit, this is worse than we thought,* he said to himself.

It wasn't some domestic dispute where a guy killed
his wife or girlfriend in a fit of anger. As a police
officer, he'd always considered a knife a particularly
vicious, and personal, weapon—not like shooting
someone with a gun. But cutting a woman there
added an element of viciousness that went beyond
rape. Whoever did this was sending a message: He
didn't like women much.

Galloway continued his examination, moving on
to the examination of the woman's interior organs,
which were normal except for the head injury that
had killed her. Based on the pattern of the injuries—the oblong bruise as well as the blow where
her scalp was split—Galloway ruled the cause of
death as "multiple blows to the head." But it was
the other injury that hung in the air like a foul
smell when the autopsy was over.

There was a murderer out there who had sexually
mutilated his victim. This was a different sort of
killer. Normal people didn't just wake up one
morning and decide to crush a woman's skull and
cut her in the most personal part of her anatomy.
If he hadn't killed before, chances were that that
sort of anger would cause him to kill again. But
where was the killer? Where was the guy in the blue
minivan?

And who was the tiny young woman lying on the
cold steel table, scarred by the pathologist's knife
as well as that of her murderer? It had been more
than twenty-four hours since she'd been brought to
the hospital, but they still had no idea who she was
or where she came from. For all they knew, she
could have been abducted from a street in Denver
or a hitchhiker picked up in another state. Her kil-

ler would be caught before they ever knew her
name.

The city of Boulder lies about thirty miles northwest of Denver and sits in a bowl nestled against the
front range of the Rocky Mountains. Although like
most Colorado cities on the east side of the mountains, it had spilled out over its natural confines into
house-farm suburbs. The old town, however, was
comprised of many beautiful neighborhoods of brick
and wood homes dating from the early part of the
twentieth century.

The Boulder population of nearly a hundred
thousand tended to be well educated and upwardly
mobile; one-third of that number were students at
the University of Colorado. Long a bastion of lib-
erals from the 1960s, many of the inhabitants had
been drawn to the area's outdoor amenities like
rock climbing, skiing, and bicycling. So it is surprising that anyone took notice of the thin man walking down a bike path that ran through one of the
neighborhoods.

Detective Norton's quick thinking had identified
a suspect, Robert Lee Riggan Jr. Now, the strategy
of asking the Denver television stations to air the
driver's license photograph of "Robert Davis" on
the television paid off twice. The first occurred
when a concerned resident called to say he thought
that he'd seen the man in the photograph walking
down the bike path. The second wouldn't be
known for several days.

Boulder had certainly had its share of murder
investigations of late. Only some five months earlier,

on December 26, 1996, the city had been shoved into the national spotlight for another murder—that of JonBenet Ramsey, the six-year-old found strangled and bludgeoned in her parents' home near the university. The case remained unsolved, and the Boulder Police Department had taken a great deal of flak for mistakes made in that investigation. This time, however, the work of its officers would be exemplary.

Shortly after 5:00 P.M., even as Dr. Ben Galloway was wrapping up the autopsy of the Jane Doe in this case, Boulder police officers Vicki Bresnahan and Curtis Johnson responded to the area and spotted the suspect. He was wearing a red-and-black checkered flannel shirt and carrying a pair of binoculars.

Bresnahan was the first to contact the suspect, drawing her gun and ordering him to place his hands on top of his head while she checked him for weapons. He was cooperative. He said he didn't have any identification on him, but gave his name as "Donald Benjamin Douglas."

Douglas said he was from California and had come to Boulder two months earlier for the rock climbing. He claimed to be on his way to meet his gay lover at a local restaurant.

Bresnahan recalled that at the morning's briefing about the Jane Doe homicide case, there'd been the mention of two tattoos. She asked Douglas if he had any. He said yes, one on his leg. She asked to see it and he pulled up his pant leg and showed her a numeral "7." She pressed him about any others, and finally he revealed "Sandy" and the multicolored rose on his shoulder.

The suspect was arrested and placed in Bresna-han's cruiser for the ride to the Boulder County jail. During the drive, he admitted to being "Robert Davis," and the driver of the van seen at the cabin.

"I didn't do it," he told Bresnahan. "It was her pimp. I know I'm in trouble, but I didn't hit her. . . . I didn't push her from the van." He asked Bresnahan if she had seen the body. "Did ya see the asphalt on her?"

The Boulder police notified Sheriff Hartman that they'd apprehended the suspect. Hartman, in turn, notified John Lauck of the Jefferson County District Attorney's Office.

Tall, brown-eyed, and balding, Lauck initially be-came a police officer in 1970 in Beaumont, Texas, because he'd needed a job. He was in college when he became engaged to his girlfriend. His folks had decided that if he was old enough to get married, he was old enough to be out on his own—which meant his college funding stopped.

A few of his classmates at the time were police officers. They told him about the opening with the Beaumont Police Department, and he'd decided there were worse ways to earn a living. He'd pushed a black-and-white for two years as a patrol officer while he finished his college education.

Two years later, he took a job as an officer with the Lakewood Police Department, a bedroom com-munity in Jefferson County, Colorado. Lakewood, like the rest of the county, was expanding rapidly and was looking for officers with college educations and street experience. He had both.

For the next six years, Lauck worked mostly as a detective in the fraud division. He liked fraud because of the challenge of trying to catch cons who spent weeks, months, years, trying to come up with the perfect get-rich scheme. He developed a knack for getting inside the heads of the cons, trying to think as they did. The best ones were great liars who knew that the secret was to tell as much of the truth as possible. They lived by their brains, and most weren't violent.

It wasn't until after Lauck quit the Lakewood Police Department and went to work for the Jefferson County district attorney in 1978 that he'd had much involvement in homicide investigations. He'd made up for it ever since.

Some were just sad cases, such as the older Hispanic man who one day had had enough of his good-for-nothing, drug-dealing son and shot him dead. When his wife raced down the hall screaming at him, he'd shot her, too. Lauck had interviewed the tiny, miserable man, and though he couldn't countenance what the man had done, he also couldn't help but feel a little sorry for him. It had been too much to take in the end, and now he had nothing but to spend his remaining days in prison.

Some were just plain evil, and it had given him a lot of satisfaction to bring them to justice. Mark Hartman and Susan Brown were a young couple who had been arrested for killing a transient—shooting him with a .38-caliber handgun and then pouring gasoline over the body and setting it on fire.

The couple claimed it was self-defense. Hartman

said he'd been changing a tire on the victim's car, a man they had met and done drugs with, when the victim suddenly came at him with a tire iron. Hartman claimed to have pulled his gun and fired up at the approaching assailant. The couple said they'd then panicked and tried to destroy the body.

Hartman had gone with Lauck to help identify the scene of the shooting, but the defendant never seemed to be able to quite pinpoint where it occurred. About a month after the murder, as the couple awaited trial, Lauck decided to find it by himself. He began by tracing the couple's known movements before and after the killing.

A local minister had recalled that a young couple, later identified as Hartman and Brown, had come to his church one evening, looking for shelter. They repaid his kindness by stealing a checkbook and other items, including a pair of blue-handled scissors.

Lauck tracked the couple from the church to a store where they had tried to pass a check but were turned down. Apparently frustrated, they'd scattered the rest of the checks in the parking lot.

As he moved on to each new point, Lauck plotted their travels on a map and used his old technique of trying to get into the minds of the people he was trying to catch. He knew they had dumped the body in an isolated area south of Denver; and he knew that on the other end of the connected dots, north of Golden, was a similar isolated area.

One Sunday afternoon, Lauck took his map and drove to an area that the dots had led him to, a dirt road that rode up and down over rolling hills in a remote spot, with few homes and few other cars. The deputy district attorneys who would be prosecuting the case, Mary Risko and Terry Gillespie, went with him, though somewhat skeptically after the detective told them how he'd arrived at his conclusion.

They reached the area and got out of the car. Lauck looked over the shoulder of the road and almost immediately saw something blue lying on the ground. It was a pair of blue-handled scissors that fit the description given by the minister. Crushed into the gravel was a pair of wire-rimmed glasses of the sort the victim was known to have worn.

Like a kid searching for arrowheads, Lauck carefully examined the ground and soon found several live .38-caliber bullets. He stepped back a few feet and saw how the ground next to where he found the bullets was discolored. He called in the crime lab technicians, who gave him quizzical looks, until their careful excavation of the discolored area turned up several spent slugs from a .38.

The discolored area was tested and revealed the presence of human blood, which was later matched to that of the victim. Lauck had found the scene of the shooting. More importantly, the trajectory of the spent slugs that had passed through the body was down—the victim had been lying on the ground when he was shot.

The pair were convicted of murder and sentenced to life in prison. Between the two, only Hartman showed any remorse or gave a reason for killing the victim. They had wanted to steal his car and rob his home of narcotics and money, which is how they'd been caught. He'd shot the victim, who had been knocked to the ground, Hartman admitted, but he wasn't the only shooter. Brown, who was into witchcraft, had taken the gun and pumped a few rounds in the still-living man "to see what it felt like."

Brown, who'd shown nothing but disdain for the police and prosecution throughout, never showed an ounce of remorse. Lauck came away from the trials believing that Hartman had been controlled by Brown, and that of the two, she was the truly evil one.

As cold-blooded as Hartman and Brown were, they could not compare to James Moulton and Ann Marie Durand. In 1985, the two lovers had killed Durand's husband, cutting off his head and burying it to make identifying the body more difficult. They'd then fled New Hampshire with Durand's three-year-old daughter, Deara Whalen.

The couple arrived in Colorado in May. Once there, they drove into the mountains, up past the town of Black Hawk, where they took a side road and found an old abandoned miner's cabin where they spent the night. When they left the area and headed south, Deara was no longer with them.

In January 1986, Moulton and Durand decided that robbing people at highway rest stops would be easy pickings. They weren't exactly subtle in their approach, killing a man at a rest stop near Pueblo by firing repeatedly through a stall door as the poor traveler sat on the toilet. The couple was arrested for that murder and authorities quickly discovered that a murder warrant had been issued in New Hampshire for the death of Durand's husband. According to authorities in New Hampshire, the couple should have had a little girl with them.

In February, a hiker made a grisly discovery, the skull of a child. A search team was organized and soon discovered a child's skeleton partly covered by large rocks. A forensic anthropologist examined the remains and concluded that they were those of Deara Whalen.

Other than assisting the lead investigator in the case, Lauck's involvement was minimal. However, this case would stay with him more than many others for which he'd taken the lead. He never got over Durand's admission of what had happened to her little girl.

While in the mountains near Black Hawk, she said, they'd decided that little Deara was too much trouble. Durand said she had tried to drown her daughter in a shallow creek, but the little girl had struggled and she had relented . . . unable to finish the deed. Moulton had no such compunctions. He'd walked over and, as Durand told authorities, "he snapped her little neck."

Eventually Moulton pleaded guilty to first-degree murder charges in order to avoid the death penalty. Durand was found guilty of conspiracy to commit first-degree murder. They were sentenced to life with enough years tacked on to ensure that they were unlikely to ever walk free again.

Eleven years later, Lauck still kept a plaster casting of Deara Whalen's skull in his office to remind him of why he did this job. Evil existed in the world and it was up to him, and others like him, to try to stop it.

Lauck sensed that he was dealing with something

evil when Burkhalter described the results of the
autopsy of Jane Doe. But it was more than that . . .
the dirt road Durand and Moulton had turned
onto from the highway out of Black Hawk was the
Old Hughesville Road. They'd spent the night in
the cabin where Jane Doe's blood had soaked into
the plywood floor. Little Deara's skeleton was discovered maybe half a mile farther up the road.

What, he asked himself as he headed out the
door and climbed in his car for the forty-five minute drive north to Boulder, *were the chances of that?*

It was almost 8:30 P.M., nearly three hours after
Riggan was arrested, when Lauck arrived at the
Boulder jail. Even then he didn't immediately rush
in to confront the suspect. First, he sat down with
Bresnahan and a half-dozen other investigators and
officers who'd had some contact with the prisoner.
He wanted to know everything Riggan had said,
most of which came from Bresnahan.

Riggan seemed to have fixated on the pretty female police officer. Shortly after being brought to
the jail, he'd been talking to Bresnahan when her
attention was distracted by a male police officer.
The prisoner yelled at her. " 'What are you talking
to him for?' . . . It was weird, it was like he was
jealous," she recalled. As though looking for sympathy, he'd also complained to her that he hadn't
eaten since before the "incident" and that he was
tired from spending the previous night hiding in a
cave in the hills.

Having heard everything they had on Riggan,
Lauck decided it was time to meet the prisoner.

When he walked into the interview room with the others, including Bresnahan, Riggan shook his head. "I ain't gonna talk to all of you," he said, "only two."

Lauck immediately recognized the con man trying to establish control. The prisoner was clever—the comment when first approached by Bresnahan about being on his way to meet his gay lover was a nifty bit of lying and demonstrated an innate knowledge of how other people reacted in certain circumstances. Gays are perceived as being passive and nonviolent. The prisoner had spent the night concocting his story and knew that the vaginal wound—if discovered—was going to be hard to explain . . . but what would a gay man be doing with a woman, much less sexually mutilating her?

Bresnahan had ignored the feint and brought in her man. Riggan was certainly an accomplished liar who thought quickly on his feet. Still, the best way to catch a liar was to get him talking and hope to trip him up.

Lauck had noticed how Riggan could hardly take his eyes off Bresnahan. He asked everyone else to leave but himself, the female officer, and Robert Lee Riggan, Jr.

With the others gone, Riggan smiled and turned his attention to Bresnahan, almost entirely ignoring Lauck. He gave the appearance of someone who really, really wanted to explain what had happened and didn't want to waste time getting to it.

Lauck tried to read Riggan his rights, but the prisoner waved him off. "She already read me my rights," he said, nodding at Bresnahan. "Let's get on with it."

"I'd like to repeat them, just to make sure you understand," Lauck said. But Riggan would have no part of it and repeated himself. "Let's get on with it."

Over the next four hours, Riggan looked at Lauck maybe three or four times. As he watched from behind a one-way mirror, Burkhalter noticed the dynamics inside the interview room. It wasn't exactly that Riggan was trying to flirt with Bresnahan. It was as though he was more confident of his ability to convince a female of his story than a male, and would then rely on the female detective to persuade her colleague.

Inside the room, Lauck was thinking that he'd seen the type before. The kind who was absolutely convinced of his ability to persuade someone that no matter how farfetched the story, he was telling the truth.

Lauck and Bresnahan were a good team, peppering Riggan with questions, and making him repeat his story to see where he was inconsistent. Sometimes they just let him ramble, occasionally tossing in a question to steer him in a direction they wanted to address.

Riggan told them that he really liked "Buffy," a prostitute he'd met on Colfax Avenue. Their time together, he said, was about more than just sex. "We had a real connection."

Riggan said he met the young woman through another prostitute. "Jo . . . Joanne . . . maybe it's Cordova. Maybe it's Jo Jo Cordova. . . . She had me hold on to her stuff, 'cause she didn't have a place to put it. . . . She's an older woman, really nice. Her ID's in the van somewhere."

He said he took Buffy shopping and bought her crack. "She had nothing. . . . She told me, 'Look, you've got to give me some underwear.' She said, 'I've got nothing under this dress.'

"We were together all day. I mean, she told me that I was the nicest guy that she'd ever met. I mean, um, she was a prostitute and all she wanted was twenty-five bucks. . . . I spent sixty-four dollars just on her tennies."

"That's pretty generous," Bresnahan noted.

"Well, no," Riggan demurred. "I liked her, and I liked Cordova, Jo Jo. I bought Jo Jo clothes, too. She stayed with me in the van for quite a while. Four or five days . . . but she wanted out."

The other girl, however, had enjoyed her time with him, he said.

"And her name was Buffy?" Lauck asked. They still had no idea who the girl was, and getting information out of the people who made Colfax Avenue their home wasn't going to be easy.

"Buffy Davis," Riggan responded. "She told them . . . she was my wife."

Riggan said he and Buffy had checked into a Colfax Avenue motel the day previous to the accident. "I paid for the room. . . . I checked in under Donna and Robert Davis."

They later went back to where "her pimp," Shane Delray, lived. Riggan said Buffy made him park and wait for her at a car wash across the street. "These girls were fucking crack heads," Riggan said, his eyes fixed on Bresnahan. "Prostitutes. The guys that took them there, the pimp didn't want them knowing where they lived . . . where they were getting crack."

"I call him a pimp," he added, "but she called him her boyfriend."

Riggan said that as he sat in the car, he could hear an argument and a struggle. Apparently, Buffy wasn't bringing home enough money. "He called her a bitch and told her she'd better be fucking taking care of business, and um . . . called her a crack head."

When she returned to the van, Riggan said, she was bleeding "a little bit" in her crotch area. "She said, 'That son of a bitch just kicked me.'" She got in the back of the van and wiped herself off with a towel he provided. She was followed to the van by the pimp who, Riggan said, he told to "get the fuck out of my van."

Smart, thought Lauck, Riggan knew he was going to have to explain why she was bleeding from her crotch. Like any good liar, he knew he was going to have to tailor his story to fit the evidence . . . and tell enough of the truth to make it seem real.

Riggan said that he and Buffy then went back to the motel. She later said she wanted to go out . . . to the mountains.

"She wanted to go to the mountains?" Bresnahan asked.

"Yeah," he agreed. "She said that she just wanted to go sit out in the mountains. She was talkin' really crazy, you know, I mean weird, weird, weird."

Buffy told him she'd been in a mental institution "for trying to kill herself and depression and all that. . . . She told me she had a kid somewhere.

But no man. And, um, she knew that she'd never get the kid back.

"Why she was tripping on that with me, I mean . . ." Riggan shook his head and didn't complete the sentence. "She got hooked on dope, and her and her old man split up, and I think that her kid is with her old man."

Riggan often repeated how much he and Buffy liked each other. "You know, I gave her forty dollars right off the bat. She only wanted thirty or twenty-five and I said, 'Look, hon . . . if you want to spend time with me so you won't have to work . . . I can pawn some of this stuff, and you can spend some time with me.' . . . You know, I just wanted to be around her. And we made love once in the van and twice in the motel room. It wasn't like . . . I mean, we took our time. In fact, she got off."

He complained that his only friends were "weird people . . . prostitutes and bums and winos. . . . I've been alone for a long time. And, uh, I do things for a lot of people, I give a lot to folks out yonder. Jo Jo can tell you that. Jo Jo lived with me in my van for a week and a half, and I never once even had sex with her."

As he spoke, Riggan kept his attention on Bresnahan and avoided looking at Lauck. He talked fast to avoid being interrupted or sidetracked. If the interrogators pushed him for more details on a subject, he'd get angry and animated and try to change the direction of the conversation. He also changed his stories.

Now it wasn't a pimp who had pushed the girl from the van. Buffy—who was wearing shorts, her new shoes, socks, and a T-shirt—jumped out of the van on Highway 119 before they reached the turn-off for the road that led to the cabin.

Over several hours, there were several variations on this story. In one, she opened the passenger door of the van and stood on the running board for "several minutes" holding a sock that contained her crack pipe in her left hand and threatening to jump before she finally did.

In another, she got high on crack in the back of the van and was talking about suicide. When she returned to the front seat, she was "real quiet for a little while. . . . And all of a sudden, she just opened the front door and got on the outside of the van. And she said, 'I'm going to kill myself.' And I said, 'No, no, no.' And you know, I looked down then, I was doing forty-five. I looked back up and she was gone."

A few minutes later, the story had grown. "I did nothing. This girl got on my door, and I begged her not to fucking jump. I told her, 'Look, don't jump. Don't jump.' And I'm slowing down all the time, trying to get her back in the van . . . and she went."

After Buffy jumped, Riggan said he could see her in the rearview mirror, lying on the highway. "So I backed up, and . . . when I got there, there's a pool of blood and she was hurt.

"She got blood all over me. I picked her up. What I was going to do was turn around and go right to Denver. I couldn't find the turnoff . . . and then I pulled off in that camping area. I was going to clean her up . . . but somebody in a black truck pulled on side, so I just left her. I figured they'd help her out."

The story was followed by another half-dozen versions of a conversation he had with Buffy after he got her to the cabin.

"I got my first-aid kit out and, uh, she was conscious. I told her I had to get her to the hospital. And . . . and she told me, 'No.' She said that she had warrants on her in New York . . . the Bronx. . . . It involved something serious.

"I told her, 'Look, I don't know what to do. I got warrants on me, too.' And I said, 'We're at this campsite where Jo Jo and me spent time.' And I said, 'You've got to get to the fucking doctor.' She was breathing real raggedy." Buffy had begged him not to turn her in.

He said that he told Buffy he was going to put her back in the van to take her to the hospital. But, "she said, 'No, just clean me up. Help me get cleaned up.' " And that's why, he said, he was dragging her to the stream.

Buffy lost consciousness after refusing to be taken to a hospital. Her breathing grew progressively worse, but for some reason he was still trying to take her to the stream to clean her up.

Riggan noted that he could have just left Buffy on the highway after she jumped and got away clean. But no, his conscience made him go back and pick her up. He'd put her head between the seats in his van so that he could talk to her on the way to the cabin.

"There was nothing I could do," he said, shaking his head mournfully. "I should have took her straight to the hospital. I should have. I got scared."

Riggan complained again that he hadn't been to

sleep for two days. He said he knew he was in trouble. "I'm looking at murder here, right?" he asked, then pointed out that the girl had been with him all day of her own free will. "I didn't rape the girl. For twenty-five dollars, I could have had her right there that morning.

"All I had to do was give her the twenty-five dollars, and I should have done it. Just 'wham-bam, thank you ma'am' . . . get the fuck out of this deal. I got a girl. She jumps out of my fucking van.

"I don't throw women out of vans," Riggan whined. "I don't beat 'em up. I don't hurt 'em. Once in a while, if I got a little money from something, I'd hook up with a prostitute."

"Why'd you take her clothes off," Lauck asked out of the blue.

The question seemed to catch Riggan off guard. He hesitated, and for one of the few times looked at Lauck with his cold blue eyes. "She asked me to," he replied with a shrug.

It was a lame answer, and everyone in the room and everyone watching behind the mirror knew it. The woman's skull had been crushed . . . cracked in half . . . she's bleeding a river from her crotch . . . why would she ask Riggan to remove her clothes, much less carry on a conversation about warrants and getting cleaned up?

But that was Riggan's story and he was sticking to it. Or, at least most of it.

For the second time in as many days, Lauck and Burkhalter left a jail together after midnight. They felt a little better than the night before. They had a suspect who they knew was lying. Now they had to put the pieces together.

Still, there was something disconcerting about Robert Lee Riggan, Jr. Call it the presence of evil . . . sometimes that was the only explanation for such a man.

Despite the late hour, Riggan wasn't through talking that night. Following the interview, Boulder police officers Curtis Johnson and Ruth Christopher transported Riggan to Gilpin County. On the way, he began talking again—a rambling, disjointed diatribe—as Christopher recorded the conversation.

"You know what?" Riggan began. "I don't even want to talk to you. Could care less. I really don't care. . . . Well, I do care; in fact, it should have been me who jumped out of the truck. It shouldn't have been her.

"I'm feeling tired. . . . I couldn't do right if I tried to, you know. Couldn't do right if I tried.

"One minute, she's telling me I'm the best guy she'd ever met; the next minute, she went stupid on me and jumped the fuck out of my vehicle. And leave me with what?"

Christopher pointed out the obvious. "Well, here you are."

Riggan ignored her and kept talking. "Spent all day boosting to give her clothes, 'cause she didn't have nothin'. . . . I should have realized that this girl was getting tweaked, and getting weird. . . . She looked back and told me she was jumping. . . . I should have yelled at her, 'Look, you know, you tell me I'm the best guy in the world, don't do this to me. Not me. Find six or seven or these other guys that you do. But please don't do this to me, 'cuz I'm just a small, petty-ass, fucking criminal, and I don't need this.' "

The prisoner looked out the window at the dark shapes of the mountains. He said he knew he should have taken her to the hospital. "I look like a piece of shit, you know. I mean I look like a piece of shit. . . . You know, I don't mind going to prison, because I'm going anyhow for check fraud, a little petty charge, again. But I don't want to go to prison with people thinking that I even hit the girl once. Because there was no need to.

". . . She told people in Sears, when we went in to pick her shoes up, that she was my wife, and I thought, you know, 'That's cool.' I really liked it. I mean that's weird that in just like twelve or fourteen hours you can actually care about somebody, but I did.

"Plus, I mean she went through over three hundred dollars' worth of crack, and I had no problem. I mean, she needed it. She told me, ' . . . If you want me to stay here, I need to do it till I fall asleep or I have to work. I'll go do a trick and you can run me out to get the dope.' I said, 'I boost more than that in a day, that's no problem. I can come up with three or four hundred a day in cash.' "

There was more silence as the road curved back into the hills he had fled two days earlier, but he couldn't stay quiet for long. "I feel fucking really rotten about not taking her to the hospital," he lamented. "You know, if I have to pay for that, I got to pay for that. But I didn't touch the girl.

"She asked me earlier what I felt about guys that had been with her. I said, 'Look . . . I been through a relationship where I had a wife that was violent . . . really sadistically violent. Jealous. You couldn't even look at somebody, and she'd start throwing pots and pans.' "

He'd never made any demands on Buffy. "I told her, 'Hey, you don't have to make love to me. I made love to a girl last night. I'm fine.' I said, 'Once a week is fine with me. I'm not into that anymore.' . . . And she said, 'Well, I need to score my dope.' "

The part he really couldn't understand, he said, was why she was holding her crack pipe in her left hand when she jumped. "Why take the pipe with you?" he asked his escorts, who didn't answer and just let him keep talking. "I haven't figured that one out at all. I was so mad, I kicked the pipe. It was laying there beside her and I kicked the fucking pipe over near the fucking guardrail."

Riggan asked if investigators had found the pipe or her blood on the highway yet. The Boulder officers said they didn't know. "Come on," he offered, "I'll show you where it is. I've been up there three times, twice with Jo Jo and once with her.

"I'll know from the bloodstain, unless we've had a horrible rain. . . . I picked the girl up, and there's blood all underneath her, so I know that if you follow along that white line, somewhere close to Black Hawk, you'll find the blood."

Riggan told Christopher and Johnson that he'd bought his van and equipped it so that he could survive a long time on his own, so that he could get away from all his troubles. But now, "I think they oughtta just lock me away, and leave me be. . . . I don't want no one around me. . . . I don't want no responsibilities and that goes for my two kids . . . 'cuz that's just bad news all the way around.

"Every time I get close to somebody, it's just bad news. Bad luck. Bad luck for me. Bad luck for them. The only way I can really survive is to be alone."

Nine

Robert Riggan, Jr.

Dennis Goodwin pulled into the motel parking lot. The day was already warm and the Nebraska afternoon smelled like fertile earth and growing things. He was in a small town, surrounded by farms, the sort of place, he thought, that a person could raise children in and not have to worry about their safety if they were out playing after dark. Or, the sort of place one could disappear in, live a quiet life.

Although he was the newly appointed chief investigator for the Jefferson County District Attorney's Office, Goodwin, a short, intense 40-year-old, was taking a backseat to Lauck and Burkhalter on this one. His job was to travel east of Colorado to learn what he could of Robert L. Riggan's past. His first stop was Nebraska to find, if his information was correct, Riggan's first wife, Judy.

Goodwin found her at a motel where she and her husband worked. He went up to the front desk and asked for Judy, who soon appeared. She was a small, attractive brunette, who paled when he told her who he was and why he was there. She already knew a little bit—one of the Denver television station's signals reached this far into Nebraska—and she'd been startled one evening to see her former husband's face on the TV screen. It didn't surprise her that he had been charged with killing a woman, she said. She was distressed, however, that he had been able to find her and disturb her peace, even if it was just through the television, and now, this visit from an investigator.

Judy was clearly afraid, even though the investigator's information showed that she'd been divorced from Riggan for a dozen years. Goodwin wondered what her ex could have done that she would still be looking over her shoulder, but it must have been pretty bad. With the memory of Burkhalter's description of the autopsy fresh in his mind, it brought back his own recollection of another man who had been accused of doing horrible things to women.

As a young criminology student at Florida State University (FSU) in January 1978, Goodwin was working as an intern for the Tallahassee Police Department when a man broke into the Chi Omega sorority house at night and killed two women and bludgeoned three others who survived. The police had a partial description of the suspect as being about five foot eight inches with brown hair. To his chagrin, the description fit Goodwin, who noticed that women would not make eye contact with him when he was walking across the expansive FSU campus.

Goodwin had been on police ride-alongs. He'd seen bodies and thought he'd developed a pretty thick skin. But this was the first time he'd felt any personal effects from a crime. His community, the place he lived and the people he knew, had been invaded by some sort of evil. That made him angry, but there was also a feeling of frustration for not being able to do anything about it.

A few weeks after the attacks on the coeds, the body of a twelve-year-old girl was found in a pigsty in another part of the state. A short time later, a state trooper pulled over a stolen van driven by Theodore "Ted" Bundy, who was suspected of raping and murdering women in Washington, Utah, and Colorado—from which he had escaped custody while being held for a killing in Aspen. He was soon connected to the murders of the girl and the coeds.

As an intern, Goodwin was given the job of transporting some of the evidence to the courthouse for hearings. It was there he first encountered the man who had caused such terror and was surprised to see, not a monster, but a trim, almost dapper, man. The first thing that struck him was that everybody—including the prosecutors and police who wanted Bundy to get the death sentence—referred to this man as "Ted." Not "the defendant," not "Mr. Bundy," just Ted, like they were talking about a naughty but likable younger brother.

As his reputation indicated, Bundy was a real charmer. Cordial. Friendly. Chatting it up with his guards. Smiling at visitors, including women who came out of curiosity or because they, too, had been charmed into the possibility of his innocence. Yet this was a man who attacked women with such savagery—including sexual mutilation—that his teeth-marks in the breast of one of his victims was what helped doom him.

Goodwin was asked to escort the surviving witnesses into the courthouse and up the elevator to the courtroom. The ride seemed to last forever, standing in silence, not knowing what to say. The women were obviously frightened that they were going to have to see their nightmare in the flesh, and he wished there was something he could tell them to make them feel better. Instead, he tried not to stare but couldn't help but see some of the scars they still bore on their faces and heads from Bundy, the man who smiled and joked in the courtroom as though in trouble for an unpaid traffic ticket.

At first glance, Bundy didn't look like a monster, but Goodwin had seen something when Ted wasn't onstage. He'd seen how Bundy's eyes turned as dark and emotionless as those of a shark swimming past the window in an aquarium. Eyes that saw other people, women in particular, as prey.

Bundy was convicted of the three Florida murders. He eventually confessed to thirty-five more, though authorities believed that number might actually be closer to one hundred. Still, it took more than ten years of appeals and legal wrangling before Bundy was executed in January 1989 in the electric chair. But that was long after Goodwin had left the state.

Approaching his graduation from FSU in May 1979, Goodwin had applied to what were thought to be the most progressive police departments in the country. Number two on his list was the Lakewood Police Department, an agency that even his professors called "the fancy department with all the college graduates and blazers"—a reference to the criteria that all officers have a minimum of a bachelor's degree and wore blazers of light blue rather than traditional uniforms.

In Lakewood, a bedroom community pressed up against the mountains northwest of Denver, he'd served six years as a patrol officer and then another eight as a detective in the Juvenile and Crimes Against Children units. The stint in the latter reminded him that Bundy, while in a class all his own, was not alone in the world.

The cases that bothered him in particular were those in which the parents—not some brutal stranger passing through—hurt their children. He couldn't imagine how someone could live with that on their conscience, and he continued to work on one case long after he left the department.

With other cases, he had more success. One involved Charles Presley, an eighteen-year-old with a juvenile record for auto theft, who was suspected of luring a little girl out of her apartment bedroom in the middle of the night and then raping her in a courtyard between the buildings. There was no telling how the incident would have ended otherwise, but another man heard the child crying and ran outside. He surprised the attacker, who jumped up and fled without his shirt. The Good Samaritan gave chase, but barefoot, he lost the suspect crossing a field.

The Good Samaritan heard police sirens approaching and panicked. He was an ex-con and there he was running around without a shirt or shoes with a little girl having been raped outside his apartment window. He dove under a car where he was found; the scratches on his body from his escape attempt made him look even worse. However, his good deed did not go unrewarded. The shirt left behind at the scene contained court documents with a name on them, Charles Presley, whom Goodwin arrested.

It was one of those cases that got better as it went along and taught Goodwin about the value of catching a defendant telling lies. Presley wouldn't talk to him, but the young man did talk to his father, who believed his son and in turn told Goodwin, trying to convince the detective of his son's innocence. In that way, Goodwin learned what Presley was going to say in his own defense as far as alibis and to explain the presence of his shirt at the scene, and the detective was able to quickly investigate and discount Charles's stories as lies. His story disputed in the courtroom by Goodwin's testimony, the young man was convicted of sexual assault and sent to prison for twenty-three years.

Goodwin had just about had his fill of more lies listening to the tape recordings of the interviews with Robert Riggan, Jr. as he headed east for Nebraska and Iowa to learn what he could about the suspect. After coming to the district attorney's office in 1994 as an investigator in that agency's Crimes Against Children unit, he'd been involved in investigating a number of homicides that became death penalty cases and had become the sort of resident expert in the office at interviewing potential witnesses should a trial move to that sentencing option.

Except under unusual circumstances, a defendant's character (except as it relates to the current case) and criminal past can't be used against him during a trial under the pretext that he should only have to defend himself against the immediate charges. To this end, defendants are often "cleaned up" by their defense attorneys and allowed to appear before juries dressed in civilian clothes to avoid having jurors judge them by their appearance or the fact that they may have lengthy criminal histories.

However, if the defendant in a capital—or death penalty—case is found guilty, the trial then moves to the sentencing phase, essentially another trial in which the prosecution and defense battle over whether the defendant should be put to death. Here, the issues of character, including his or her participation in other, possibly related crimes, are allowed into evidence. Therefore, investigators for both sides beat the bushes looking for examples— good and bad—to support the arguments of the attorneys they work for; the only difference is, investigators for the prosecution are required to turn over everything they find to the defense, and the defense has no such burden.

The prosecutors assigned to the Riggan case, senior deputy district attorney Dennis Hall and deputy district attorney Pete Weir, had already discussed the possibility that they would seek the death penalty. The sexual mutilation of the victim had pushed this murder to a whole new level of brutality. However, the prosecution team was feeling its way through what were uncharted waters. In most states, the decision to sentence the accused to death or life in prison following these mini-trials was left up to the trial juries. The Colorado legislature had recently taken that decision from the backs of the jurors and created three-judge panels to hear the sentencing arguments and render a decision. The idea was that judges would be more likely to follow the letter of the law, rather than be swayed by emotional arguments. The Riggan case was slated to be one of the first to go before the panel of judges, but no one knew how that might change their strategy. The prosecutors and investigators decided that it was better to learn all they could about Riggan.

That meant that the investigators needed to move, and move quickly. Goodwin had learned the hard way in previous death penalty cases that if the prosecution team didn't get to the potential witnesses, the defense attorneys' investigators would. Even family members of defendants would often talk candidly about the defendant with prosecution investigators if they got there first, but if the defense investigators beat them to it, they could convince the witnesses that their counterparts were only "trying to kill" their son, or brother, or friend. More than one door had been slammed in Goodwin's face as a result of being too slow.

A few days after Riggan was apprehended, Goodwin found himself in a car heading east on Interstate 80. There hadn't even been enough time to listen to the interview tapes at the office, so he'd made copies and listened as he drove across the Great Plains.

In late spring, the world outside the car was a vibrant green as the crops of corn and wheat and soy began to sprout. The countryside was so full of life, which seemed a cruel irony to Goodwin as he listened to Riggan whine about how he was being falsely accused while hardly mentioning the girl he'd been with who was now dead.

At least they now had the name of their victim: Anita Paley. How they got the name made a strange case even stranger. The information had come from a prostitute named Joanne Cordova, who'd been in contact with Burkhalter. She'd supposedly spent some time with Riggan just prior to Paley's death and was going to be an invaluable witness. But the strange part was that, according to Burkhalter, she was a former Denver cop. He wondered how somebody who apparently had so much going for her could have fallen so far . . . but that would have to wait.

The first stop in Goodwin's travels was the small town in Nebraska. Boulder sheriff's detective Norton's work had produced an extensive history of Riggan's criminal background, including the fact that he had twice been arrested for sexual assault. Nothing apparently had ever come of the charges, but one of the victims was Riggan's second wife, Sandy. Before he got to her, Goodwin wanted to talk to the first wife, Judy, who had also shown up in the records.

Judy said it had been years since she'd had any contact with Riggan. She wished it had stayed that way. She lived in a nice home now, with a good man for a husband with whom she was raising a happy family of kids, including the two sons she'd had with Riggan.

Now she was frightened. She'd thought that she would be hard for anyone to find outside of her family. Obviously, however, Goodwin had no trouble. "You found me, what's to say he won't," she told him. Despite her fear, she was willing to help by telling her story.

Some of the events leading up to their meeting, Goodwin wouldn't learn until later. Riggan didn't last long in the Navy, a period of time during which his criminal nature was quite evident. In June 1978, he was arrested for contributing to the delinquency of a minor, a young female. That was followed a month later with an arrest for armed robbery during a drug buy. While in the brig, he threatened to commit suicide and superficially cut his wrist. That got him transferred to the hospital from which he soon escaped and went AWOL before he was caught and brought back.

Riggan was certainly a talker. He even got several California state congressmen involved when he accused his superiors of being on drugs and having him beat up. Nothing, of course, came of the allegations. It was just a Riggan smoke screen, but it demonstrated that he had a way of convincing almost anyone of almost anything.

He was still blowing smoke in 1980 when he claimed to have fallen down a ladder on a ship and injured his head. He reported hearing voices commanding him to harm himself. It was determined later that the only injury he'd suffered was hurting his knee when he fell down some steps . . . but at the time it got him sent to the Navy hospital from which he went AWOL again. This time, he would be absent for six years, even though he managed somehow to get himself marked "present" at roll call and even got his paychecks sent to him at his father's address in Iowa.

Judy met him in 1983 when they were both working at a nursing home in Cheyenne, Wyoming. He said his name was Curtis Eugene Reimers. He was a real charmer who could talk his way into or out of any situation. But he seemed nice and treated her with kid gloves.

The gloves came off on their wedding night, June 4, 1983. Throughout the wedding and reception, he was the solicitous, loving bridegroom. But when he got her up to their hotel room, his demeanor changed. She was now his and he expected her to submit to his desires.

Sitting across from Goodwin, her head down and voice quiet, Judy paused. It was obvious to him that she was struggling not to cry. Finally she pulled herself together enough to go on. Her new husband had tied her to the bed and then forced her to have anal intercourse.

"I told him it hurt, but he wouldn't stop," Judy said in almost a whisper. When the nightmare of her wedding night was at last over, he told her she was "the coldest cunt I ever fucked."

The tears were coming unchecked now, and Goodwin gave her the time to recover. He was beginning to get an idea of why this pretty young woman was so afraid, but there was more to come.

Reimers, the only name she would know her husband by for a long time, reverted the next morning back into his old charming self. From then on, her marriage would resemble a roller-coaster ride of emotions in which he would be nice and loving, and then, often without warning, another side of him would erupt.

A year after their wedding, she said, they'd moved to Douglas, Wyoming. He quit his job, bought a big-screen television, and would sit home all day watching porn movies and drinking with his buddies while she worked, even though she was pregnant. In June 1984, a daughter, Ann, was born.

Judy hoped that the baby would settle her husband down, but he had other plans. He tried to get her to go for wife swapping and having a male friend to come over for three-way sex. When she wouldn't, he'd curse her and sneer degrading things about what he said was her lack of sexuality. Then he might disappear for several days and refuse to say where he'd been.

Although he didn't have a job, Reimers always seemed to have money. She soon discovered why, when he began involving her in all sorts of scams from getting a houseful of furniture by applying for credit under fictitious names to having her sign up for welfare under false pretenses.

Reimers seemed to have what she thought was an unusual interest in guns, and this from a woman whose father was the police chief of a small town in Wyoming. He sometimes threatened her with them, though usually in a subtle way, but enough that one day she called the police to respond to the trailer where they lived so that she could gather her things and move out safely.

She should have stayed away, she told Goodwin. But Reimers didn't easily give up something he considered his property. He turned on the charm, begging her to come back, promising to change . . . and she relented. Almost immediately he suggested that they move to Phoenix, Arizona, for a fresh start. He wouldn't even let her tell her family that they were going.

Judy's father grew alarmed when he couldn't locate his daughter and put out a national advisory to other police departments to be on the lookout for her. He grew even more worried when he discovered that Curtis Reimers was actually a man named Robert Riggan. What did this guy have to hide?

The couple were eventually found in Phoenix, where Riggan was still using the Reimers name. While in Phoenix, Judy told Goodwin, her husband would not allow her to make any friends or have a driver's license. He'd disappear, sometimes for several days at a time, but if she asked him where he'd been, he'd explode in anger. Despite his sexual proclivities, her husband was insanely jealous, accusing her of sleeping with any man whom she even dared talk with. At the same time, she began getting telephone calls from women asking for "Bobby," some even saying that this Bobby owed them money for sex.

Judy began to worry about her own safety one day when a mysterious fire broke out in a china hutch they had in their trailer. Normally, she and the baby would have been in the trailer, and maybe trapped by the smoke and flames, but that day they'd gone out.

Two days after they were found in Phoenix, Riggan moved his family to Everett, Washington, near Seattle, and changed his name to Tom Stone. He continued to run scams for money and goods. If he felt the heat was about to come down on them, they'd move . . . sometimes leaving all their household goods, most of them acquired under false pretenses, anyway.

In December 1985, the family was living in Portland, Oregon, where a second child was born. With bills coming in from the hospital, Riggan moved his family back to Des Moines and an apartment in a poor part of town. Back on his home turf, the anger and meanness he'd demonstrated in the past escalated. If Judy used the wrong false name, he would hit her. If she failed to respond sexually in the way he demanded, he'd hit her for that, too. The blows were never to the face—he was too smart, even in his rages, and careful not to cause injuries that someone else would notice; the blows were always to her ribs, or the side and back of her head. He kicked her several times in the crotch, drawing blood. The verbal abuse was nearly as bad. She was a whore, and he was sure she was sleeping around behind his back.

Riggan lied like some people breathe. He told her he was a Vietnam veteran who'd been wounded in combat. He apparently had a good line for just about everybody, even prostitutes who continued to call her demanding money for services rendered to her husband.

Riggan seemed to delight in tormenting her. The projects were infested with rats, which found their way regularly into the apartment, where she feared they might harm her or her children. "But if I complained," Judy said, shuddering at the memories, "he would kill one with his bare hands and throw it at me."

One day, Judy finally decided she'd had enough of the name-calling, the blows, and the thrown rats. "I thought, 'Anything is better than this,' " she told

Goodwin. "I told him, 'I can't take it anymore, I'm leaving.' "

Riggan's response was to pick up an Uzi submachine gun and riddle a living room wall with a stream of bullets. "He said, 'If you ever try to leave me again, that will be you, you fuckin' cunt.' "

As she got further into her story, Judy paused often to wipe her eyes and take a deep breath before plunging on. The pause was particularly long as she prepared to tell the investigator about the day her husband sent her on an errand to the store. When she returned and walked into the bathroom, she saw her husband holding their infant son underwater in the bathtub. He hadn't heard her return and so she got a good look before he noticed her rushing to the aid of the child. He was definitely holding the struggling child's head beneath the water, but he explained that the child had slipped while he was trying to give him a bath.

Again, Judy knew that she should leave her husband before he killed her or one of the children, but she didn't know how. The memories of the submachine gun bullets peppering the walls, and his threat that she would be next if she left, were too fresh. To be honest, she didn't want to believe that her husband—the sweet-talking charmer who'd swept her off her feet—would try to drown his own child. But she knew he had, adding, "For a long time after that, Michael would scream if any man came near him or even if I wanted to bathe him," she said.

As if it would make her forget what she'd seen, Riggan soon moved his family to Montana. Once again, he left a trail of angry creditors, including family members and friends, whom he'd ripped off.

In Montana, he had Judy apply for welfare again, but this time she was turned down, which earned her a beating from her husband.

Riggan moved them to Denver, where he thought it would be easier to get welfare and run more scams in a larger city. She tried to be a good wife, give him what he wanted, but nothing seemed to appease him or temper his anger. He was beating her up as often as twice a week, she told Goodwin. He seemed to have a thing, even in her presence, of stopping to talk to prostitutes in Denver's seedier sections.

One day, after knocking her around, he turned on their son, Michael, and beat him with a running shoe. Finally Judy had had enough and called the police, as well as a cousin who lived in the city, to come rescue her. But it wasn't so easy getting away from Robert Riggan Jr.

Three days later, Riggan kidnapped his daughter, Ann. He called Judy and told her that she would have to have sex with him and promise to take him back if she wanted Ann. Afraid for her daughter's life, she agreed and submitted to his sexual demands when she met him. But once she had her child, Judy wouldn't take him back. Neither did she go to the police. She was married to him and didn't think the police would believe she was anything but an upset housewife. Instead, she called her parents and asked them to come get her and take her back to Wyoming.

Judy said it wasn't until much later that she learned that her husband had done worse than coerce sex from her or kidnap her daughter. Apparently, her husband had carried on an old family tradition. Many years later, when she was a teenager, Ann revealed, "He raped me, Mom."

The words hung in the motel room air. Judy's voice was low, sad, and resigned. After a moment, she went on to the finish. Riggan stole a car and tried to follow her and his children to Wyoming, but he was arrested for vehicle theft in Casper. She never saw him again, or at least she was never sure she had, though there were times, still, when she would turn and think she caught a glimpse of him. He had called her several times after their divorce . . . which had frightened her, not so much because of what he said, but because no matter how often she moved, or changed her telephone number, he always seemed to be able to find her.

Finally she'd settled in the Nebraska town to live quietly and thought she'd finally rid herself of Robert Riggan, Jr. Yet even here, he'd found a way to insinuate himself into her life.

Goodwin left Judy at the motel. This was just the first interview and already he had no problem believing that Riggan was the sort of man who could easily kill a woman and leave her body in the woods. As he drove his car, heading farther east, he had a feeling that this opinion of Robert Riggan would only grow.

"You must be the PO-lease."

Goodwin looked up at the obese woman sitting in a wheelchair on the front porch of the dilapidated wood-frame house who had called out to him when he was hardly out of the car. "And you must be Henrietta," he replied.

Whatever he believed about Riggan, Goodwin was realizing that this case had a variety of characters that the most fertile mind in Hollywood would have a hard time imagining: Joanne Cordova, the cop-turned-crack-addicted-prostitute, Robert Lee Riggan, Jr., a man who'd killed rats with his bare hands and used them to torment his own wife.

Now, here was Henrietta who, Goodwin learned, was apparently Riggan's half sister. He'd found her through yet another interesting character, a man named David Marker, who was the president of a college in Iowa, and yet had some sort of friendship with Riggan. Oddly, Marker had reported his sports car stolen, but when Riggan was apprehended in it, he'd refused to press charges. Marker told Goodwin that he found the high school dropout to be an interesting fellow, "well read" he said, and considered him a sort of reclamation project. Marker was friendly and told Goodwin how to find Henrietta who, he said, was the last person Riggan had been living with before leaving for Colorado.

"I drove all the way from Colorado to talk to you," Goodwin told her now as he walked up to the porch.

"Well, then you oughtta get to it," she said with a smile.

Goodwin took a seat and surveyed his surroundings. He'd been warned by the Des Moines police, whom he'd contacted to say he was in town, that the area he was in was one with the highest crime rate in the city, a drug neighborhood whose inhabitants didn't think much of the police. The yards, if they could be called that, were littered with a variety of flotsam and jetsam—from automobile parts to shopping carts—whatever came to rest on a piece of property for a few hours was left there apparently forever.

The house where Henrietta lived was in an equal state of disrepair. What little paint was left on the structure was flaking off, and such a stench emanated from the interior that Goodwin was relieved not to be invited inside to talk. Henrietta herself sat in a creaky old wheelchair that appeared to be in danger of collapsing beneath her bulk. He didn't realize it at the time, but he was looking at a younger version of Riggan's mother, Vernice, who, her daughter told Goodwin, had died in 1993.

Henrietta wasn't surprised that her half brother was in trouble with the law. However, she found it hard to believe he was guilty of killing a woman. "He might hit a man," she said, "but I don't think he'd hit a woman." But she didn't ask to know any details of the murder and seemed more concerned that "Bobby," as he was known to the family, had taken one of her bedspreads when he left. She wanted to know if she could get it back.

Other than Bobby's penchant for petty crimes, Goodwin didn't learn a lot from Henrietta, except for the address of his father, and that the Riggan family seemed to be a tragedy waiting to happen.

Henrietta's son was in prison for sexually molesting a young girl. She made no excuses for him, it was just a fact. Her daughter, Theresa, however, had been a saint. But, Henrietta told him tearfully, she'd been murdered in 1978—shot down in the street near the house.

Goodwin would have liked to ask what the shooting was about. Judging by the occupants and visitors who tromped in and out of the house where Henrietta rented a room, giving him the eye, he figured it was likely drug related. But he could tell that aspect of the Riggan family history was something Henrietta wasn't going to discuss with him.

Goodwin's next stop was a little farther out in the countryside, where Robert Lee Riggan, Sr. lived. While not such an urban blight, the man's yard mimicked those of its city cousins with an assortment of debris, including an old rusty lawnmower that appeared to have been abandoned right where it had quit in the midst of tall weeds.

The house was cluttered, but it wasn't dirty and didn't smell when he was invited inside. A motley collection of dogs and cats—some known and others not—rambled in and out at will.

Goodwin's host was tall and skinny. The detective figured he must be in his eighties, but he said he was still doing manual labor for other people in the neighborhood. Some of the reason for that was his son, said the elder Riggan.

Bobby was a scam artist, he said. "He'd bar-rah money from friends of mine on some sob story or t'other, and never would pay 'em back." The old man complained that he'd spent his life savings and was still taking on work too strenuous for a man his age to make up for Bobby's thieving ways. He suspected him of starting a fire that had burned his home to the ground.

Henrietta and her brother, George, were his dead wife's children. "But they ain't mine," he said. They had been fathered by his wife's brothers.

What's more, he said, he'd caught his son in bed having sex with Bobby's stepniece, Theresa, when the boy was a teenager.

Bobby had mistreated and beat his second wife, a Des Moines girl named Sandy, and neglected the two children they'd had together. "I'd go over to their house and there'd be flies swarmin' all over the baby's eyes and nose, but he wouldn' do nothin' about it."

Robert Riggan was worried about his comments getting back to his son, who, he said, was violent and unpredictable. "He tol' me he was gonna kill me, or git someone else to do it. . . . He says he's killed people before."

Bobby had called him about the trouble he was in . . . something about a girl jumping from his van. "He said he tried to save her."

Goodwin found Sandy living in a Des Moines apartment complex. She wasn't in the first couple of times he stopped by, but she called him in the evening. She wanted to know first of all who he was with: the prosecution or the defense attorneys. She didn't want anything to do with Riggan or his attorneys but invited him over when he explained that he worked for the other side.

Sandy was short and attractive, a lot like Judy . . . and the victim out in Colorado, Goodwin reminded himself. She was worried about what "Bobby might do" if he found out she was talking to the police, but on the other hand, she wanted to help. So the next four hours, he sat in her kitchen and listened to how another woman had suffered at the hands of Robert Riggan Jr.

One night in April 1988, Sandy was walking down a Des Moines sidewalk on her way to work when a man stopped her. He asked if she knew where the federal building was located. Sandy, just seventeen, did her best to give the man, who said his name was "Bob," directions. When he continued to express confusion, she invited him to accompany her to her job, where someone might better be able to help him.

When he got the directions he was after, Bob asked Sandy if he could have her telephone number and address. She hesitated. He was older, by eleven years it would turn out, and, she thought, ugly. But the more he talked and teased, the more she started to like him. At last, she relented.

Just like he said he would, Bob dropped by to visit the next day. He was funny and obviously taken with her when he insisted that she go out with him. Their romance blossomed quickly.

Sandy was a girl from the wrong side of the tracks and a high school dropout, but he treated her like she was the most intelligent, desirable woman in the world. The boys she had gone out with were interested only in getting into her pants. Bob was interested that way, too, but he also spoke to her about other things, and listened when she wanted to talk. He had such great stories, telling her that he worked for "Naval Intelligence." She didn't know whether to believe him, but she didn't really care. Nor did it matter to her that her parents didn't like him. She wanted to party and Bob was a party guy.

His favorite thing to do was shop. He liked new things like nice clothes, which he also lavished on her, but he especially loved electronics equipment like stereos. It stemmed from growing up poor, he explained to Sandy. There were a lot of kids in his family, he said, and he'd felt deprived and angry his whole childhood. "My clothes were always shitty-looking."

Except for such short-lived outbursts, Riggan wasn't especially forthcoming about his early years. His natural mother had died when he was young, he said, and he hated his stepmother. She was mean, he said. Whenever he got into trouble, she'd cut a switch from a willow tree and beat him with it. He wasn't the only one she'd hit. His stepmother was extremely jealous, he said. If his father so much as talked to another woman, she'd beat up her rival and "call her a whore."

The name seemed to be a favorite term for women who came near the men in her family . . . at least according to Bob. Soon after he and Sandy met, he took her over to his parents' home. The visit seemed to go well enough, but as Bob drove Sandy home, he blurted out, "My mom's a bitch."

"Why?" Sandy asked, wondering about the sudden invective.

"She called you a whore," he said.

Sandy would never know if what he said was the truth. Every time they visited his parents after that, his "stepmother," who only much later did Sandy learn was his real mother, never said anything rude or out of place. She wasn't especially nice to her, but then she didn't seem especially nice to anyone, including her son.

Riggan talked Sandy into running away to California with him. Somehow he'd got his hands on a fancy new sports car, and she'd happily climbed in for the trip west. He knew a lot of people in California and they went to party after party, sleeping wherever they ended up that night. He seemed to be able to talk his way into and out of anything. When they were in San Diego, he marched her into an accounting office at the naval base and pretended to be an officer. He told the clerks that she was the wife of a fellow officer who was out at sea, and that she was pregnant and needed an "emergency loan." He pulled that scam off three times at $500 a pop.

However, his luck seemed to run out when he was pulled over by the police and arrested for car theft. They also found an old warrant for escape from Wyoming. The police wanted to know what he was doing with such a young female. Riggan told them that he was "rescuing" her—that when he met her, she was working as a prostitute and living with two male drug addicts.

The police discovered that Sandy had been reported as a runaway and soon she was on her way back to Iowa. They sent Robert Riggan to Wyoming, where once again, he managed to get by with a slap on the wrist. He was sentenced to 270 days in jail, 180 of which were suspended. As soon as he got out, he returned to Iowa, where he fetched Sandy and they were on the road again.

Sandy was soon pregnant with their first child, and the couple was soon wed. She believed that

Bob Riggan was the man she would grow old with, especially after he tattooed her name on his shoulder along with a multicolored rose. If there was anything that told her the future might not work out that way, it was the fact that Riggan was an inveterate petty criminal. They traveled all over the country—California, Montana, Arizona, Nevada, Washington, and Colorado—living off his scams. He wrote bad checks or used stolen credit cards to "buy" what he didn't just simply shoplift.

A regular chameleon, he sometimes passed himself off as a lawyer, or as a doctor and her as a nurse. The number of people, including well-educated professionals, who believed whatever story he told them, never ceased to amaze her. He would steal a car by walking into a dealership and asking to take a test drive, leaving his never-ending supply of false identification behind as his assurance that he'd return the vehicle.

From time to time, they'd return to Des Moines, where in April 1989, agents of the Bureau of Alcohol, Tobacco, and Firearms (BATF) responded to an advertisement in the newspaper for someone selling submachine guns. The ad had been placed by Riggan. Undercover agents contacted Riggan, who showed them an assembled Sten Mark II submachine gun, as well as parts for more of the guns. Identifying themselves, the agents told him they believed the guns were illegal and asked him to turn them over, which he did. They told him that if he tried to sell similar weapons again without a permit, he'd be arrested.

On June 1, 1989, Sandy gave birth to Robert Lee Riggan III. But neither the fact that he was the father of a newborn nor that he was not licensed to sell machine guns stopped Riggan's criminal behavior. On June 9, police officers in Omaha, Nebraska, saw a white male displaying submachine guns to street gang members. According to the police reports, the youths appeared to be fifteen to sixteen years old. The man was accompanied by a teenage boy and driving a hatchback car with Iowa license plates. They pulled the car over. In the back of the car, the officers could see the assembled weapon and several boxes of machine gun parts, enough for eighteen more guns. The police arrested Riggan, who gave them the false name of Michael Roe, a mentally retarded man he'd known while in the Seattle area.

An ATF agent interviewed Scott, the fifteen-year-old brother of Sandy, who said Riggan had received the guns via UPS from a company in Nevada. He said he had assisted loading the boxes and accompanied Riggan to Omaha. The Omaha police charged Riggan, who in July 1989 served ten days for the offense, with giving false information to the police.

The gun charges they left to the federal government. Through his court-appointed attorney, Riggan contended, "I saw an ad in *Shotgun News,* a national magazine, for gun kits. My father-in-law bought them through the mail from Global Sales, a company in Las Vegas, Nevada.

"Global told us that the guns did not need to be registered, and I believed them because they had a letter from the head of BATF. When the BATF agent in Des Moines came to my house and told me that selling them was against the law, I didn't believe them because Global Sales was still selling the guns.

"I took them to Omaha to sell them to pawn-shops. Omaha police officers saw the gun boxes and one gun I assembled for display purposes in the back of my car when I stopped at a grocery store. The display gun was clearly visible and I made no attempt to conceal that gun or the gun boxes."

On September 14, 1989, a Nebraska grand jury indicted Riggan on two counts: that he was not licensed to transport such weapons across state lines; and that he transported submachine guns across state lines that were not registered to him in the National Firearms registration record.

On September 29, 1989, Riggan was arrested on the federal gun indictment. He was released on his own recognizance on October 6, but he screwed up and was taken back into custody on November 3, 1989. In jail, he was prescribed Meloril, as well as Narvane and Cogentin—common treatments for depression.

In April 1990, when he pleaded guilty to one of the charges in exchange for the second being dropped, his wife was pregnant with their second child. In June, Sandy gave birth to Thomas Santana Riggan in Des Moines; a month later, young Thomas's father was sentenced to five years in prison. However, he was allowed out in September while his case was appealed.

Despite so much hanging above his head, Riggan seemed unable, or unwilling, to change his ways. In October of that year, Sandy said, Riggan picked up a nine-year-old girl, posing as a friend of the family, at her school. Instead of taking her home, he drove her to a remote area in the countryside, where he exposed himself to her and molested her before returning her to her family. The incident was reported to the Des Moines police. For unknown reasons, Riggan was never contacted about the allegations, nor were charges ever filed.

Even the feds, when they went looking for him after he lost his appeal, had him slip through their fingers. Riggan, using the alias of Mike Roe, and Sandy had moved to Denver, where she got a job at a Denny's restaurant while he continued his life as a thief.

Her husband was changing, Sandy told Goodwin. He was gone from home a lot, sometimes all night. She suspected that he might be seeing other women. But asking him where he'd been would only make him go into a rage. To make matters worse, he was constantly accusing her of cheating on him. "You're a whore," he'd rant and demand to know who she was seeing. His accusations began to escalate into hitting her, and once he kicked and stomped her badly enough that she was afraid he was going to kill her. He was always remorseful after such an incident, so she always gave him one more chance.

She went into work one day and the manager asked to talk to her privately. The police had come by, he said, looking for Mike Roe. They said he was a suspect in a car theft and a sexual assault case. They said he'd been accused by a prostitute over on Colfax Avenue of raping her.

Sandy confronted Riggan, who denied he knew

any prostitutes or had raped one. "They're looking for Mike Roe," she said.

"It must be another Mike Roe," he answered.

She didn't believe him. All she wanted was to get away from him. She was tired of being called a whore and of being hit. She was tired of always being on the run from the police, knowing these latest accusations would mean having to pick up and move again. But she didn't know what to do.

In August 1991, he beat her so severely that she called the police who showed up and arrested him. A quick search turned up the federal warrant and he was soon on his way to a federal penitentiary in Colorado.

When her husband was arrested, Sandy called her mother and asked her to come to Denver to help her move back to Iowa. Riggan tried to stop her from leaving town by telling the Denver police that she was a bad check fugitive. The police pulled her over, but quickly ascertained that all they had were two frightened women who were terrorized that Riggan had found a way to reach out from behind prison walls. They sent the pair on their way.

Even living in Iowa didn't prevent Riggan from calling Sandy as much as fifty times a day. He used U.S. Navy phone lines, corporate telephone cards, and an unused telemarketing number he obtained somehow. Insane with jealousy, he would demand to know who she was "fucking." He just knew there must be other men. She was, after all, a whore.

Sandy's parents moved her again, this time to

Eliot, Iowa, to stay with her grandparents. They hoped he would not be able to find her. But even from prison he traced her and began calling different people in the town—complete strangers—wanting to know if they'd seen Sandy and, if so, did she have a boyfriend? The strange contacts were reported to Sandy's grandparents, who complained to the police, but even trying to block his calls from prison didn't work. He'd just go through a third party.

One day, the telephone rang and it was him. Sandy told him that it was over. She didn't want to be with him anymore. He wouldn't listen. If she left him, he said, he'd find her when he got out. And when he found her, he was going to kill her. He told her stories he'd supposedly been keeping from her—that he'd been shot in the face in Mexico during a drug deal and that he'd killed a father and son and then set their car on fire with their bodies inside on the Arizona-Mexico border. He'd killed, he said, and he'd kill again if necessary.

Frightened, Sandy moved back to Des Moines with her children. She rented a tiny apartment in a seedy neighborhood, hoping to disappear into the masses. It was hopeless. One hot, muggy day in August 1992, when Sandy was home alone with her two young sons, Riggan showed up.

"Come on, Sandy, open the door," he whined when she refused to let him in. "We need to talk."

"I don't want to see you no more, Bob. Go away," she pleaded.

At last, he acted like he accepted her decision. Then he asked if he could please use the telephone to call for a ride.

Desperate to get him out of her life, she tried to hand him a cordless phone through the partly opened door. Suddenly he shoved hard, knocking her back. Before she could react, he was behind her with an arm around her neck.

"You're coming with me, bitch," he snarled. He dragged her into the kitchen, where he picked a large knife up off the counter.

Forcing her into the bedroom, he pushed her to the floor and tied her hands behind her back with the sash from a bathrobe. He told her he was going to rape her "in the ass." Then he picked up their youngest son, Tommy, just two years old. Holding the knife behind the toddler's back, he said, "I'll use it if I have to."

Sandy wasn't sure if the threat was directed at her or her son. Robert's face was flushed and he was sweating profusely; his eyes looked wild and dangerous. "Okay, I'll go," she said. She was faced with the dilemma of whether to take the boys or leave them. She was afraid he might harm them if they went, but it was a bad neighborhood and she didn't want to leave them alone, not knowing how long it would take for someone to find them if something happened to her. She decided to keep them with her.

The four walked out of the house. The boys were clothed only in their diapers, but Riggan had thrown a winter coat over Sandra to hide the fact that her arms were tied behind her back. As they moved toward his car, they were seen by Sandy's landlady.

The older woman looked puzzled by the strange

procession. It was awfully hot to be wearing a winter coat. "Everything okay, Sandy?" the woman asked.

Sandy looked at Riggan, who was staring hard at her, sweat dripping from his brow, while the hand with the knife moved in his pocket. "Yes," she replied. As they proceeded to the car, she turned her head toward her landlady, who was still watching, and mouthed the words "No" and "Call the police." She had no idea if the woman understood.

Riggan drove them out into the Iowa countryside. He kept alternating between begging her to come back to him, bursting into tears, and threatening to use the knife if she didn't do as told. She tried to tell him the relationship was over, but he wouldn't listen.

The farther down country roads they traveled, the less traffic Sandy began to see. Just rows and rows of green cornstalks, until at last he drove through a field and pulled up in front of an old abandoned shack. He ordered her to get out and walk into the shack, leaving the boys behind in the sweltering car.

The shack, perhaps an old toolshed, was so dilapidated as to be hardly standing. She could see the fields outside through gaps in the slat walls; some parts of the roof had caved in revealing the hot blue afternoon sky. The floor was dirt and debris. She wondered if she would die in this horrible, lonely place.

Waving the knife, Riggan told her to cooperate if she wanted to live. He untied her and told her to remove her pants while he fumbled to drop his. As he raped her, he cried, cursed, and pleaded with her to come back to him. She didn't resist; there was no point. Her boys needed her to stay alive.

As he forced himself on her, Riggan kept demanding that she come back to him. She knew that he was reaching the breaking point.

"Yeah, okay," she said, as he finished. "I'll come back. Now calm down."

The words were a tonic. He was immediately happy, as if they had both looked forward to the moment that had just passed. She'd see, he said, it'd be just like old times. He escorted her back to the car, and even opened the door like a gentleman.

Riggan was so convinced that he'd changed her mind that when they got to Sioux City, Iowa, he left her and the boys in the car while he went into a mall to get some money. He also left the keys.

As soon as Riggan was out of sight, Sandy hopped into the driver's seat, started the car, and took off. She drove to a motel and called her father and told him what had happened.

"Call the police," he said. She did, but the police couldn't find Robert Riggan at the mall.

It wasn't for another month that Riggan was caught in Denver and sent back to Iowa to face charges of sexual assault and kidnapping. The case never came to trial. Even though he was in jail for raping her, Riggan continued to call Sandy as if the charges were just a misunderstanding that would soon be cleared up. Afraid that he'd get out and come after her, she told him that she was still willing to get back together.

In the meantime, Sandy still faced the everyday challenges of being an impoverished single mother.

She and the boys were living on welfare, the bills were stacking up, and the gas company was threatening to cut off service.

One day, she read an advertisement in the newspaper for a massage parlor. The management was looking for new trainees and said an employee could make $500 a week. Riggan happened to call that day and she ran it by him. Despite wanting to be free of her husband, in some ways she was still the teenager he had once controlled so thoroughly.

"Sandy, you have to watch out," he cautioned. "Places like that will have you doing other things besides massage. I don't think it's a good idea."

"But it says I can make five hundred dollars a week," she said. "I'll just go see what it's about."

The next day, he called again. He'd been thinking. If she went to work at the massage parlor, she could post his bond on the rape charge that much sooner. Then they could be together again. He had decided to give his permission.

Sandy applied for the position, even though it meant performing the service in the nude and giving "full" massages. It took a couple of weeks, but in the end, she couldn't resist the money and twice agreed to have sex with clients.

Riggan guessed what she'd done. "You whore," he sneered over the telephone. She had always been a whore, he said. She was a whore when he met her, and a whore now.

Sandy protested. Why was he being so mean? He'd known what working in a place like that might lead to; he'd given his permission. She had two little boys to take care of. He'd certainly never provided for them. What was she supposed to do?

Anita Paley, 22, had only been a prostitute for a few weeks before she was murdered. *(Photo courtesy Jefferson County, Colorado District Attorney)*

Paley with her daughters at Christmas in 1994.
(Photo courtesy Jefferson County, Colorado District Attorney)

Barely alive when found, Paley's bleeding head had
swollen to the size of a basketball.
(*Photo courtesy Jefferson County, Colorado District Attorney*)

Abandoned miner's cabin in Colorado woods
where Paley was attacked.
(Photo courtesy Jefferson County, Colorado District Attorney)

Evidence tags mark the places where spots of blood were discovered outside the cabin.
(Photo courtesy Jefferson County, Colorado District Attorney)

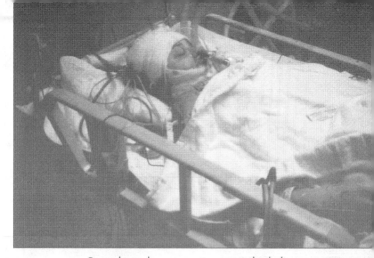

Brought to the emergency room by helicopter,
Paley was rushed into surgery.
(Photo courtesy Jefferson County, Colorado District Attorney)

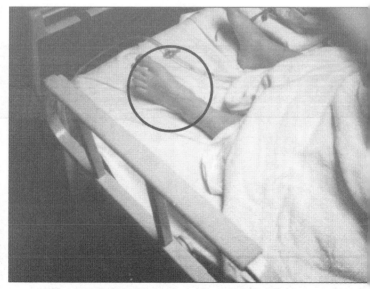

The tattoo of an Egyptian ankh on Paley's left foot was the
most prominent identifying mark on her body.
(Photo courtesy Jefferson County, Colorado District Attorney)

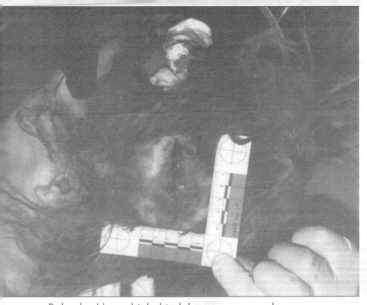

Paley had been hit behind the ear so severely,
it fractured her skull.
(*Photo courtesy Jefferson County, Colorado District Attorney*)

Police found the blue Chevy mini-van seen speeding from
the cabin in a motel parking lot.
(*Photo courtesy Jefferson County, Colorado District Attorney*)

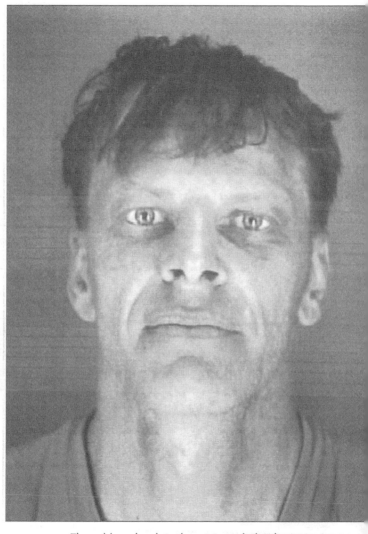

The address book in the mini-van led police to
Robert Lee Riggan, Jr.
(*Photo courtesy Jefferson County, Colorado District Attorney*)

Riggan dropped out of high school in the tenth grade to join the Navy. (*Photo courtesy* Denver Rocky Mountain News)

Joanne Cordova, 38, identified her friend Anita Paley as the victim after seeing a television news story about an attack on an unknown woman. (*Photo courtesy Jim Sternfield*)

Joanne Cordova, 5, was raised in a close family. (*Photo courtesy Joanne Cordova*)

A good student and cheerleader, Cordova, was the victim of sexual abuse by neighbors. (*Photo courtesy Joanne Cordova*)

Cordova ran away from home at 17. (*Photo courtesy Joanne Cordova*)

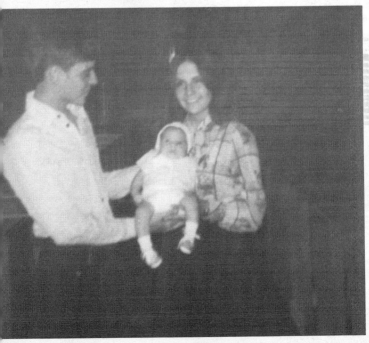

Cordova, 18, at the baptism of her first child with then husband James Shannon. (*Photo courtesy Joanne Cordova*)

Joanne Cordova was a member of the July 1983 graduating
class of the Denver Police Academy.
(*Photo courtesy Joanne Cordova*)

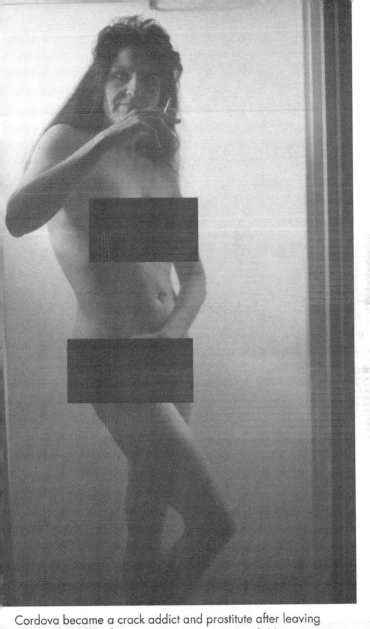

Cordova became a crack addict and prostitute after leaving the police force. (*Photo courtesy Jim Sternfield*)

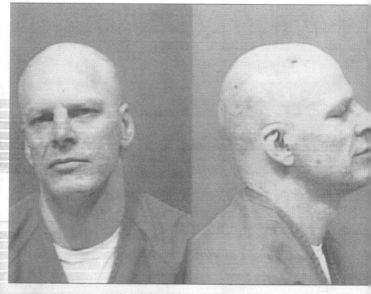

Riggan was charged with two counts of first degree murder
for the death of Anita Paley.
(*Photo courtesy Jefferson County, Colorado District Attorney*)

A styrofoam head was used at Riggan's trial to show
the position of Paley's wounds.
(*Photo courtesy Jefferson County, Colorado District Attorney*)

Chief Deputy District Attorney Dennis Hall was the lead prosecutor at Riggan's trial.

Investigator John Lauck of the Jefferson County, Colorado District Attorney's office was the lead detective investigating the murder of Anita Paley.

Chief Investigator Dennis Goodwin of the Jefferson County, Colorado District Attorney's office traveled to Iowa to research Riggan's background for the case against him.

Investigator Jim Burkhalter was a 30-year veteran of the Denver Police Department, before joining the Jefferson County, Colorado District Attorney's office.

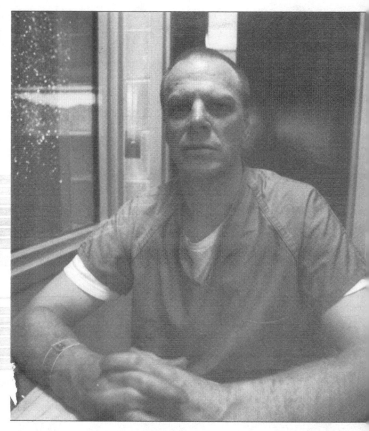

Riggan in visitation cell at the Jefferson County Jail on the first day of his death penalty hearing in April 1999.
(*Photo courtesy* Denver Rocky Mountain News)

It didn't matter. She was a whore and his defense attorney would rip her apart on the stand, he said. After all, who would believe a prostitute who cried rape. Just wait until he got out; then she'd wish she never betrayed him.

Sandy was stuck in a no-win situation. She quit the massage parlor after she got caught up on bills, but she knew that she was in worse trouble. The police had not been able to find the knife she said Riggan took from her house. Worse, the landlady who had seen her and Riggan, and had called the police, had disappeared. No one knew if she'd been threatened, or maybe worse, but the only witness who could back up Sandy's story was gone.

The deputy district attorney prosecuting the case told Sandy not to worry. They'd find the landlady. But a week before the trial was scheduled, they still had not located the woman.

Sandy decided then that it was over. No one else was going to step forward to help her. She wasn't going to take the witness stand and then have him come after her if he got off. She decided that she wasn't going to cooperate, and the prosecutor had no option except to drop the charges.

After being released from jail, Riggan continued with the telephone threats and name-calling. Sandy had a new boyfriend and Riggan wasn't the sort to take on a man. He told the couple he would plant a bomb in their car someday, but he never followed through.

Instead, he continued to make his living as a criminal, mostly shoplifting electronics equipment to re-sell at pawnshops. He went by a number of different aliases and had identification cards in case he was stopped by the police. He never forgot Sandy, or what he considered her betrayal. Apparently, he decided to take it out on the sort of woman he considered Sandy and Judy to be . . . a whore . . . a hooker . . . Anita Paley, Goodwin thought as the young woman reached the end of her story.

The investigator wondered how many other victims there might be. He'd felt a chill go up his spine when Sandy described the scene of her rape . . . an isolated dirt road . . . an old abandoned shack. It was as if Riggan were reliving that event with Anita Paley . . . only something had snapped and he'd killed and mutilated her. Of that, he was sure.

Sandy told him that Riggan had called her from jail to tell her about the trouble he was in. He said the girl had jumped from his van.

Goodwin could see that she hoped that was the truth. She'd indicated that she was afraid of her ex-husband. Not like Judy, who was fearful of even being in the same room with him, but more than that, she was worried what he'd do if he found out she'd been talking to the police. Still, for all she'd been through, the investigator could tell that she still had strong feelings for her ex. And whether it was due to loyalty or fear, he was not going to win her over entirely.

Nor would Goodwin be able to win over the last person he needed to contact in Iowa: Robert Riggan's sister, Rosie.

He'd met several other relatives who had interesting stories to tell about Riggan, including several who recalled that as a teenager, he'd once baby-sat for a child relative who'd had heart surgery. Ever after, the child had phobic reactions to being bathed. Recalling Judy's recollection, Goodwin wondered when Riggan first began entertaining murderous thoughts. Others told him that Riggan had been abusive to animals—that he'd kick them around if they didn't do what he wanted.

Rosie, on the other hand, was defensive on behalf of her brother. She was a tiny slip of a woman, sort of mousy. Her home and yard in the countryside were neat and tidy, almost compulsively so. When he called, she'd invited him over, anxious to give her views on her brother, knowing that others might not have been so kind.

They'd had a horrible childhood, she said, telling Goodwin about the filthy living conditions, the lack of love, the sexual improprieties, the whippings Bobby in particular endured, and the fire that had scarred his face and the cruel taunts of the other children. She acknowledged that he'd been in trouble with the law most of his life. But, she said, he wasn't the sort to hurt a woman. Nor had she known him to hurt animals, she said. In fact, his only friend in childhood had been a dog named Goofy, whom he'd adored.

Some of what Goodwin was being told, she said, wasn't true. For instance, it was their father, she said, who had been caught in bed with Theresa, not Bobby. Her father was an old pervert who drilled holes in the ceiling of the bathroom to watch Theresa and even his own daughter take baths.

Rosie said she'd been lucky. Her second husband

was a good man, who treated her and her children well. No one had ever reached out to Bobby like that . . . otherwise things might have been different.

Bobby had called her from jail. He told her that the girl had jumped from his van. She'd also heard—she couldn't remember where—that the girl had her throat slashed. "Which Bobby would never do," she said. "I might believe that he'd beat somebody up."

If Rosie's purpose had been to convince Goodwin that her brother was not capable of murder, she failed. As he headed back west to Colorado that evening, the one thought that kept recurring was that for most of his life Robert Lee Riggan, Jr. had never faced any real consequences for anything he'd done . . . which was quite a lot . . . but maybe now, it had all caught up to him.

Ten

Jane Doe may well have remained just another unidentified murder victim, just a piece of evidence in a murder trial, her own, but otherwise consigned to a pauper's grave and quickly forgotten. But it was revealed that she had a name, Anita Paley, and a family, because after a couple of days of wrestling with her fear and her conscience, Joanne Cordova had stepped forward.

She had wavered several times, arguing with Jimmy who insisted that it was the only right thing to do. She knew that, but she was still afraid—even though Bob Davis, or Robert Riggan, was in jail. What if she had to testify against him, but he wasn't convicted? He'd probably come looking for her. Revenge was something any street person understood. They also understood that being labeled a snitch, a rat, a police informant, could be a death sentence. It didn't matter that the cause was just; the way the thinking went on the streets, someone who went to the cops regarding one crime, might go to them for another.

Joanne Cordova was a street person. That was never more clear to her than the day she was walking down an alley with a hooker friend, who was pushing a shopping cart loaded with all her worldly possessions with no place to go, and it was still more than Cordova had. Her life was in danger, every single day . . . she didn't *need* to invite more trouble. But she had also once been a cop, sworn to protect and serve. She'd fallen a long way down since those days when she dreamed of catching a killer, of being the hero, but not so far that she couldn't remember how much pride she felt when wearing that uniform.

Anita Paley had been a friend. A young woman who had her troubles, but did not deserve to be murdered. She didn't doubt that Paley would have tried to get her clothes back for her . . . street people, particularly other prostitutes, looked out for each other. Now Cordova thought that she owed something to Paley . . . and maybe owed something else to herself.

With Jimmy prodding, Cordova called her old partner and friend from her days on the Denver Police Department, Pat Jones. She occasionally saw Jones on the streets. He was always after her to get off the drugs and away from the streets, but he'd never looked down on her, and she knew she could trust him.

Jones drove to meet her at Jimmy's house. She told him how she knew both the victim and the suspect.

"Ah, Jo, what are you doing?" Jones said, shaking his head. "Why are you still doing drugs? You could have been killed." That was as far as the lecture went. He said a friend of his from his police academy days, Jim Burkhalter, was working on the case. "He's a good guy," Jones said. "You can trust him."

Cordova told him to have Burkhalter give her a

call at Jimmy's. A short time later, she heard from
the investigator. First, he wanted to know if they
were even talking about the same woman. He asked
her to describe Paley. Burkhalter was quickly convinced that they were talking about the same
woman. He grew more interested when she told
him about spending several days with Riggan before
the murder. "We need you to come here so we can
talk to you," he said.

On Monday, she borrowed Jimmy's car and drove
the fifteen miles to the Jefferson County District
Attorney's Office building. When she got up that
morning, she was convinced that she was doing the
right thing, but the closer she got, the more she
started to doubt herself. There was fear, yes, but
there was something almost worse. Embarrassment.
She had been a police officer, for God's sake, and
here she was now, a crack-addicted prostitute.

Cordova had resisted getting high before leaving
for the meeting. Now, as she pulled into the parking lot, she wished she could and had to struggle
against the desire to withdraw into a protective bubble and remove herself from the situation. She
needed a mask but had brought no drugs with her.
She would have to do this . . . or she could run.
The decision was to stay . . . but not as a confiden-
tial informant, not as someone who talked to the
police for money or, perhaps, a deal on an impend-
ing criminal case. She had a couple of minor legal
issues for which she could have used a good word
to the prosecutor in another county to clear up,
but she was determined to do this for the right
reasons, or not at all.

Inside the building, she was escorted to a conference room, where she was introduced to those present including senior deputy district attorney Dennis Hall, as well as investigators John Lauck and Jim Burkhalter. They thanked her for coming, and also on behalf of Anita's family. Because of her, they'd been able to contact Paley's stepfather, Paul Bibaud, and tell him what had happened. It was bad news, but that was better than Anita disappearing without a trace.

Just to be sure, they showed her a photo lineup from which she easily picked the mug shot of Robert Riggan as the man she had known as Bob Davis. For the next few hours, the investigators and the attorneys had her go over every moment she spent with Riggan and how he'd met Paley. Then they had her go over it again—every statement, every move, every expression. They were particularly interested in how his personality had suddenly changed, and his demands for violent, demeaning sex.

As she went into details she would have just as soon forgotten, Cordova felt her face flush. For the price of a little cocaine, she'd let herself be used and abused like some old dog. *I wonder what they think of me now.* She forced herself to recall everything from those few days from his comment "They think I'm just a normal guy," to the shopping trips, to his rage when she asked where he'd been, to making tuna fish sandwiches with that long, thin blade. She'd heard that Paley died of head injuries, but little else, and many of the questions she didn't understand the reason for. There were some memory lapses because of her addiction, but she amazed the investigators and attorneys with her eye and ear

for detail, down to quoting Riggan's description of
the cabin as his "favorite place in the whole world."
She even told them about the vision she'd had of
herself lying facedown in the stream and the feeling
that something evil had been watching her from
the woods.

Throughout, they treated her with respect and
were as delicate around the issues of prostitution
and sex as they could be, given the circumstances.
When they finished and she rose to leave, Burkhalter, who would obviously be the one she would be
dealing with the most, politely asked, "Can we call
you?" She appreciated that courtesy and the fact
that, no matter what they might have been thinking
about her character, it wasn't betrayed by their faces
or demeanor. They only said that they needed her
help and hoped that she would cooperate. She
found herself saying that she'd do whatever she
could . . . being labeled a snitch, be damned.

She walked back out into the afternoon sun that
day feeling good about herself. Clean. For the first
time in far too long, she had taken a step back up
the hill from which she had tumbled. She knew it
would be a long climb, but she was determined that
the first step would not be her last.

Goodwin's report back to his colleagues regarding Riggan's past got the wheels spinning even
faster: the abused background, the compromised
sexual boundaries as a child, the violence—sexual,
physical, and emotional—toward his wives, the fires
he'd been accused of setting, the reports of animal
cruelty. Childhood sexual abuse combined with fire-

setting, animal cruelty, and bed-wetting were, the investigators knew, seen by psychologists as warning signs of a future serial rapist or killer. They thought it was unlikely that at age thirty-seven, Riggan had suddenly started picking up hookers, crushing their skulls, and cutting their vaginas. It wasn't long before they began to hear more that convinced them they were on the right track about Riggan.

Some of the reports came courtesy of Joanne Cordova, who had talked some of the other street people who knew Anita Paley and had contact with Robert Riggan into calling Burkhalter. In that way, the investigator met several people: Shane Delray, who backed up Cordova's story that Paley claimed Riggan had raped her the day before her death; Prostitute Debbie Johnson, who told him that Riggan had talked about taking her to the mountains but then raped her anally while threatening her with a knife; and prostitute Char Fitch, who also added to Cordova's credibility with her own recollection that Riggan had wanted to take her to his "favorite place in the whole world" and had seen a blunt-ended ax in the van that wasn't there when criminalist Vicki Spellman examined the vehicle.

The Des Moines police came up with another lead. A thirty-eight-year-old hooker named Pamela Kay Hart, who complained that Riggan had tied her up at knifepoint and raped her, too. Goodwin read the reports and then found Hart in prison, who gladly told him about her "date" with his suspect.

On January 9, Hart said, she was hanging out at a homeless shelter in Des Moines when another resident, who acted as a pimp for the hookers, approached her. "A guy outside wants a 'date,'" the small black man said.

A crack-cocaine addict, Hart was happy to get the business in order to support her habit. She walked out the front door and met a man who introduced himself as "Bob." He'd parked his truck, a red Toyota 4-Runner, in a hospital parking lot across the street.

Bob offered Hart dinner, crack, and money to return to his motel with him "to party." She agreed and got in the truck. When her date continued past the street where the motel was located, she began to worry.

"Where you going?" she asked.

Bob pointed to a black bag behind the seat. "I have to drop that off at my boss's house first," he said.

Mollified, Hart sat back. Bob drove into a residential area. When he started down a dead-end street and the houses stopped, she grew nervous again. He parked near railroad tracks with no houses nearby.

Suddenly he reached between the seats and pulled out a knife. Holding the blade against her throat, he ordered her to climb into the backseat. "I'm going to kidnap you and take you off the streets," he said. "Cooperate or you'll be punished."

Bob tied her hands and feet with a nylon rope. When she struggled, he grabbed her around the throat. "You want to die?" he snarled.

He wasn't talking about rescuing her anymore. He was cursing and calling her names. "You whore," he spat. Waving the knife, he demanded oral sex. When he tired of that, he pushed her over on her stomach and raped her from behind. He was rough and when she screamed, he yelled, "Shut up, mother," and gagged her.

After he finished, the anger seemed to drain from him. He cut the ropes off and threw them out the window. He explained that it was "fun" to intimidate and then dominate a sexual partner. "It was all just a fantasy," he explained.

Bob kept her with him as he drove around. He repeated that he was going to kidnap her for her own good and take her off the streets. If she "co-operated," she would "have it made." He'd take care of her. Why would she want to be a prostitute, anyway? He told Hart that he had to meet someone named "Sugar Bear." He drove to a bar, where he got out and walked up to a black Cadillac.

Hart had not tried to escape. Her date had calmed down and was talking about buying her things. In her crack-starved mind, she thought maybe Bob would come around and pay for what he had stolen. The deed was done . . . it wasn't like a prostitute could go to the cops and cry rape. By the time Bob found Sugar Bear and she saw the pair walking toward the car, she decided that she was tired of waiting and that Bob was a little scary. He'd left the keys in the truck, so she hopped into the driver's seat and took off with Bob and Sugar Bear in hot pursuit.

Hart noticed the truck's gas gauge read empty. When she felt she had enough separation between herself and her pursuers, she pulled over, got out of the truck, and started walking. From a couple of blocks away, she looked back and saw Bob get in the truck. He attempted to drive off, but the vehicle stalled. He got out and walked quickly in the opposite direction.

Hart found her way to a convenience store, where she called her husband. She wanted money, but he wouldn't help. A short time later, she solicited an undercover Des Moines police officer and was arrested for prostitution.

"I was just raped," she complained to the two officers taking her in for booking. "I want to go to a hospital and get checked out." She said she knew where the suspect, Bob, left his truck. So on the way to the hospital, the officers swung by where Hart had last seen her supposed assailant. When he saw the truck, one of the officers recognized it as matching that of a reported stolen vehicle.

A cab pulled up behind the truck and a man got out with a gas can. Hart yelled, "That's the guy! That's the guy who raped me!"

When the man saw the police officers approaching, he veered and acted as if he were walking up to a house. Warned that he might have a knife, the officers pulled their guns. "On the ground!"

The man sprawled on the lawn. "I'm just visiting my friend . . . he needs gas," he said.

"That your truck?" an officer asked.

"I don't know whose truck that is," the man answered.

The lie didn't last long. The officers patted him down and found the Toyota's keys in his pocket. "I borrowed it from a friend," the suspect said, changing his story.

"What's your name?" an officer asked as Bob was handcuffed and read his rights.

"Gary," Bob replied. "Gary Dean Emrick."

"Gary's" fingerprints came back as a match for Robert Lee Riggan, Jr. Cases were filed against Riggan for theft of a motor vehicle and sexual assault. A knife fitting the description of the one described by Hart was found in the truck and white nylon ropes were discovered near the railroad tracks. The police photographed the rope burns on her wrists.

Nothing ever came of the sexual assault. The investigating officer, Goodwin noted, had written on his report that the victim would not make a good witness in front of a jury. The Jefferson County investigator didn't understand the rationale. They'd found the ropes, they had a knife, they had the photographs . . . the victim had led them to the suspect, who just happened to be driving a stolen truck . . . and they hadn't even tried to make a case. If nothing else, the idea that someone would violently rape a prostitute when for a few dollars he could have had what he wanted, should have sent up a red flag that maybe, just maybe, this guy bore a little extra investigating—maybe even turning up the old sexual assault charges brought against him by his wife Sandy. But once again, Riggan slipped through the cracks like oil.

Hart, on the other hand, was sentenced to two years on the prostitution arrest. A few months later, a warrant was issued for Riggan when he didn't appear in court to face some minor forgery charges, but he was no longer in Iowa. He was on his way to Denver, where he arrived May 7, 1997. Ten days later, a novice prostitute named Anita Paley was dead.

* * *

The Jefferson County investigators sent their information out on a national crime computer with photographs of Riggan, a list of the more than a dozen places he had lived since leaving Iowa to join the Navy, his proclivity for befriending and then victimizing prostitutes, and the possibility that he had sexually mutilated his victims. The response surprised the investigators. If the victims had been good girls from families who demanded police action, there would have been numerous inquiries. They knew that prostitutes turn up dead in big cities all the time, but apparently when they died or simply disappeared, no one cared enough to investigate for very long even in the unlikely chance that someone reported them missing.

Or if the police were investigating prostitute murders because of something like sheer numbers, they apparently weren't interested in Riggan. For instance, the Green River Killer was suspected in forty-nine murders of (mostly) prostitutes, whose bodies were dumped in remote rural areas near Seattle from 1982 to 1984, when the attacks suddenly stopped. Riggan had been in and out of that area during that time, but no one seemed to care.

There were a few responses, some of which asked for more information and then were never heard from again. Des Moines even called with a report of a prostitute having been found murdered near some railroad tracks. The Des Moines detective said it probably meant nothing . . . the body had been there for a while, and from what they estimated to be the approximate day of death, they thought that Riggan was in jail.

Goodwin, who was becoming less and less im-

pressed by that department, wondered how the
other detective could be so sure, but he never
heard anything more about it. Pamela Kay Hart said
she'd been taken to the railroad tracks. She was
street smart and not particularly enamored of the
police, but when he talked to her and compared
what she said to the reports, she never wavered
from her story.

In the meantime, the investigation in Colorado
was moving along. Sheriff Hartman and his deputies had taken Riggan to the highway the Sunday
following his arrest to point out where he said Anita
Paley had jumped from the van. They walked hundreds of yards in both directions from the spot but
found no pools of blood, large or small, on the
highway, nor had there been rain to wash blood
away. There was no sign of a crack pipe stuffed in
a sock lying next to a guardrail, either. The Jefferson County investigators did get a chuckle when
Hartman told them that Riggan had asked if he
could wear his "running shoes" for the little excursion . . . a request that was denied.

Two security guards who worked in the Black
Hawk area reported having seen a dark blue minivan with Wyoming plates parked in an otherwise
empty casino parking lot about 5:30 in the morning
of the day that Paley was found by the stream.
There was no sign of a struggle, no blood in the
lot. Lauck and Burkhalter were skeptical about the
report, mostly because they couldn't figure out why
Riggan would have stopped in the well-lit lot—it
was a little exposed as a place for a sexual encoun-
ter—unless he wanted to see how badly she was
hurt.

The investigators had returned to the scene of the crime and noted that if Riggan was taking her to the water to clean her up, he'd passed on the first and best access to the stream. Instead, he'd pulled her to a place where the bank to the stream was much steeper and more difficult to reach.

Once again, the Boulder police helped out with a good piece of detective work when a burglary was reported three days after Riggan's arrest. An older couple claimed that someone had broken into their travel trailer, which they had been in the process of loading for an upcoming trip. The thief had stolen some items, including a red-and-black-checkered shirt and a pair of binoculars, and left some other clothing behind. He'd also apparently spent the night drinking their root beers and eating chips.

Normally, such a report would not have caused much of a stir and would have gone unnoticed. But it so happened that Officer Curtis Johnson, who responded with Bresnahan to help arrest Riggan, also responded to this scene. He remembered that Riggan had been wearing a red-and-black-checkered shirt and binoculars. Crime scene technicians were called in who spotted dark stains on the clothing left behind by the thief, which turned out to be Paley's blood, and lifted Riggan's fingerprints from the root beer bottles. Once again, Riggan, who claimed to have spent the night hiding in the hills without food, water, or sleep, had been caught in a lie.

Their progress was a mixture of good detective work and a whole lot of luck: first, Sosebe and Johnson driving past the cabin at just the right time. Otherwise, Riggan might never have become a suspect. Then an observant citizen had spotted him walking down the bike path, presumably headed for a highway and a way out of town. Followed by Officer Johnson responding to the scene of an otherwise unrelated burglary. And, of course, Joanne Cordova, without whom they might never have been able to identify Anita Paley, or found the people who could trace Riggan's movements and moods in the days preceding her death.

Cordova had proved to be invaluable, but the investigators, particularly Burkhalter, who knew her best, worried that she might never make it to trial. As a Denver detective, Burkhalter had eventually transferred out of homicides and into the sexual assaults division. Quite a number of reported rapes came from prostitutes.

Many of those reports were for what the detectives in the unit referred to as "no pays," in that the girl only considered it rape when the customer couldn't come up with the cash. Burkhalter knew that such women sometimes told the truth. He'd once investigated a claim by a hooker who said she'd been tied up, raped, and held against her will for three days. Her whole story sounded preposterous, but he'd checked out her story and found the home in east Denver where everything—including the bondage equipment—was just how she had described it. He arrested the owner for sexual assault and kidnapping.

The case illustrated what a dangerous life these women, most of them drug addicts, led. If it wasn't disease or an overdose, they never knew when they might run into the wrong man. He might be a pimp, or a drug dealer, or the member of a gang. Or, he might look like an accountant but get his jollies by hurting or even killing women. Prostitutes were easy targets. They'd jump into cars with strangers, and few people missed them when they were gone—certainly not enough to call the cops when that might attract the wrong kind of attention.

Denver had its share of men who preyed on prostitutes. In 1988, a religious zealot named Vincent Groves was arrested and convicted of the murder of two prostitutes whose partially clothed bodies had been found lying beside rural roadways, strangled to death. He was suspected of as many as seventeen more . . . almost all hookers he had picked up on Colfax Avenue.

Groves had already served time for killing a seventeen-year-old girl in 1981 when he was twenty-eight. A bright, articulate, and overtly religious man, Groves had actually driven his truck to the Jefferson County Sheriff's Office with the dead woman's body in the back cargo area. He claimed she'd died of a drug overdose, but an autopsy revealed she'd been strangled. He was convicted of second-degree murder, but he served only five years before being released in 1987. When he got out of prison, Groves married a woman he'd met as a prison pen pal. She was even more religious than himself, and he believed that she was so pure that he wouldn't have sex with her. Instead, he went to prostitutes, whom he then strangled.

Over a period of a half a year beginning in August 1994, there had been a string of prostitute killings in Denver. The first had been forty-two-year-old Karen Kastning, whose nude body was found in a vacant lot; she had been strangled. In December, nineteen-year-old Belinda Bridgmon's body was discovered in a cardboard box inside a Dumpster. Known as "Little Bit" and "Shorty" on the streets, Bridgmon had been born a dwarf. She was only three feet ten inches and looked more like a child than a woman. She was killed by a boyfriend in an argument over who smoked an unfair portion of their crack-cocaine stash. The boyfriend, Charles Weatherall, was convicted.

However, Groves and Weatherall were the exceptions in that they were caught. Kastning's killer was never caught. Nor was anyone brought to justice for slashing open the throat of thirty-three-year-old prostitute Susan Boston and leaving her body, nude except for thigh-high stockings, propped up against a fence. A man named Jon Morris was a suspect in the killing, as well as that of the August 1996 murder of transient Norma Fisher. Morris was never charged, though he was later arrested and convicted for the rape and murder of nine-year-old Ashley Gray, whose crack-addicted parents had allowed him to take a trip to the store with their only daughter. Morris had killed Ashley and, like Belinda Bridgmon, left her in a Dumpster like so much garbage.

The prosecution of prostitution rape cases was often dropped for reasons beyond the control of the police and prosecutors, including the lack of cooperation from the victims. The women often refused to sign statements, or they invariably failed to show up at court for hearings and trials. If all they were after in the first place was revenge for getting stiffed by a customer, then it was enough to have cried rape and caused the john to get hassled by the police. But few ever took their troubles to the police, especially if their beef was with another street person rather than some lonely husband driving in from the suburbs. There was a code on the streets among the people who inhabited its dark places: Don't go to the police . . . no one trusts a "snitch," and out of self-preservation for their criminal ways, the rule was if you snitched, you could expect to die.

Sometimes a prostitute might get help from her pimp if she was having trouble with a customer or another street person. Some also carried weapons and weren't afraid to use them. Most just accepted the occasional rough stuff, stayed away from the cops, hoped that they wouldn't meet the next Vincent Groves or Charles Weatherall or Jon Morris, and carried on with their desperate lives.

Joanne Cordova was one of these. Burkhalter and the others feared for her life—not just because they needed her as a witness, but because she was a likable, compassionate woman who had caught them all a little off guard with her intelligence and charm. They had all wondered what could have caused someone with so much going for her to lose herself, though they'd seen enough of what drugs could do to anyone to understand better than most.

In coming forward, Cordova had taken that first step back up the hill. But it was not as though she changed overnight, if indeed she could ever change. Just weeks after Paley's murder and her interview at Jefferson County, Cordova was back over at a drug dealer's house trying to explain how a few grams of crack he'd given her to sell had been stolen from her bag. The dealer didn't believe her. His accomplice, a large white biker, jumped up and spit in her face.

Cordova had learned to put up with a lot of abuse on the streets, but being spit at was too much. "You know I have one felony left," she yelled, referring to the "three strikes and you're out" rule for habitual criminals. "I don't want to use it on someone like you."

The biker stepped back, but the next thing Cordova knew, the dealer had sprayed her in the face with Mace. Gagging and nearly blinded, she realized with terror that the biker had pulled a long hunting knife. At the sight of it, another prostitute who had been at the house announced that she was leaving. "And if Joanne's missing when I get back, I'll know you killed her and I'll go to the police," she said.

The two men apparently thought better of killing her in the apartment. They left the house, cursing her and giving her dark looks that seemed to say, "This isn't over."

When they left, Cordova called Burkhalter. As far as she knew, the men were waiting for her outside somewhere, and in a few minutes, she would be just another hooker with her throat slashed in some alley. All over a few hundred dollars' worth of crack.

Cordova explained what had just happened to the investigator. "I'm leaving now," she told him. "If I die, Jim, I want you to report what I told you."

"Let me send an officer," he suggested.

"Absolutely not," she replied. If he did, everyone

would know she was cooperating with the police. She'd be just as dead.

"Do you want to report it?" he asked without much hope. He knew the code of the streets.

"No. Not unless I turn up dead," she replied. With that, she hung up the telephone and walked out into the night.

Eleven

Robert Lee Riggan, Jr. was charged with two counts of first-degree murder for the death of Anita Paley. Count One contended that he killed her after deliberation. Count Two, called a felony murder charge, contended that he killed her in the furtherance or to cover up another felony, in this case, sexual assault with whatever blade they believed he used to slice her vagina. Either charge could result in the death penalty—by lethal injection in Colorado—which Jefferson County district attorney Dave Thomas announced that his office would seek, or life without the possibility of parole. The hard work of actually prosecuting the case, however, fell to senior deputy district attorney Dennis Hall, who would be the lead, and deputy district attorney Dana Easter, a former registered nurse, who had spent her career thus far prosecuting sex crimes and was brought in on this case for her experience with that, as well as medical matters.

Mild-mannered and boyish-looking, with a secret passion for racing vintage race cars, Hall was often the man Thomas called on to handle the most complicated cases. This was his first murder case since the 1996 conviction of Thomas Luther for the 1993 murder of Cher Elder.

Luther was a suspected serial killer, linked to the death of several other women both in Colorado and other states. But the judge in that case had disallowed any testimony about Luther's "prior bad acts," including convictions for two brutal rapes and the more circumstantial evidence in the other murders.

The rest of the case was comprised of many small, separate pieces and Hall had serious concerns about whether the case could be won without the jury understanding that Luther preyed on women because that was his nature. In the end, Hall, and his co-counsel, Mark Minor, had swayed eleven of twelve jurors to vote for first-degree murder. However, such decisions must by law be unanimous and the twelfth juror, a fifty-five-year-old Catholic housewife, had refused to go along with anything more than second-degree murder. The judge had then ordered the jurors to follow an obscure law and find the defendant guilty of the lesser charge.

It was both a victory and a defeat for Hall. Luther, who was also still serving time for a rape in West Virginia, received forty-eight years in prison and an additional fifty from a later attempted murder case in Denver; he would be off the streets for the rest of his life. But the murder of Cher Elder had been particularly brutal and the hiding of her body for two years had tormented her family, and justified asking for the death penalty. Public outrage over the holdout juror had in part been responsible for changing Colorado law so that if that case had gone to trial, the outcome would have been up to a three-judge panel not the jurors.

The trial had been bitter and emotionally draining. Hall was only half joking when he told his colleagues that he was refusing any trial involving "blood or semen" from his caseload. This was his first since, and he wondered—after listening to the investigators about Riggan's past—if he had another serial sexual predator on his hands. It would have been one thing if Riggan had simply gone into a rage and hit Paley hard enough to kill her. But there was the cut, and like his investigators, Hall didn't believe that a man waited thirty-seven years to take up sexually mutilating prostitutes.

In particular, the story of Riggan's second wife, Sandy, being taken at knifepoint down a dirt road to a cabin in an isolated spot in the country was just too similar to the circumstances surrounding the death of Anita Paley. It was as though he were re-creating the scene . . . and maybe it was the sort of scene he'd created again and again. If so, Hall wondered, why did Sandy and Joanne Cordova survive? They both told the investigators that when Riggan went into a rage, they'd recognized the danger signals and given in to his requests, calming him with their words and their bodies.

Maybe Anita Paley, who didn't know Riggan well and was new to prostitution, didn't recognize the danger signs. According to the reports, Riggan enjoyed raping women, even those he didn't have to, and there was his affinity for anal sex. Taking all of this into account, the prosecution team had come up with a theory: Paley, either frightened by Riggan's fantasy or repulsed by his demand for anal sex, tried to escape. They felt she may have jumped or fallen from the van in the attempt, though not at high speed as Riggan had claimed, causing the minor scrapes and bruises she had on her body. Riggan had then run her down and struck her—perhaps with the missing ax seen by Char Fitch or even just a rock, of which there were plenty in the mountains—on the side of her head. He'd then quickly put her into the van with her head between the front seats where the blood was found and driven her to the cabin. In the dark, he might not have realized how badly injured she was, but he had "paid" for sex and he was going to get it. He'd removed her clothes, pulling the red panties off with her shorts, but it had to have become increasingly obvious that Paley was badly hurt, her head swelling like a basketball. Thwarted, enraged, he'd decided to cut her deep inside—and after a few mistries, he carefully inserted the blade and then sliced.

It wasn't a perfect theory. Only two people knew what had really happened and one of them was dead and the other was denying everything. True to his nature, Riggan was proving to be less than a model prisoner. There were conflicts between him and other inmates over who would be the boss of the cell block. He would accuse his fellow inmates, with some justification it would turn out, of talking to the guards about him. He threatened to get revenge by cutting them with a broken coffee cup or stabbing them with a pencil.

Riggan constantly whined that his rights were being violated and found a sympathetic television news reporter to air his grievances in a series of jailhouse interviews. As if still able to manipulate a gullible public, he claimed to be a lawyer and threatened to file class-action lawsuits. But his big mouth also got him into trouble, such as when a deputy heard him bully another inmate by saying, "I'll bash your head in just like I did hers." One inmate even came forward to contend that Riggan confessed to killing Anita Paley in the process of telling yet another inmate that he was not afraid to kill to remain boss of the cell block. Riggan had also revived the story he'd told his wives about killing a father and son at the Arizona-Mexico border and burning them in their car.

Several weeks after his first appearance in court, Riggan fired the public defender appointed to represent him. The public defender's office had been trying to work out a plea bargain for second-degree murder, but Riggan wanted a trial and decided he'd represent himself.

As such, Riggan had the same right to call Hall to exchange information or attempt to work out a deal as would any lawyer. He called often and the conversations often lasted more than an hour. However, the conversations were rarely of much use other than as insights into Riggan's character. Mostly, he just wanted to complain. "Why do you want to kill me, Dennis?" he whined when the district attorney's office announced it would seek the death penalty.

In another telephone conversation, he asked, "When did my violent tendencies start?" Then he answered his own question by saying that his father used to "kick the shit out of me and my sister." The old man also had tried to rape his former wife Sandy, he claimed.

Riggan stuck to his story about Paley jumping

from his van. But there was always that one detail that he could not, or would not, explain when Hall repeatedly asked, "If she jumped out of the van, how do you explain the vaginal wound?"

The defendant's only attempt at an explanation was to go back to his story that her pimp had kicked her in the groin, but he soon realized that would not fly. He'd read the reports and neither the OB-GYN specialist, Dr. Cohen, nor pathologist Dr. Ben Galloway, had seen the sort of damage, such as bruising, to the exterior of her vagina that would have indicated her having been kicked. Plus, a kick hard enough to damage the inside wall of her vagina would not have caused the neat, surgical-like incision.

After he gave up on the kick by the pimp, Riggan said he wouldn't tell how it happened. Then he changed his mind and said that he might "some day." Finally, during one call in the late summer of 1997, he explained that the wound was caused "by my big dick. When I get excited, I can really rip a woman."

Still, Riggan conceded that the "big dick" theory, or any other that he could dream up, wasn't going to win over a jury. "You've got me by the balls, Dennis," he told Hall. "The jury isn't going to believe my story. . . . I don't think I'm gonna win; that vaginal wound's going to do me in."

As the summer drew to a close, Riggan seemed to give up. He said that if convicted, he wanted the death penalty rather than life in prison, "if I can get it quickly. . . . I'm tired of livin'. I don't wanna appeal."

Hall, however, was becoming concerned that Riggan was making no attempt to work on his defense. Not because he was worried about Riggan, but he didn't want to try the case over again if an appeals court ruled that more of an effort should have been made to get him to work with a lawyer. He knew that Riggan was clever and it crossed his mind that the defendant was representing himself because he was banking on getting another trial if he lost this one.

In September 1997, Hall wrote to Riggan advising him that he needed to come up with his list of mitigating factors should the case get as far as the death penalty phase. During such a phase, the prosecution presents "aggravators"—reasons the defendant should be put to death, such as the crime being particularly "cruel or heinous"—while the defense, in this case Riggan, presents reasons, or "mitigators," that he should be spared, such as a rough childhood that rendered him incapable of choosing between right and wrong.

"I must discourage you in the strongest terms from proceeding without counsel," Hall wrote to him. "To put this as bluntly as possible: GET A LAWYER."

Hall also expressed his concern to district court judge Frank Plaut, who had been appointed to the case. He told Plaut that he thought Riggan should be examined to determine if he was competent to stand trial, much less act as his own attorney.

In his advisement to the court, Hall said he suspected that Riggan was "manipulating" the system to "cause his own destruction." While the government was seeking the death penalty, it was still Hall's ethical obligation to bring Riggan's lack of effort to the attention of the court. Riggan's emotional state, Hall told the court, fluctuated wildly. At times, he'd break down crying, making statements like "nobody but these prostitutes cared about me." In other conversations, he would suddenly become "enraged for no apparent reason and scream obscenities and threats."

Hall believed that Riggan suffered some sort of "mental disease or deficiency" that made it "impossible for him to engage in the exchange of information. . . . It is clear . . . he is doing nothing to prepare." Instead, he said, Riggan was "obsessed with the sexual conduct of his ex-wife."

Throughout their conversations, Riggan had demanded that investigators be sent to Iowa to "investigate" Sandra's relationships with men. "She's a whore," he said over and over. "She's a whore!"

Finally Hall had grown tired of hearing this particular complaint from Riggan. "What's that got to do with this case, Bob?" he asked, exasperated.

"It has everything to do with this case," Riggan shrieked over the telephone. "It has everything to do with it."

Hall wasn't the only one having to deal with Riggan's outbursts. Depending on his mood, Riggan at times had to be carried into court hearings by deputies, struggling against his shackles and raining curses on all involved, particularly Judge Plaut, who sometimes also ordered that the belligerent defendant be removed from the courtroom.

The sixty-six-year-old Plaut had just been appointed to the bench in the fall of 1996 after a forty-year career as an attorney mostly involving civil litigation. In his time on the bench, Plaut had developed a reputation as a hard-nosed, no-nonsense jurist. He was up at the crack of dawn to run his miles, and he also ran a tight courtroom. He was known to have attorneys who complained too vociferously about his rulings escorted from his courtroom.

The Riggan case was his first murder trial. As such, he was warned by his colleagues on the bench to prepare himself emotionally. "Death is different," they said, even in the trial phase. Every little mistake, every ruling, every utterance, would be under the microscope. The flow of paperwork would be enormous. If the prosecution won, he would be part of the three-judge panel that would decide if Riggan received the death penalty or not. For it was his luck that the Riggan case was slated to be the first death penalty case to go to trial under the new law.

Plaut acted on Hall's recommendation and appointed a psychologist to examine Riggan. The psychologist determined that Riggan was mentally competent to stand trial. However, there was a second question, whether Riggan was competent to represent himself. From what the judge could gather, the trial would hinge a great deal on the testimony of medical experts, perhaps DNA testing and other complex issues. He didn't think Riggan could learn what he needed to know to address those issues, much less know the law and be able to conduct the examination and cross-examination of witnesses. He decided that Riggan needed lawyers.

Because Riggan had fired his earlier attorneys

from the state public defender's office, Plaut felt he needed to go outside the normal channels to find counsel for the defendant. He turned to a volunteer group known as the Office of Alternative Defense Counsel. From among them, he chose Colorado Springs attorney Dennis Hartley, a former marine and Vietnam veteran, who'd handled dozens of other murder trials.

Hartley had a reputation as a tough, pugnacious litigator. He brought in another attorney, Nathan Chambers, as co-counsel. Although younger, Chambers also had plenty of experience with a couple dozen murder trials under his belt and himself had a reputation of being willing to challenge anyone, including a judge.

Plaut told Riggan of his decision. The defendant didn't like it, but he accepted it. There were times Hartley and Chambers would wish that he hadn't.

In July 1998, Plaut ordered a second psychiatric examination to determine if Riggan was capable of understanding the charges against him and helping his lawyer to defend him against the charges. Riggan was getting more and more difficult to work with. Although Hartley and Chambers filed hundreds of motions and fought the prosecution motions at every step, Riggan sometimes accused them of being in cahoots with the district attorney's office. In open court, he accused them of being liars and worse, and if Plaut tried to intervene, Riggan would turn his foul mouth on the judge as well, who at last decided a second examination was necessary.

The examination was conducted by Dr. Robert Ruegg of the Colorado Mental Health Institute in Pueblo. He began by talking to Andrea, a paralegal in Hartley's office who offered the opinion that the competency issue had been raised because of Riggan's wild mood swings. She said that she'd talked to the defendant on the telephone when at times it had taken him a few seconds to go from calm and rational to cursing and belligerent.

Riggan, Ruegg wrote in his report, would often fly into rages, "demanding action on issues that were personally important to him but not relevant to the defense of his case. He is demanding and controlling and claims he could do things faster and better than his attorneys. . . . He interferes with his defense by calling potential witnesses and scaring them into hiding."

Ruegg talked to Chambers, who said Hall had originally raised the issue of Riggan's competency because he wanted to represent himself. At first, he and Hartley and Chambers did not think the competency hearing was necessary. However, they'd since found Riggan extremely difficult to deal with. At times, he would be reasonable. "At others, he flies into abusive, threatening rages and is unable to respond to the issues being addressed," Ruegg wrote. "He is obsessed about his ex-wife Sandy and her activities that have nothing to do with his defense."

However, when Ruegg went to talk to Riggan, Chambers insisted on being present for the examination. Ruegg asked him to give Riggan whatever instructions he needed to before they began and then to remain out of Riggan's view and not communicate with him verbally or by gesture. The attorney refused and said he would interrupt at any point he felt it was necessary.

Furthermore, Chambers wouldn't let Riggan give Reugg his account of what happened to Anita Paley. The attorney knew that if Riggan changed his story again, it would appear in Reugg's report and might be used against his client. Nor would the attorney allow Riggan to talk about his past psychiatric history. They did talk a little about Riggan's abused childhood. His parents, he complained, liked his older sister, Rosie, better and he got less attention.

Ruegg noted that Riggan did not recognize "personal space" when talking or passing by others. However, "he was pleasant, cooperative, talkative and engaging. He was articulate, using appropriate grammar and vocabulary. . . . He seemed slightly inappropriately unconcerned about his legal situation except when the issue of the death penalty was being discussed. Then, he seemed appropriately serious, but the sudden appearance of this concern seemed incongruous."

Riggan, the psychologist noted, did not trust his attorney, but "this is an attitude, a part of his personality, and not evidence of mental illness." The defendant said that the competency issue had been raised in part because "he sees himself as a person who will never give in or bow down, even when the court expects him to."

Chambers soon cut off the interview, and Reugg had to learn much of Riggan's past by reading Goodwin's reports. Based on this "limited evaluation," Ruegg wrote that he believed that Riggan had both an antisocial and narcissistic personality disorder. He also believed that given a more thorough evaluation, Riggan would meet the criteria for "psychopathy," a subset of antisocial personality "marked by such features as remorselessness, cruelty, premeditated violence, criminal versatility, parole violation, glibness, superficial charm and lack of guilt . . . with poor institutional adjustment, worsening or no benefit with psychological treatment, recidivism and future violence and sexual crimes."

As for his legal capacities, Ruegg wrote, "Mr. Riggan understands the elements of the justice system . . . and how they apply to him. . . . He has a problem with his temper, but his history indicates that he was able to hold it in abeyance in order to carry out his exploits and deceptions when doing so served his purposes.

"I have therefore found, within the scope of this limited evaluation, no sufficient reason to believe that Mr. Riggan is suffering from a mental disease or defect that renders him incapable of understanding the nature and course of the proceedings against him or of participating or assisting in his defense."

In the late summer of 1998, the trial was at last drawing near. In the year since the murder, the investigators had continued to learn more about Riggan's past. For instance, following his arrest in Wyoming in November 1986 while attempting to follow Judy in a stolen car, Riggan had "attempted suicide" in the Douglas jail. He was never in any real danger—having "hung" himself while sitting in a chair, but when he started complaining about imagining odors and hearing voices, in particular that of Joe, a deceased Vietnam war veteran, he was sent to the state hospital. There it quickly became apparent why he'd acted so strangely when he escaped.

Nearly eight years after walking away from the Navy, Riggan was discharged in January 1988 and transferred to the Veterans Administration Medical Center in Knoxville, Iowa. The doctors there diagnosed him with schizophrenia, but then promptly, just four days after his arrival, discharged him to his parents' home.

In March 1988, Riggan sought care at the Des Moines Veterans Administration Medical Center. Although he was there on his own free will, he became belligerent, argumentative, and demanding. He threatened to hurt or kill the admitting physician. He was admitted and voluntarily transferred to the psychiatric ward at the Knoxville medical center the next day. Within hours, and against medical advice, he left again. His discharge diagnosis was an adjustment disorder with "mixed disturbance of emotions." A few days later, he met Sandy.

The prosecution team also learned that Riggan had been unable to control his bowel movements as a child and young teen. It answered one of the questions that had been bugging them since they'd gone through the van and discovered dozens of pairs of clean underwear, some of it brand-new and still in its packaging. They wondered if encopresis was a good enough substitute for bed-wetting when it came to matching the criteria for a serial killer in the making.

Two of Riggan's fellow inmates came forward to say that Riggan admitted to them what he'd done when they were in jail together in April 1998. One said Riggan told him that "the last person I killed, I beat her brains in." This was significant because there had been no news reports about the exact cause of Paley's death.

According to handwritten notes made by the second inmate, purportedly after each conversation, Riggan claimed he had been paid to kill Buffy and that he bought her $400-a-day's worth of crack so she would "hang around long enough for him to 'get a piece of ass' and set his 'trap.' "

In the van, on the way to the mountains, Riggan tried to have sex with Buffy, but she refused. "He said she thought he was gross. He said it 'got messy,' and he 'cut her to the bone' with a fishing knife." Riggan also reportedly told him, "Trust me, no one would ever have had sex with her again."

Somewhere along the route to the mountains, the inmate wrote, Buffy jumped out of the van to get away and Riggan had to stop and "whack her upside the head" to subdue her. Then after he was spotted by the couple in the black truck and chased by the police, he ditched a hammer in a Dumpster, because "it had her blood all over it."

Riggan told his fellow inmate that he wished he could explain the woman's head injuries better. He was worried that there was no good reason for him taking her into the cabin "and that his expensive lawyer better figure that part out." According to the inmate's notes, he also bragged that he was involved in ten other murders in other states, but only this one had come back to haunt him.

"Most people don't care about drug addicts disappearing," Riggan reportedly complained. "Why are they making such a big deal about this one?"

Twelve

The trial of Robert Lee Riggan, Jr. opened with the Jefferson County courtroom 5-C gallery nearly empty of spectators—just a couple of reporters, a few curious courthouse employees, and a private investigator who worked for the defense team. The only other people in the courtroom were the jurors, Judge Plaut, a court reporter, several deputies, the prosecutors and their investigators Lauck and Burkhalter, the two defense attorneys, Riggan, and a pretty young blond woman who sat next to him. The more cynical courtroom observers noted that it had become a regular defense tactic in Jefferson County—particularly in sexual assault cases—to have a pretty young woman, with no apparent professional reason for being present, seated next to the defendant, as if to show the jury that he was no danger to females.

Other than those paid by the state to be at his side, Riggan had no friends or supporters in the gallery. Nor was there a grieving family, or tear-stained friends, not even silent street people, sitting in the gallery behind the prosecution table for Anita Paley. Her family lived back East and had told the district attorney's office that such a trip would be a financial hardship. They'd come if they were needed to testify during the death penalty hearing. To any outside observer, however, it appeared that no one really gave a damn what happened to Anita Paley or Robert Riggan.

A jury of fourteen was picked—four women and ten men, which included two alternates. The jury was comprised of homemakers, businessmen, a young male college student, a man who had just retired from the Marine Corps after twenty-five years of service, a male systems analyst, and a statuesque blond flight attendant, who caught the eye of every man in the courtroom when she took her seat in the middle of the jury box.

They could tell from the questions asked during voir dire, the jury selection process, that this would be a difficult trial to sit through. They were relieved in one aspect when told that it would not be up to them whether the defendant lived or died. That terrible decision would be left to a three-judge panel and, Judge Plaut said, shouldn't be part of their deliberations. He went on to explain his role as that of a "gatekeeper" who decided what evidence they would be allowed to hear or see. This, he said, was to protect the defendant's rights, not hide important facts from them. The jurors were told that they were to base their decision only on what they heard from the witness stand and what was accepted as an exhibit.

The prosecution had taken several hits in pretrial motions. The jurors would not hear of Riggan's past, unless introduced by the defense, including his treatment of his wives or the rape of Pamela

Kay Hart. They wouldn't learn that although the DA's investigators had looked, there was no record of Anita Paley having any outstanding warrants in New York, as Riggan had claimed she said.

Plaut had ruled that the prosecution could call the inmate witness who claimed that Riggan had told him about beating in the brains of his last victim. However, the second inmate, who'd written that Riggan had "cut her to the bone" had backed out when the prosecution wouldn't give him a deal, and the judge had ruled that his prior statements and journal would not be allowed into evidence because the defense attorneys could not cross-examine him on the witness stand.

The judge had ruled that the prosecution could not introduce Anita Paley's comments to Shane Delray—overhead by Char Fitch and told that same day to Joanne Cordova—about having been raped by Riggan "in the mountains." Nor would the jury hear Riggan's comments to Hall while acting as his own attorney—comments such as how his "big dick" had ripped Paley. Nothing about his obsession with his ex-wife Sandy's sexual activities that he claimed had "everything to do with this case" would be allowed.

In September, Plaut had again asked Riggan if he still wanted to represent himself. Riggan said he did if he would have the same resources available to him as the prosecution. The judge noted that there was only a month to go before the trial and that he had "two excellent attorneys" who had done a lot of work, so Riggan agreed to proceed.

Hartley and Chambers didn't care whether Riggan wanted them. It would have been easier if they actually got along personally with their client, but this was not likely with the abrasive, confrontational Riggan. It wasn't necessary to the case, however. They were there only to do the best they could by Riggan. All they asked of their client was that he not waste their time and resources by sending them down blind alleys or chasing lies. Otherwise, they were too busy trying to save his life to worry about the character of their client.

"Frankly, I'm not interested in what my client has to offer except for a statement of the facts and an explanation of the surrounding circumstances," Hartley said in an interview with the press. He never let on how much he truly disliked his client.

Dana Easter, a tall, soft-spoken woman, opened for the prosecution. She began by noting that if not for the "fortuitous" timing of a couple on their way to work, Riggan would not have been seen dragging Anita Paley up a trail.

After he was caught, Easter said, Riggan had come up with "a strange tale" of the young woman jumping from his van and then, mortally wounded with a massive head injury, begging not to be taken to a hospital. The evidence, she added, would show that Paley's death was not accidental, and she was confident the jury would find him guilty as charged.

In plain, unemotional language, Easter laid out the chronology of events. She and Dennis Hall had talked about their strategy and decided that they needed to keep their case as straight and simple as possible so that the jurors could see through the smoke and mirrors the defense was sure to throw up. The prosecutors would stay away from emotional appeals—the facts of the case, the photographs of Anita, would be emotional enough.

On the other hand, Dennis Hartley, who opened for the defense, jumped right into theatrics. A short, balding man in cowboy boots, he rose to his feet and paused looking at the floor as if lost in thought. "Ladies and gentlemen, it is my pleasure to represent Robert Riggan," he said at last, sweeping a hand back to indicate his client sitting at the defense table. "And it is my pleasure BECAUSE . . ." He paused to let the word settle in and then lowered his voice almost to a stage whisper. ". . . he is not guilty."

Riggan had run that morning back in May 1997, Hartley continued, only because he had warrants for his arrest back in Iowa and didn't want to return to prison. He developed friendships with prostitutes "because they don't say a lot or ask a lot of questions." Among those prostitutes, he said, was Joanne Cordova, "a former Denver police officer who in May 1997 was a hooker addicted to crack cocaine . . . and Anita Paley, who in the days before her death had become suicidal and obsessed with religion." It was important to note that Riggan had claimed "from Day One" that Paley had jumped, he said.

Up to this point, Hartley's opening had gone pretty much as the prosecution had expected. The big question, the challenge they waited to hear, was how the defense would explain its biggest problem: the cut in Anita Paley's vagina. Other than Riggan's reference to the size of his penis or the pimp kick-

ing her in the groin, they'd heard no logical explanation for the record or off the record for that
injury.

Now, however, Hartley said he had one. "These
street ladies have an odd habit," he continued.
They carried their extra drugs and money in metal,
plastic, and glass containers "where if [they are]
stopped by police, it cannot be found." They carry
these containers "as gross as it sounds," he said,
"in their vaginal vaults."

Hartley went no further with the "vaginal vault"
theory at this time, but it was obvious that he in-
tended that when all was said and done, the jurors
would understand that Paley had jumped from the
van, and that the impact of hitting the highway had
caused one of these containers to break, slicing her.

It was all the prosecution team could do not to
let their jaws drops open. *Where in the hell had that
come from?* they wondered. Riggan had never mentioned any such thing, and he'd been with her for
a couple of days. Neither had Dr. Cohen mentioned
finding any sharp objects inside the woman.

Hartley moved on. The evidence, he said, would
show that Paley's brain was damaged on both
sides—the "coup" and "contra-coup" injuries,
which could only be caused when her "moving
head struck an immovable object . . . the road."
Or, the defense attorney continued, the sort of injury a boxer receives when struck in the chin but
suffers the more serious injury when his brain slams
against the back side of his skull.

Bob Riggan wasn't guilty of homicide, he concluded, because Anita Paley wasn't murdered. Her

death, he said, was nothing more than "an unfortunate suicide."

After the opening statements and a brief recess, the prosecution opened its case with the testimony of Amy Johnson and Jason Sosebe. The murder of Anita Paley had also killed their relationship, which wouldn't survive past the trial. Johnson, in particular, had been moved by the death of the young woman so close to her own age. She and another neighbor had brought flowers to the cabin, and she had erected a little monument at the spot where Paley had been left beneath the pine tree. Her tears on the witness stand as she described what she'd seen would be the only tears shed for Anita Paley in the courtroom.

As Easter had outlined in her opening, the prosecution marched chronologically through their witnesses: the police officers and detectives who took part in the initial investigation. Sheriff Bruce Hartman testified that when he arrived, the woman had moaned but was unconscious. When asked, he reported that a thorough investigation had not located any blood on the highway, nor had there been any rain.

Vicki Spellman was called to the witness stand to describe the crime scene, using photographs to point out the pools of blood in the cabin, the floorboards of which had been torn up and brought into the courtroom still darkly stained. Continuing with her investigation of the scene outside the cabin, Spellman laid the foundation to counter Riggan's contention that he was dragging her to the stream to clean her up. If that had been true, the criminalist noted, he had bypassed the easiest and closest access to the water.

Dr. Stuart Levy was called to the stand to describe the head wound. He said he could not say "one way or the other" that the patient had received more than one blow, nor could he say "with absolute certainty" what had caused the injury.

On cross-examination, Hartley got him to concede that the injury could have been caused by "ejection from a moving motor vehicle." However, the doctor countered, he thought that if the wound had been caused by an impact with the road after jumping from a vehicle moving forty-five miles per hour, "there should have been more of an abrasion around the stellate laceration." Levy admitted that he had seen a contra-coup injury in the head of Anita Paley. Hartley again used the imagery of a "boxer hit on the left side of his chin, but the problem being to the right side of the brain."

On redirect, Easter showed Levy a photograph of Paley's head wound, to demonstrate that there was "very little" abrasion. He noted there was no abrasion on her left ear, which—given its proximity to the head wound—should have been damaged when hitting a broad, flat surface like a road.

Dr. Harvey Cohen testified next.

"First, have you seen other vaginal lacerations?" Easter asked.

"Many," Cohen replied.

"Have you ever seen one like this?"

"No."

"What would you usually see?" Easter asked.

"Most would be jagged," Cohen replied.

The instrument that had caused this injury, he said, had to be "very sharp." Consistent with a knife? He agreed with Easter.

Countering Hartley's "vaginal vault" theory, Easter questioned the doctor as to whether he'd found any "foreign debris . . . any glass fragments or sharp objects" in the woman's vagina or the blood that came from there. He hadn't and what's more, he said, he would have seen it if it had been present.

On cross-examination, Hartley tried to get Dr. Cohen to agree that a violent fall could cause an object made of plastic or glass and placed in the vagina "for safekeeping" to break and cause an incision.

"I have a hard time visualizing that," Cohen said. "It was a very precise cut."

"But could it happen?" Hartley pressed.

"I said I have a hard time visualizing that," Cohen repeated. "The vagina is very well protected."

Cohen elaborated on his statement when Easter asked about it on redirect. The vagina, he said, "is a very elastic organ" and protected by the muscles and bones of the pelvis.

"Can you visualize the blow it would take to break something in there?" Easter asked.

No, Cohen replied. Especially, he pointed out, when the same blow wasn't hard enough to break her hip, back, or leg bones.

"What about from a kick?" Easter asked.

Cohen shook his head. "It was not the sort of injury you see with kicks."

Both doctors had testified in a detached, professional manner. However, Cohen's resolve slipped away when he quietly recalled the image of the hardened emergency nurses in tears.

"Will you forget this case very soon?" Easter asked.

"No," he said, "not for a very long time . . . if ever."

Following the other doctors, pathologist Ben Galloway testified to his findings at the autopsy. As he answered Easter's questions, he showed no trace of the emotions he'd felt when he discovered the cut. Only those who knew him were aware that he was still profoundly troubled by this particular wound.

Contradicting what was clearly going to be important to the defense case, Dr. Galloway said he didn't see a "contra-coup" injury. He said the bleeding on the opposite side of the brain from the wound was not caused by the impact of slamming against the skull, but by "gliding abrasions," which are caused when the brain shifts position in the skull, such as by rapidly turning the head, tearing tiny blood vessels. The rest of the bleeding on that side, he said, was caused by Dr. Levy's attempt to relieve the pressure.

Galloway wouldn't budge from that position under a fierce cross-examination by Hartley. What's more, he said, it was his medical opinion that the victim's head was stationary when it was struck by a moving object. . . . In this case, an object that hit her more than once.

The prosecution case shifted to the comments and contradictions Riggan made during his interviews with Boulder police officers Vicki Bresnahan and John Lauck testifying. The result was the picture of a man who lied as easily as some people breathe, and was clearly more concerned about lying to the police than he was about the young woman he'd left in the mountains with a shattered head.

Shane Delray was called to the witness stand. He swaggered into the courtroom wearing white cowboy boots made of reptile skin, a big silver belt buckle, and a button-down shirt opened almost to his navel to reveal several strands of thick gold chains. The swagger was an act. He had been expressing increasing apprehension to Jim Burkhalter as the trial approached. Rumors flew like birds on the streets and changed like chameleons. . . . His cooperation with the prosecution in this case, he explained, might get him shot before he had a chance to say what he was doing.

No one really knew what he was other than a sometime musician. Those same rumors had it that he was a pimp or a drug dealer. Delray told Burkhalter that none of that was true. He was trying to help girls like Anita Paley and Joanne Cordova get off the streets. He dressed like he belonged on the streets because that was a way to gain the trust of these women. Whatever he was, he gained a small measure of respect from Burkhalter, with whom he'd mostly dealt, because despite his reservations he did not run.

Delray made a big show of his disdain for the proceedings, lounging back in the witness chair, and looking as though each question took an immense physical effort to answer as he slowly leaned forward to speak into the microphone before sinking back to wait for the next question. Most of his answers were yes or no . . . he wasn't happy about not being able to testify about Paley's rape claim, but he still conveyed the image of a young woman who wanted to get her life back on track.

On cross-examination, Hartley got Delray to also admit that Anita Paley was a troubled woman who tried, albeit not very hard, to kill herself, and on the last day he saw her, spent her time reading a Bible.

"Have you ever known prostitutes to carry their drugs in their vaginal cavities," Hartley asked.

"Yeah," Delray responded, though he looked puzzled.

It was a point for the defense theory. However, on redirect by Easter, Delray said that he never knew Paley, who had only been involved in prostitution for a couple of weeks, to use that method of safe storage. Even if she had, he added, the common container was nothing more than a plastic sandwich bag.

Delray was allowed to step down and the courtroom grew quiet. The moment the court watchers had been waiting for had arrived . . . the appearance of the former Denver cop who'd become a prostitute.

"The people call Joanne Cordova," Easter announced.

Thirteen

It had taken Joanne Cordova months to grasp that Anita Paley was really dead. The girls who worked Colfax Avenue rarely stayed around long. They were always talking about going somewhere better . . . back home . . . another city . . . off with some trick who promised to take them away from it all. In some ways, Anita had simply gone out the door one day and not come back, no different than many others.

It wasn't until Lauck and Burkhalter took her to the old cabin in the mountains, several months after Paley's death, that it sunk in. They were walking back down the path near the stream, returning from the meadow where Riggan had left her alone that day, when she noticed a small white cross with a bouquet of flowers next to a tree. She thought it was the sort of thing a child might have erected over the grave of a pet. She passed on by but looked back just as Lauck approached the tree. She was surprised when he suddenly knelt in front of the cross and bowed his head.

"What is that?" she asked.

"Didn't you know?" he replied. "This is where we found her."

That's when it hit. *Anita's not gone . . . she's dead.* Cordova burst into tears.

Burkhalter put his arm around her and helped her back to the car. It was a nice gesture. She appreciated the way the district attorney's office—from the investigators to the witness advocates to Dennis Hall and, later, deputy district attorney Dana Easter, whom she was told would handle the questioning of her during the trial—treated her. Cordova didn't kid herself, she knew they considered her an important witness in their trial. But still, they could have subpoenaed her, forced her to testify. They didn't need to be so kind.

Char Fitch and Debbie Johnson had both taken off rather than testify. It wasn't just that she was afraid of being labeled a snitch, Fitch had said before she disappeared, she just couldn't deal with the idea of being in the same room as Robert Riggan. "I don't . . . I just think he's evil." The district attorney's office had issued warrants, but the two prostitutes couldn't be found.

So it was left to Joanne Cordova to be the lone representative of the women from Colfax Avenue who'd crossed paths with Riggan. At times, she wasn't easy to find . . . having no permanent place to stay at first. Burkhalter had to leave messages at Jimmy's that he had more questions and hoped she would call. She always did, though she didn't always understand why they were so interested in some aspects, such as the shopping trips (What sort of panties did Riggan buy her and of those, which had she left in the van? Or, what kind of knife did Riggan give her to make the sandwiches?).

Some questions at first confused and then frightened Cordova. For instance, Burkhalter asked her a lot about anything Riggan said about his travels before coming to Colorado. Had he mentioned other cities? Other women?

"Do you think he's killed other women?" she asked when she realized what this line of questioning meant.

"We think its a real possibility," he replied.

She'd answered the question as best as she could, but all the while in the back of her mind, a small voice cried out, *Oh my God, it could have been me.* She would wonder why she had been spared. *Why Anita and not me?*

As the day of the trial approached, Joanne Cordova began to have second thoughts about testifying. She tried to rationalize skipping town. She didn't *know* that Bob Davis, or Robert Riggan or whatever his name was, killed Anita. *What if he's innocent? What if he's not, but the jury lets him off and he comes looking for me? What if everyone thinks I'm a snitch? They don't really need me. . . .* Riggan was the family name of the owner of a large local construction company and suddenly she was afraid—aided in her paranoia by crack—that Robert was a son and they'd use their money to get her killed.

The danger wasn't all paranoia. That summer had been a particularly violent one for Cordova, and she worried that her number was up. She'd talked back to one gang member, demanding he respect her, until he hit her so hard he knocked her down; then he'd forced her to perform oral sex on him while her head was still buzzing.

Most of the danger had come from a man known simply as 51-50, which she understood to be California police call numbers to indicate a mentally ill person. Crazy. The man was one of the main crack dealers in the Capitol Hill district and known for protecting his turf, and enforcing his rules, with a baseball bat. He was big and black, not quite six feet tall, but probably weighing close to three hundred pounds.

Cordova never knew how he would react to her from one day to the next. Often he seemed to trust her more than he did his compatriots—the men who stood guard in his crack house—even more than some of his relatives. For instance, he trusted her to hold on to his crack supply if he needed to leave, knowing she wouldn't do any and would fight to protect his assets. Of course, he'd reward her with some of the drug.

But he could turn mean with little provocation or notice. He sometimes referred to her as "the PO-lease," having learned her past. He might say it in jest, but other times, he issued it as a challenge and looked at her suspiciously, as if trying to decide what to do about her. *Maybe,* he accused, *she was just pretending to be down and out. Maybe,* he said, *she was really working undercover.* He knew better and Cordova wasn't worried that he'd hurt her for that particular reason. But there were always other men around when he talked like that, gang members and drug dealers, who didn't know her but gave her hard looks that made chills run down her spine.

Cordova's mouth and maybe the pride she was recapturing from her cooperation with the Jefferson County investigators got her into trouble also. She didn't like to be ripped off or treated like she didn't matter, and she would stand her ground when any other hooker, and many of the men, would have backed down.

One day, she accused 51-50 of selling her and a friend $300 worth of *woo*, or fake crack. She banged on his door and demanded either crack or her money. He appeared and told her to go away. The man with her got the hint and took off, but Cordova demanded satisfaction. "Or I'm going to start yelling and then all of your neighbors will know what you do here," she said. "And somebody might even call the cops."

Then 51-50 produced a sawed-off shotgun that he leveled at her head. "Take off, bitch, or I'll blow your fuckin' head off," he snarled.

Cordova yelled back. "Pull the trigger, if you think you can."

It was insanity. They both yelled at the same time with only the screen door between them. His eyes grew larger, sweat appeared on his brow. "Back off, bitch, I'll do it," he screamed, thrusting the gun at her. "I'll do it."

Cordova saw his finger tense on the trigger. She knew then that she was going to die . . . there, outside a crack dealer's house because of $300 worth of a drug that had already ruined her life. *What the hell,* she thought, *if God wants me to die now, why fight it?*

The storm passed. 51-50 dropped the barrel of the shotgun and pursed his lips. "You're one crazy bitch," he said, and turned away from the door, disappearing into the gloom of his drug den.

Cordova didn't get any satisfaction that day. No crack. No money back. She didn't care anymore as she walked away, dazed by the realization of how close she had come to dying.

For a time after that, 51-50 seemed to treat her with more respect. When he said, "Uh-oh, here come the PO-lease," it was in a teasing manner, but the friendly chatter didn't last.

One afternoon, she called him looking for crack. He told her to meet him and led her into the laundry room of an apartment complex. She'd told him that this time she wanted to try the crack before she bought it. Suddenly his massive hands came up and before she could react, his fingers were wrapped around her throat. "I'll murder you, bitch," he thundered, his eyes wild, spittle coming from his mouth as he cursed and grunted and choked her to the ground. "I'll murder you, bitch."

Joanne Cordova believes that she died that day. She saw herself as though from another place in the room, helpless and still as the huge black man strangled the life out of her. She might have left her body there, but that tiny voice in her mind kept saying, *Hold on to life. Hold on to life.* She felt her body convulsing, but somehow managed to pull the money she brought out of her pocket. 51-50 took the money and eased his hold. "Scream and I'll murder you, bitch," he threatened. As soon as his hands were off her, she screamed. She couldn't help it; she'd never been so terrified in her life. Fortunately, 51-50 took off running.

Later, after she'd recovered, Cordova called Burkhalter and told him what had happened. She made him promise not to do anything about it. If she disappeared, she wanted him to know that it wasn't because she'd decided not to cooperate. If she wound up down at the morgue, she wanted him to know why.

Joanne Cordova knew that if she did not sober up, she would die soon, nothing more than a dead crack-addicted prostitute who'd lost any vestige she'd had of self-respect. She'd be just another Anita Paley, only the police might never find her killer.

Thinking about Anita Paley, Cordova's mind turned to the only people outside her small circle of friends like Jimmy and Shane who had treated her decently . . . the people in the Jefferson County District Attorney's Office. She knew she owed it to them to clean up her act. They had respected her and now she wanted to earn that respect. She couldn't be a police officer anymore, but she could respond like one.

Cordova entered Samaritan House, a Denver facility run by Catholic Charities, where she could get drug counseling and a safe place to stay with three good meals a day. They found her a job, too—not much of one, but more than she'd had for many years. Samaritan House had strict rules against drug use and late nights, so with the counselors' help, she weaned herself from crack and stopped selling her body.

Quitting prostitution was easy; she'd only done it to support her drug habit. Getting off crack was much harder. . . . She slept a lot and sweated the poisons from her body as her skin crawled. Not a day, and hardly an hour, went by that she didn't crave a fix, but she was determined that she would appear at this trial sober and clear-headed.

However, as the trial day approached, Cordova's

resolve weakened. Jimmy was on her about it being her "civic duty." It wasn't that she didn't want to, she told him, but she was frightened of what the reaction on the streets would be. She decided she needed to ask the criminal world for its permission to testify, and that meant pleading her case to 51-50, a man who had tried to kill her just a few weeks earlier.

Cordova hadn't seen 51-50 since that day, and she was trembling when she walked up to the door of his crack house. The house was typical for its kind. Young boys stood on the street corners and sidewalks acting as lookouts for the cops and rivals. Inside, other young men watched out the windows. Guns were present everywhere . . . assault rifles and handguns. 51-50 was sitting in his big easy chair, a semiautomatic 9mm handgun on the table in front of him. There was no telling what he was thinking behind his broad, scarred face.

"I need to ask a favor," Cordova began, as though she were a serf making a request of the local baron. She talked about Anita Paley . . . about her children . . . and how she had not deserved what happened to her. She explained what was happening and why she felt she needed to testify. . . . *I'll owe you forever.* . . . Other men in the room scowled at the mention of courtrooms and police.

The big man in front of her had not reacted, but Cordova felt that she was losing the argument . . . and if she did, she might lose her life for even thinking about becoming a snitch. "If he killed your sister, I'd testify for her," she pleaded. "He killed my friend, and I need to be there."

51-50 was a hard man in a hard world. He wouldn't hesitate to kill to protect his turf or business interests. But at the mention of the word *sister,* his features softened, though Cordova had no idea if he even had a sister. "Do what you need to do," he said, although not without a caveat, "so long as that's all you do."

Conversations stopped and heads turned as Cordova walked down the fifth-floor hallway of the Jefferson County courthouse. She smiled at those who met her gaze and tried to look confident, though she felt weak. She'd seen them nudge each other as she approached, knew what they whispered as she passed. *Used to be a cop . . . Colfax hooker . . . how did that happen?* With an effort, she kept her head high as she walked on toward the courtroom where thirty-nine-year-old Robert Lee Riggan Jr. waited for his trial to resume.

Dressed in a conservative cobalt-blue suit with a white blouse buttoned to her throat, she looked like a businesswoman. Her thick dark hair was pulled back from her face, emphasizing her high cheekbones and deep-set dark brown eyes. Her nose was slightly crooked—it had been broken by another prostitute a few weeks earlier. *All you have to do is tell the truth,* she reminded herself. *Don't get defensive.*

When she was a young cop, Cordova had dreamed of a day like this. A day when she would march into a courtroom as a key prosecution witness fighting to convict a killer. The defense attorney would attack, of course, but she would deftly turn aside his cross-examination and, speaking calmly and directly to the jury, testify for the victim. Then the jury would find the defendant guilty, justice would be served, and she would be the hero. Now, as she was sworn in, she just wanted to get it over with.

Cordova took her seat at the witness stand, smiled briefly at the jury, and turned expectantly to Dana Easter, who asked, "Did you know Anita Paley?"

"Yes, I did."

"How long?"

"I would say not more than a couple of months."

"Could you describe her?"

"She was a petite white woman with blond hair, approximately shoulder length, and she had light-colored eyes," Cordova replied. "She was about five-two, muscular but still petite."

"In the week that ended with her death, did you meet a man that you spent some period of time with?" Easter asked.

"Yes, I did. His name was Bob."

"Can you describe him, please?"

"He's in the courtroom."

"All right, if you would just point him out."

Cordova turned to where Riggan sat and looked at him for the first time. He sat with his head down, staring at this feet. "He's the gentleman sitting at the defense table," she said, pointing briefly.

Under questioning from Easter, Cordova described meeting him and his "wife" Debbie and how he'd gotten her attention the next day by honking. "He said he was looking for me. I was kind of taken aback. I didn't realize that anybody had an interest in me like that. So when I asked

him why he had been looking for me, he said that
he had bought me some clothes.

"He asked me what I wanted to do, and I told
him that I wanted . . . that I wanted to do some
drugs."

"And what kind of drugs did you want to do?"
Easter asked.

"I wanted to do crack cocaine."

As she answered each question, Cordova remembered to turn and address the jury, making eye contact. *Just like I was taught.*

"Okay," Easter said, nodding. "And how would
you describe your relationship with cocaine in May
of 1997?"

"I was an addict."

Joanne Cordova described their visit to the lake
that first afternoon with Riggan and how his van
was so meticulously arranged. "He had enough
camping gear for a crew."

"Do you remember the next day?"

"I believe we went to the mountains . . . to Bob's
'favorite place in the whole world.' "

"How do you know that?"

"He told me. We went to a place, it was an old
abandoned cabin." As she talked, Cordova thought
about the stream beside the path that led to the
meadow. "When we got there, Bob opened a Co-
rona. I sipped on that and fell asleep."

"Did he stay with you?" Easter asked.

"No, he did not," Cordova answered. "I don't
know at what point he left, but I woke up and I
was alone."

"Did you stay and wait?"

"No, I got scared being up there in the mountains alone, not even knowing where I was. So I walked back to see if the van was still there."

It was all coming back to Cordova. The fear . . . the vision of herself lying facedown in the stream . . . the feeling that something evil lurked in the woods, sizing her up.

When Riggan returned, Cordova said, she asked him, " 'Why did you leave me?' And he became angry that I had asked him . . . that I had questioned his whereabouts. . . . I felt uncomfortable, so I told him that I needed drugs and then we left."

"And was it ever your plan that you would have sexual intercourse in that clearing?" Easter asked.

Cordova felt her face blush. She forced herself to look at the jury to give her answer. "I never discussed it, and I wouldn't," she replied. "He said, 'Before we go back, can we do this?' I just wanted to get it over with. I just wanted to get back to Denver. I did have sexual intercourse with him in the van."

She wished Easter would ask her why she complied so she could tell the jury that she was afraid. She wanted to tell them about how he didn't ask to have sex with her . . . it was a demand . . . for doggie-style, whether she wanted that or not. But the prosecutor didn't ask those questions.

"Did he remove his clothing?" Easter asked.

Cordova knew that the prosecutor was not trying to humiliate her, but she still felt ashamed. "No, he did not. . . . He was on his knees and he said that he just wanted to have sex doggie-style, and he just kind of pulled his pants down . . . I turned over and that was it. He didn't take off any other clothes." The sex, she said, was rough . . . he'd cursed her and ignored her cries when he hurt her.

The next time he bought her crack, he demanded sex in the parking lot. "He said, 'You got your rocks, and I want to get my rocks off now.' " He was getting angrier and angrier until she suggested they return to the mountains, where, she said, he'd pulled into a construction site and again demanded that she comply with his wishes. "I was not appreciative of that at all. However, I knew that the situation was that he wasn't just going to give me free crack. And I knew at some point that I would have to do something and that was, you know, the sex, so I knew I was just going to do it anyway."

Again, he insisted on doggie-style sex and again he didn't bother to remove his clothes. "He was just right in the middle of it, he was kind of . . . I felt this . . . I don't know if it was anger or what it was, but it was just a real aggressive move and it was just a real aggressive thrust, if you will."

Throughout Cordova's testimony so far, Riggan had sat with his head down, only occasionally looking up as though bored. He looked up now when she talked about his sexual aggressiveness and shook his head before bowing it again.

Joanne Cordova related how they'd run out of gas and he'd blamed her. "I stayed in the van because he demanded that I have these tuna fish sandwiches ready when he came back."

"What did he give you in order to make these sandwiches?"

"He gave me this long, skinny knife . . . what I

would consider a knife to like gut fish with," she replied, "and tuna fish and bread and mayonnaise."

Easter walked over to where the exhibits were kept and picked up People's Exhibit 48, a fish fillet knife. The knife had already been shown to the jury when a criminalist testified that although a spot of Anita Paley's blood had been found on the outside of the sheath, no blood was found on the inside. Nor had the knife been wiped, the expert had testified, making it unlikely that this was the blade that had been used to cut the victim.

"Let me ask you if you remember seeing the defendant in ownership of this knife?" Easter was taking a chance. If Cordova identified this knife as the same one she'd used to make the sandwiches—a knife the jury knew was probably not the weapon used on Paley—then they still had no murder weapon.

Cordova was puzzled. She had not been told the nature of Paley's injuries beyond that she'd been struck in the head. She had no idea why Easter would be making such a big deal about what knife she had used to make the sandwiches, but she looked at the blade. She hoped she wasn't messing it up for the prosecution when she answered honestly, "No, that one does not match. There's definitely a different knife that I used for tuna fish, which was a lot thinner and a little more curved."

Without knowing it, Joanne Cordova had just delivered a blow for the prosecution. They didn't have the knife that they believed had been used on Anita Paley, and there had been only the knife Easter held in her hand in the van. Now the jury could be expected to realize that a knife was missing—a knife with a thinner, more curved blade that Cordova had used to make the sandwiches . . . and could have been used on Paley, after which it had been discarded.

Easter moved on to People's Exhibit 35, the lacy red panties that had been found intertwined with the gray shorts in the cabin. "Do you recognize these?"

This time, Cordova nodded, though again she wondered what this question was about. "That's the style of panties bought for me by Bob."

"So they appear similar?"

"Yes, but the ones I had were still on the hanger and still had tags on. I didn't take any of the tags off."

Easter nodded, apparently satisfied with the answer. She moved on to a clear plastic bag that held a number of personal effects. Cordova identified the contents as her check-cashing card, her identification card, and her Social Security card. There was something else that caused her to pause for a moment and fight back tears for the first time. She looked up and smiled at the jury as she added, "And I can see my picture . . . a little picture of my daughter."

It was late afternoon when Dana Easter finished her questioning of Joanne Cordova and Judge Plaut called a recess until the following morning. The prosecutors were pleased. Cordova had handed them the knife, not physically but certainly the existence of one that was now missing. Her statement that she'd never worn the red panties, which were

stained and had obviously been worn with the
shorts found near the pool of Anita's blood in the
cabin, meant that they'd been on the murdered
woman.

The defense attorneys had nearly blown a gasket
when the prosecution introduced a drawing Cordova had made for them the previous day of a
blunt-sided ax she'd seen in the van, which like the
knife she'd used, was missing. As important as those
points were, however, it was the portrait she'd
painted of Riggan as a conniving liar, a violent, sexual predator, that had damaged the image of the
clean-cut man in sweaters and slacks the defense
had put forth.

As he had with the Tom Luther case, prosecutor
Dennis Hall had considered trying to introduce
Riggan's "prior bad acts" regarding his wives and
Pamela Kay Hart into evidence. There was a provision in the law, written with sex crimes in mind,
that allowed such previous history. But judges were
reluctant to grant such damning material, as had
the judge in the Luther case. Riggan had never
been convicted of those other rapes and abuse, so
the prosecutors knew it was unlikely that such evidence would be allowed under the provision. They
had decided their energies could be better spent
elsewhere.

They would have to rely on the prostitutes who'd
met Riggan just before Anita Paley's murder to por-
tray him as he really was. After Char Fitch and Debbie Johnson disappeared, the judge had ruled that
their previous statements would not be allowed, because they couldn't be cross-examined. Only Joanne

Cordova had stayed and given them what they needed from the witness stand.

Cordova was not at all what they had expected. Most of the prostitutes they'd run into were hard, jaded women looking out for themselves and no one else; most had very little going for them. Cordova, on the other hand, was obviously intelligent and friendly. She made no attempt to disguise what she was—a crack addict and a prostitute. It was a shame what the drugs had done to her.

Burkhalter in particular knew that at some level Cordova wanted them to recognize that she was in a way acting as a law enforcement officer. She'd often told him that her days as a police officer were the best in her life and he'd just as often thought that she must have been a fine officer . . . one who should have been still rising through the ranks. But it was too late for that, and like the others on the prosecution team, he could only hope that this trial, her efforts to stay sober and do the right thing, was a turning point in her life. They had all come to like and respect Joanne Cordova.

Dana Easter thought that Cordova had come off as credible. Her embarrassment and humiliation at some points in the questioning were obviously not feigned, and unlike Riggan, her story had not changed from the first time she told it. Now she would have to face the defense attorneys.

When she reported to the courthouse the following morning, Joanne Cordova was pleased with how the first part of her testimony had gone. She'd been careful to make eye contact with the jurors, as she'd been trained to do at the police academy, and they had paid close attention to her answers. A rather striking blond juror seemed particularly attentive, nodding each time a point was made and taking notes on a legal pad.

But as Cordova walked down the hallway to the courtroom again, she felt her heart start to beat faster. She smiled at the gawkers, but it seemed a phony, nervous smile . . . as though she were trying to look out from behind a mask again. Only now she didn't have any drugs to help keep it in place. The defense attorneys were about to have their turn at her, and she knew they'd be casting stones. She was no longer a cop, shielded by a badge and the respect it bought.

Joanne Marie Cordova was a prostitute and a crack-cocaine addict whose fall from grace would be laid bare by the defense. It wouldn't matter that she had stopped using crack and wasn't turning tricks anymore. She felt alone and ashamed, fragile as a robin's egg, and she didn't know how she would hold up under the defense attorneys' attack.

She did know she had to try—for Anita Paley, who was so alone in the world that no one had come to the trial of her accused killer . . . not even much of the press, although this was a death penalty trial. The empty rows behind the prosecution table, normally reserved for the victim's family and friends, spoke volumes about the tragedy of Anita Paley's life.

Still, this wasn't just about Paley. Cordova had told everyone from 51-50 to Burkhalter that she was doing this for her friend, and because she could have just as easily been Riggan's victim. In reality, she'd stayed and dealt with her fears because she knew that in the end, this trial was about redemption for Joanne Cordova.

As she approached the courtroom doors, she saw a tall, well-dressed man leaning against the opposite wall. She recognized him as one of Riggan's defense attorneys, Nathan Chambers. She smiled timidly and murmured, "Good morning."

Chambers nodded, though he didn't smile. "Good morning," he replied.

Cordova turned and walked through the heavy wooden doors. As Chambers moved to follow, he was asked what he'd thought of her testimony the previous day. He shrugged. "She's a whore."

Court was convened and Cordova was again called to the witness stand. Judge Plaut turned and reminded her, "You understand that you're still under oath?"

"Yes, sir," she answered, and turned to smile at Chambers as he rose for the cross-examination. *Just tell the truth*, she thought. *Don't get defensive. Oh God, I don't want to be here.*

"Good morning," Chambers began.

Cordova nodded. "Good morning."

"Yesterday afternoon, you testified for close to an hour, I would guess, about events that happened in May of 1997, correct?" Chambers asked.

"Yes, sir," she answered, turning her head to the jury, "that's correct."

"And so your testimony is about events that are a year and a half ago almost?"

"That's correct."

"And because of the passage of time, your memory is, in some respect, foggy?"

"No, it's not foggy," she said, shaking her head.

"You're absolutely clear on all details?" Chambers asked, raising an eyebrow so that the jury could see his skepticism.

"I'm clear on details. However, I'm not . . . I'm not clear on the chronological order of things."

"Okay." Chambers nodded. "That's what I meant. It's a little bit hazy?"

"Yes."

"And during this period of time in May of 1997, you were addicted to crack cocaine?" Chambers asked.

Uh-oh, she thought, *here we go*. "That's correct."

"And you were using quite a bit of the crack cocaine during that period of time, using it regularly?"

Cordova forced a smile and nodded to the jury. "Yes, I was using it regularly."

"Every day?"

"Pretty much."

"And so when many of the events that you testified about yesterday were actually happening, you were using crack cocaine or [were] high on crack cocaine at the time the event was transpiring?"

"Part of the events, that's correct."

"How were you supporting yourself in May of 1997?" Chambers asked innocently.

Cordova smiled again, though there was a pit in her stomach. She looked at the jury, in particular the pretty blond woman and wondered what she would think. "I was working on the street in prostitution and also off the street in what you might call a call-girl status." *There, it's out*. She noticed the blond woman was writing something on her pad. *I just want this to be over*, she thought.

"Okay," Chambers said, sounding as if she'd just told him she was the dogcatcher. "And how long had you been doing that in May 8 of 1997?"

"One month."

"One month?" Chambers repeated, a half-smile on his face.

"Yes."

"So April of 1997 is when you began . . . prostitution?"

"Probably," Cordova said, pausing a moment as if to view a calendar in her mind. "Yes, that's correct."

"And you spent several days with Bob [Riggan] in May of 1997, correct?"

"That is correct."

"And you were with him voluntarily?"

"Yes, I was."

"He didn't force you to be with him?"

"No, he did not."

Cordova repeated her story about how they'd met. "And you wanted some crack cocaine?" Chambers asked.

"Yes."

"And so you went and you procured crack cocaine?"

She concentrated. "My memory doesn't serve me correctly. I mean, I can't recall if we actually went and got some crack cocaine at that point or not."

"You had crack cocaine that day, correct?"

"I don't recall. Let me see." She shook her head. "I don't recall having done crack cocaine that day."

"And Bob gave you the money to buy crack cocaine?"

"That is correct."

Chambers asked about the afternoon at the park. "And that was a pleasant experience?"

Riggan looked up. Cordova nodded and smiled. "That's correct."

"In fact," Chambers said, himself turning to the jury with his back to Cordova, "at one point you thanked Mr. Riggan for being so nice to you?"

"Yes, that's correct."

The questions turned to the shopping trip. "And at those places Bob got some clothes for you?"

"Yes, he did." She wondered about all the softball questions, knowing the other shoe had to drop sometime.

"And again, during this day, you were obtaining and smoking crack cocaine?"

"I believe I did almost every day that I was with him."

"Now, you talked about some articles of clothing that Mr. Riggan got for you?"

"Yes, sir."

"And he got you several pairs of panties?"

"That's correct."

"And you were shown People's Exhibit thirty-five, and you said that these panties were at least of the same design as the kind he bought for you?"

"That's correct."

"These panties, however, were actually too big for you?"

"Yes, as were the rest of the panties that he purchased."

"Apparently, Mr. Riggan didn't know your clothes size any better than you did?" It was a joke and everyone in the courtroom laughed, including Cordova, who answered, "Apparently not."

"Now, you knew Ms. Paley also; is that correct?"

"Yes, that is correct."

"She was a smaller woman than you?"

"In stature, yes."

"So clothes that were too big for you were way too big for her?"

"She had a much more muscular build, and she had more of a buttocks. But I'm not—"

Chambers interrupted. "So you wear the same pants as her?"

"I wouldn't be able to fit into anything that would fit her around the waist."

"Because she was smaller than you?"

"That's correct."

Chambers asked her about the clothes and watches Riggan had purchased for her. "So he got items for you that were worth several hundred dollars, accurate?"

"Pretty close."

"And that was something he did for you not in exchange for sexual favors? Just did it?"

Joanne Cordova nodded to the jury. "That's correct."

"In fact," Chambers said, again turning his back on her to face the jury, "if he had wanted to purchase sexual favors from you, he could have done it for a much cheaper price, correct?"

The suddenness of the question caught her off guard. "I wouldn't say a much cheaper price by the amount of time I spent with him. However, I didn't look at that as such when I got in his van. I looked at the crack cocaine."

"Right," Chambers said. "You wanted the crack cocaine?"

She agreed, wondering where this was leading.

"Ms. Cordova, I don't mean to be indelicate here . . . ," Chambers began to say.

"Oh, no," she said, almost involuntarily.

"Since you were working as a prostitute," Chambers continued, "what did you charge for your services?"

"One hundred dollars per half hour of my time," she said, trying to smile, this time not looking at the jurors but feeling their eyes on her.

"That's pretty pricey, correct?" Chambers asked. "More than other people were charging?"

"I'm not familiar . . . I'm not accustomed to asking other women what their prices are," she answered, trying to sound more nonchalant than she felt.

But Chambers wouldn't let up. "You were certainly familiar with other prostitutes working in the area?" he asked sarcastically.

"I don't know what they charged," she retorted.

"You were familiar with their habits?"

"I was familiar with a lot of their habits, because I lived with them. But, I mean—"

Chambers didn't allow her to finish. By now, the exchange was growing heated and they were almost talking on top of each other. "For instance," Chambers shot back, "like Char Fitch—"

Before Cordova could counter, Judge Plaut held up his hand. "If each of you would allow each other to finish your statement, I think it would be easier on the reporter." The two were like bull elk competing in mating season, charging, withdrawing, then charging again.

"Char Fitch was working as a prostitute," Chambers began again. "You were familiar with her habits?"

"A lot of her habits," Cordova agreed. "However, as far as money, that's something that . . . I wouldn't ask you how much you have in your pocket."

"Okay," Chambers said, nodding. "Anita Paley, you were familiar with her habits?"

"A lot of her habits just from being around her."

"So if Bob had simply wanted sex, he could have got it for less than the amount of goods that he gave you?"

That, she thought, *was a low blow.* She felt humiliated, cheap. "As I stated before, no," she said, getting angry and letting it show. "Actually, I don't believe he would have been able to get it for less than the amount of the goods he gave me simply because of the amount of time I spent with him, several days multiplied—"

Chambers jumped in. "That wasn't my question. Please just answer my question."

Cordova calmed herself to answer. "No, he would not."

"How much time do you spend with a john?" Chambers asked sarcastically. "Do you typically spend five days with a john?"

"No," she answered. "Typically, I haven't—"

But again Chambers didn't let her finish. "Typically, very short? Half an hour or an hour, right?"

Cordova was finding it harder to give her answers to the jury and look them in their eyes. "There's no typical. It's just, you know . . . ," she said, groping for the words. ". . . I mean, I can remember charging five hundred for a night—"

Chambers was relentless. "You can remember charging twenty bucks for fifteen minutes, too, right?"

The statement hurt and she answered angrily again, "No, I cannot."

Joanne Cordova didn't know how much more she could take along these lines, but then Chambers moved on to another subject. "You and Mr. Riggan eventually went to the mountains, up to a cabin?"

"Yes, to the area of the cabin," she said. "I never went into the cabin."

Chambers repeated the story that she drank a beer and fell asleep and when she woke, Riggan was gone. "And you were afraid?"

"Yes, I was."

"You were paranoid?"

"I might have been," she agreed.

"You had been using crack cocaine?"

"Yes."

"You're familiar with the effects of crack cocaine?"

"Yes, I am."

"Tell the jury how you smoke crack cocaine. How is it ingested?"

"Crack cocaine is put on either a metal pipe, glass pipe, or aluminum pipe with some type of screen, which may be a Chore Boy or Brillo," she explained, as if talking about a science experiment. "It's then melted. It's ingested into the lungs, absorbed by the cilia of the lungs, goes to the bloodstream, then to the brain, and you get high."

"And what's the effect?" Chambers asked, obviously expecting a simple answer.

A moment later, jaws were dropping all over the

courtroom. Investigators Burkhalter and Lauck, however, smiled. They knew Joanne Cordova was no dummy.

"Its effect," Cordova said, turning to the jury as she recalled the information she'd looked up regarding cocaine in the public library, "is that it releases dopamine, which is an endorphin, into your brain so that you get that good feeling immediately."

Even Chambers seemed taken aback and at a loss. He recovered, though, and asked, "And when you come down from your high, what's the effect?"

"I've never had physical withdrawals."

"There's a craving for more cocaine, though?"

"There's absolutely a craving for crack. That's the market's intention."

"And there is frequently, when you're using crack, intense paranoia?"

"That's one of the psychoses of cocaine usage."

"And that's something you've experienced?"

"I have experienced paranoia on occasion," Cordova agreed. "But I've been using it long enough to differentiate between paranoia and reality at this point."

"The fear and paranoia, that fear at the cabin was because of the crack cocaine?"

"Absolutely not, because I hadn't gotten high that day." She shook her head.

"You just told the jury you did." Chambers scowled.

"That I got high that day?" she asked.

"Yeah," Chambers answered.

"But I hadn't—at that point of the day—got high."

Chambers tried a new line of attack. "Ms. Cordova, how many felony convictions do you have?"

Cordova sighed; he was leaving her nothing. "If my memory serves me correctly, I believe I have four or five felony convictions," she replied.

"Tell the jury about those."

Cordova recounted them all. The police test she'd cheated on. The high-speed police chase. The credit-card-company theft. A drug conviction.

The trial suddenly ground to a halt when Riggan began squirming in his seat and his attorney Hartley announced that he needed a break because of a "stomach ailment." Actually, under the stress of the trial, Riggan's encopresis had returned and he'd often had to ask to be excused. Several times, he barely made it out of the courtroom before he voided his bowels.

While the court waited for Riggan to return, Cordova was allowed to step down from the witness stand. She took the opportunity to go over to the prosecution table to ask for a drink of water.

Chambers complained to the judge. "Ms. Cordova was still technically on the witness stand. . . . But she was conversing with Mr. Hall in the courtroom. I object to that and move for a mistrial."

Cordova paled. *Oh God, what have I done.* Hall explained the circumstances. "I did not discuss her testimony."

Plaut denied Chambers's request. Riggan returned and Cordova was directed to return to her seat.

"Would it be fair to say that crack cocaine has had a dramatic impact on your life?" Chambers asked.

"Absolutely," she replied, this time without smiling. "Without a doubt."

"The felony convictions is one aspect?"

Cordova nodded. "Anything having to do with anything criminal is absolutely one effect. . . ."

"You used to be a police officer; is that correct?" Chambers asked. The jury looked at Cordova with revitalized interest.

Cordova nodded sadly. She was beginning to feel defeated. She had tried so hard, but she was being stripped bare. "That is correct."

"And you lost that job?"

"No, I did not," she answered. If he was going to take everything, she was going to make him be accurate.

"You didn't?"

"No, sir, I did not."

"Weren't you fired when you obtained that first forgery conviction?"

"No."

Chambers rolled his eyes at the jury. "You weren't fired when you obtained that first forgery conviction?"

"No, sir, I was not fired."

"You were allowed to resign?" Chambers asked.

"No. I chose to resign on August 1, 1985, that's correct."

"I see." Chambers smirked. "You chose?"

"That's correct," she replied.

Chambers took a shot. "The Denver Police Department was anxious to have a forger on their force?"

Before Cordova could answer, Judge Plaut raised his hand. "All right," he growled. "That's argumentative. Please move on."

Chambers, clearly frustrated, asked, "You're familiar with the practice of women who are addicted to crack cocaine?"

"In general, I said I am familiar with some of the practices."

"Is this a way of saying yes?" Chambers said, rolling his eyes again.

"No," Cordova shot back.

Again, the judge intervened. "Just a minute. Mr. Chambers, she answered your question. It wasn't a yes, but it was a responsive answer. Please move on."

Chambers demanded that he be allowed to make a record. The witness, he said, was not cooperating and the judge was allowing her to get away with it.

"All right," Plaut acknowledged. "But I'm not going to allow this to continue. So I'm asking you to ask relevant questions and move along in your cross-examination."

Chambers flushed. "I need to make a record now, Your Honor."

"No, you don't," Plaut answered. "Please move along."

Chambers refused. "I need to make a record immediately," he said, his voice rising.

Plaut was unmoved. "Mr. Chambers, please proceed with your questions."

Angry, Chambers returned to his cross-examination of Cordova.

"You know that people who are addicted to crack cocaine are very cognizant about keeping their crack and other valuables safe?" he asked.

"That's correct," she replied.

"They want to make sure that when they're stopped by the police, the police won't find them?"

"Or if they're approached by any criminals, so that criminals won't take their drugs," she added.

"They want to know that if they're stopped by the police, the police won't find the drugs?" Chambers repeated, enunciating each word slowly.

"Is that a question?" Cordova asked. Now she was feeling as though she were gaining the upper hand.

"Yes," Chambers sighed.

Cordova smiled. "Would you repeat your question, please?" she asked pleasantly.

Chambers stared at her for a moment as though dumbstruck. Then he asked the question again. "They want to be sure that if they're stopped by the police, the police won't find the drugs?"

"It's my experience that in reference to the police they get rid of the drugs," Cordova answered. "But in reference to other drug users, they would tend to hide the drugs. Does that answer your question?"

Chambers shook his head. "It does not, so I'll ask it for a third time. If the police stop them, they want to make sure the police won't find the drugs."

Cordova nodded. "By throwing them, yes."

"And by other means?" said Chambers.

"If I was approached by the police, I would not choose to keep any drugs or paraphernalia on my person," she answered. "I would do everything I could do to get rid of them, but around other drug addicts, it would be a different story."

Chambers gave up trying to get her to independently say what he wanted her to say. "Women frequently store their crack cocaine and other valuables in their vaginal cavities, correct?"

"Occasionally," she answered.

"They use many different types of containers to do that?"

"I've seen a couple of different types," she agreed. She wondered what this had to do with anything.

"Plastic containers?" Chambers asked.

"Plastic wrap," Cordova answered.

Plastic wrap wasn't going to do the defense any good. "Plastic vials?" Chambers asked.

"I've not seen a plastic vial to date, but it's possible."

"Metal containers?"

Cordova nodded. "I've seen metal. . . . Small, round containers."

Defeated, Chambers dropped the subject. He asked about Riggan wanting sex in the clearing that day. "And you did not want to do that?"

"No, I didn't."

"And you told him you didn't want to do that?"

"That's correct."

"And so he complied with your wishes?"

"He respected that."

"He backed down from his desires and went to the van?"

"Yes, he did."

"And you had sexual intercourse in the van?"

"Yes, we did."

"And after doing that, you drove back to Denver?"

"That's correct."

Chambers noted that they then drove back to Denver and obtained more crack. "Mr. Riggan stated that after you obtained crack cocaine that he wanted sex?" he asked.

"He wanted to 'get his rocks off,' " she answered.

"He wanted to do it right there?"

"Right where we were," she agreed.

"But you didn't want to do it right there?"

"I didn't want to do it at all, but I did."

"So you didn't want to do it right there?" Chambers repeated.

"I didn't want to do it at all or right there."

Chambers scowled. "And Mr. Riggan honored your wish?"

"He became very angry," Cordova replied.

"He honored your wish?" Chambers repeated.

"Yes, he did."

"Didn't force you to do anything?"

"No, he did not."

"You suggested that you go to the mountains, correct?"

"That's correct, sir."

"And Mr. Riggan honored your request?"

"That's correct."

The two argued about whether she agreed to have doggie-style sex with Riggan. Then Chambers complained that Cordova had drawn a picture of the missing ax for the prosecution but only described it for the defense investigator. The prosecution should have had to turn that over much sooner so that the defense could have prepared an objection. Such an argument normally would have been made outside the hearing of the jury, but Chambers was angry and complained again, "This is a discovery violation, Your Honor."

Now Plaut was angry. "The jury is instructed to disregard that. Mr. Chambers, you know better than that. Please don't do that again."

Chambers flushed. "I need to make a record, Your Honor."

"You will when I say you will," Plaut replied. "Please move to another area of questioning."

Chambers refused and started arguing, at which point the judge excused the jurors and asked Cordova to step into the hallway. With them gone, Chambers accused the judge of being unfair. Easter countered that Chambers was trying to intimidate Cordova. "And it's causing her some difficulty in answering the questions. So I just want the record to reflect that if the court has limited Mr. Chambers's cross-examination, it's been because of improper examination, which includes tone and manner."

Plaut admonished Chambers. "I'm sure you don't like the idea that this court is going to continue to run this trial, and it's not going to be run by any of the lawyers.

"I can assure you, since I've admonished you several times off the record and now on the record, that if you continue to act in a way that the court finds detrimental, whether it's intimidating to the witness, or because it's contrary to something that the court's just ruled on, I will tell you about it. I will tell you about it very firmly, and I will tell you about it in the presence of the jury. I don't have enough time to send this jury out each time you do something inappropriate.

"If there's been any prejudice toward your client this morning, it is my firm belief that the record will reflect that it was caused by counsel and not by the court."

With that, Plaut ordered the jury and Joanne

Cordova to return. Then, as if nothing had happened, he asked Chambers to proceed with his questioning. The defense attorney seemed to have had the fire taken out of him and he soon ran out of questions.

Easter, however, had a few more, to address some points made by her counterpart. "Ms. Cordova, you were asked a number of questions about the type of container that is used in order to hide crack in a woman's vagina?"

Still puzzled, Cordova nodded.

"What types of things are most commonly used?"

"Any type of plastic whatsoever from a grocery bag, toilet paper, Kleenex. Just anything that's handy."

"Okay. You have seen metal containers?"

"Maybe a month ago, I saw a metal container."

"And you are aware of the habits of the other women, including Anita Paley, is that right?"

"That's correct."

"Did you ever see Anita Paley save or hide her crack cocaine or anything else, for that matter, inside her vagina?"

"No, I didn't," said Cordova, shaking her head. "It would be highly unlikely because she didn't have enough money to guard or to save."

"What did she usually do when she got her crack?" Easter asked.

"She smoked it. That's how little she had."

"Okay. What's the size of containers that you were referring to?"

"I would say a container no more than a half an inch in height and maybe a maximum of three quarters of an inch in diameter. They're very small."

Easter nodded. She had one more question. "Ms. Cordova, did you show Bob the cabin, or did he show it to you?"

"Oh, he absolutely showed it to me," she said. "It was his favorite place in the whole world."

At last, it was over. As Joanne Cordova stood to leave, she looked at Riggan. He was staring at her, and though she couldn't be sure, she thought he mouthed the words "I'm sorry" before looking back down at his feet.

For a moment, she felt pity for him and wondered what demons he had to deal with. Better than most, she knew that the seeds of self-destruction were often planted early in life. Then she remembered Anita Paley. They all made choices, good and bad. Cordova had to live with hers, and Riggan would have to live with his.

Fourteen

October 20, 1998

The defense opened its case by calling Christine Clark Hunter, a registered nurse who was present in the surgical intensive care unit when Anita Paley was brought in. The main purpose of her testimony was to note that the abrasions on the victim's body appeared to be "road rash," a malady Hunter was familiar with as part of a medical team that cared for injured riders on an annual bicycle tour in the Rocky Mountains.

Hunter was followed by Triena Harper, an assistant coroner for Jefferson County, who had first been called by the prosecution to testify that Paley's abrasions and bruises were not consistent with that of other victims she'd seen who hit the pavement at a high rate of speed. She'd also testified that such victims usually broke bones.

Hartley, however, had insisted that Harper dig more thoroughly through the records to locate cases in which victims who died had suffered relatively little damage except for the injury that killed them. However, most of those deaths had occurred at relatively low speeds and by people dressed in long sleeves, even leather jackets, and pants, which Hall noted on cross-examination.

"In your experience, ma'am, would it be fair to say that the extent of a person's external injuries—and by that I mean scrapes and abrasions—would have at least something to do with the speed at which they hit the pavement?" the prosecutor asked.

"In most cases, yes," Harper replied.

"And would it be fair to say that the extent of the person's external injuries would also depend upon the kind of clothing they were wearing?"

"That's correct."

"And based upon that same experience, do you think you have in your mind an idea of the average external injuries that a person would get if they hit the road at forty-five miles an hour?"

"Yes."

"Would it be fair to say that based upon your observations the injuries to Ms. Paley were below the average of the injuries you've seen from persons who have hit the road at about that speed?"

"Yes."

The defense called their investigator, Jennifer Gedde, a law student, who spoke about the warrants out for Robert Riggan in Iowa. These were the reason, the defense was contending, that Riggan "panicked" and left Paley when spotted by Sosebe and Johnson.

Gedde also testified that when she interviewed the inmate who had testified for the prosecution that Riggan told him he beat in the brains of his last victim, the inmate told her he wasn't sure if

Riggan was referring to what the authorities accused him of doing or what he had actually done.

Although she wasn't present during Joanne Cordova's testimony, Gedde said she'd interviewed her and was told that prostitutes sometimes stashed crack pipes, pillboxes, even cigarette lighters in their vaginas. Shane Delray, she said, told her that he did know that Anita stored her crack there, though he didn't know what container she used.

Hall attacked Gedde's testimony in order. First, he got her to admit that the warrants for Riggan were "in-state," meaning that Iowa didn't consider them significant enough to extradite the person in question if located in another state. He then turned to the investigator's interview of Joanne Cordova.

"Isn't it true she was talking about the manner in which women smuggle items into jails?" he asked.

"She also spoke about when women are in fear that they may be searched or in fear that their items may be stolen on the street," Gedde replied.

"Ma'am, you don't think that women are afraid of being searched for cigarette lighters, do you?" Hall asked.

"I'm unaware of whether they would be frightened about that," Gedde answered.

"So when Ms. Cordova talked about cigarette lighters, what she meant was smuggling things into jails, right?"

"With regard to cigarette lighters, that's possible, yes."

"Did any of the kinds of items that Ms. Cordova describe have any kind of a sharp edge?"

"Depending upon the status of a crack-cocaine pipe; if it were glass, it might have a sharp edge."

Hall wasn't worried about the crack-pipe-in-the-vagina theory. Riggan's own statements were that Anita Paley had been holding the pipe in her hand and that he'd kicked it aside later. "She didn't describe any metal objects that would have a cutting edge, did she?"

"Not that I am aware of, no."

Hall then turned his questioning to the inmate's testimony. "How many times have you interviewed him?"

"Specifically, I've contacted him three times," Gedde replied. "I would consider two of those to be interviews."

Hall stood with his arms folded across his chest. "Now, Ms. Gedde, the original interview with the police was tape-recorded, was it not?"

"Yes, it was."

"And you had a copy of that tape recording, didn't you?"

"I had a transcript of it, yes."

"And despite the fact that you had a transcript of his taped interview, you chose to contact him on those separate occasions?"

"Yes."

"And on each one of those occasions, he was somewhere in the Department of Corrections, was he not?"

"Actually, on two occasions, he was in the Department of Corrections, and at one point, he was in the Jefferson County jail."

"Now, Ms. Gedde, are you familiar with the term 'snitch jacket'?" Hall asked.

"Yes, sir," she said. "Typically, a snitch jacket is something that is placed upon an individual within the Department of Corrections concerning they are providing testimony on an individual who's facing criminal charges."

"And the way that a person in the Department of Corrections gets a snitch jacket is oftentimes having someone come to the prison facility and interview him, right?"

"Actually, that's not my understanding," she said smugly. "Usually, someone gets a snitch jacket from having been placed on a witness list or having been endorsed as a witness in a case."

"And the fact that you as an investigator for someone contacted this man three times would give the other inmates some kind of an idea that maybe he was a witness, wouldn't it?"

"There were only two times that I contacted him in the Department of Corrections," Gedde replied, then apparently realized that the jurors would see her nit-picking for stonewalling and answered, "You're correct."

Hall nodded and looked down at the floor, his chin cupped in his hand as if immersed in deep thought. "Now life for someone in prison who has a snitch jacket is often kind of unpleasant, is it not?"

"I can't speak from personal experience," Gedde obfuscated.

Hall ignored the sidestepping. "And you knew that by contacting him those two times in the Department of Corrections, you might well give him a snitch jacket; you knew that, didn't you?" It was an old defense trick to contact a government witness in jail to make him think twice about cooperating, but he needed the jurors to realize that, too.

"That's a possibility."

"And oftentimes people who have snitch jackets ultimately become somewhat reluctant to testify; isn't that true?"

"They can be."

"Now, Ms. Gedde, in his tape-recorded statement to Corporal Thorpe [the deputy at the jail], the inmate wasn't talking about what the charges were against Mr. Riggan, was he?"

"Objection," Hartley said. "Unless she heard the tape—"

Plaut answered, "Well, I thought that foundation had been laid." He allowed Hall to continue and the prosecutor repeated his question.

"I don't believe that he says that Mr. Riggan was talking about his charges . . . I don't believe that," she replied.

Hall asked if it would refresh her "recollection" if he provided a copy of the transcript. He directed her to page 1619 of the discovery. "And doesn't he say on this page, 'He said, "The last person I killed, I beat her fucking brains in." ' Isn't that what he says?"

"Yes."

"He's not talking about the charges against him there, is he?"

"At that point in that interview, no," Gedde admitted.

Hall took a seat having done his damage, but Hartley counterpunched. "Ms. Gedde, in your experience do inmates always tell the truth when they're trying to make a deal with the DA?"

"No, they do not," she answered.
"Are they trying to procure a favor?"
"Sometimes."

Although Gedde had concluded that portion of
the defense case, Hall and Easter knew that what
happened next would determine the outcome.
Their own case was a puzzle . . . lots of little pieces
they had hoped to fit together for the jury. As a
result, they hoped to give, if not a complete picture,
at least most of an overview. Joanne Cordova had
been wonderful. A real hero in their eyes. Riggan's
statements to the police and the inmate had certainly damaged him. But in the end, they knew the
rest of this case would come down to a battle of
the expert witnesses and would be won or lost on
how well they were able to cross-examine the defense witnesses.

The first of these especially rankled the prosecution team. Expert witnesses—people accepted by
the court as having specialized education and experience in a particular area—are used all the time
in trials by both sides. Some of these experts will
even testify in one trial for the prosecution and
then another trial for the defense. They're supposed to render objective opinions, but they also
know which side butters their bread.

What upset the prosecution about the defense's
next witness was that he worked in law enforcement
in another state. Here, he was to be a paid gun for
the defense. His name was Dr. Chris Lee Sperry, a
forensic pathologist like Dr. Galloway. Sperry
worked for the Georgia Bureau of Investigation and

was the chief medical examiner for the state of Georgia. As he explained it to the jurors, the Georgia bureau was similar to the FBI, except limited to Georgia as an agency "that deals with investigation of all sorts of different crimes . . . usually assisting local law-enforcement agents throughout the state."

"How many autopsies have you performed?" Hartley asked.

"Personally, as of last week . . . I myself have performed 4,082 autopsies," he replied. In this case, he'd been asked by Hartley to examine the autopsy report and the toxicology report, as well as the photographs that were taken of the autopsy. And "evaluate, first of all, what injuries she had and how those injuries may have occurred."

"After reviewing the material in this case, were you able to form an opinion as to cause of death?"

"Yes."

"And would you tell us with a reasonable degree of medical probability what that opinion is?"

"My opinion is that the cause of death in this case was the complications of severe brain swelling and brain injury that occurred when this lady's head was moving and struck a fixed, unmoving surface." He said he reached that conclusion because the victim had suffered a coup and contra-coup injury.

Handing Sperry enlarged photographs from the autopsy, Hartley asked, "Doctor . . . were you able to form an opinion as to whether or not Ms. Paley died from one or multiple blows to the head?"

Sperry nodded. "Ms. Paley died as the consequence of one blow that initiated on the upper left side of her head, and this is what resulted in the fracturing of the skull and also a severe brain injury."

The Georgia pathologist referred to the photograph of the stellate laceration on Paley's scalp. He said there was "extensive associated scraping and bruising of the tissues around this laceration." Aware from reading the reports that Galloway did not agree, he repeated his assertion that the wound included extensive scraping and abrasion that would "bleed profusely."

Was the wound consistent with a hammer, tire iron, or pipe hitting a stationary head? Hartley asked.

"No, it is not consistent with those."

"Why not?"

The pattern of the wound would have been different, he said. A weapon would have left a distinct mark, indicating its source, and "the fracturing pattern beneath such an injury will usually be a depressed or crushed-in fracture rather than just a linear fracture as was exhibited here."

The oblong contusion behind the left ear that Galloway thought was caused by a separate blow, Sperry contended was actually bleeding into the soft tissues caused by the fracture. Again, and unasked, Sperry repeated that in his opinion "her injuries are all consistent with exiting a moving vehicle," including the "road rash" abrasions.

Hartley moved on to the toxicology report that indicated that cocaine and its by-products were still in her body at the time she died. "If the evidence showed that Ms. Paley was discovered approximately six-twenty, the morning of May 16, 1997, and she died approximately six forty-one P.M. on May 16, 1997, what significance does that have?" the defense attorney asked.

"The fact that there was still cocaine in her blood at the time she died means that, working backward, there was a massive amount of cocaine in her blood when she was found," Sperry replied.

"Assume for a moment that Ms. Paley kept drugs or other material in her vaginal vault," Hartley said. "Assume also that Ms. Paley exited a moving van at approximately forty-five miles an hour. Could that have caused her vaginal injury?"

Easter objected. "That calls for speculation." Judge Plaut overruled her.

"Yes," Sperry said.

"What is the nature of vaginal tissue when it is subjected to force?" Hartley asked. "What does it do?"

"It will tear in a splitting fashion. . . . The wall of the vagina has a great deal of elastic tissue, because it's built really so that babies can be born." A hard enough blow, he said, might have caused that elastic tissue to stretch until it tore in a neat line.

If a knife had been used to cause the wound, Hartley asked, wouldn't he have expected to see cuts on the outer parts of the vagina? Yes, Sperry replied.

Under questioning, the pathologist said he'd seen thousands of accident victims and that "long bone fractures" were actually uncommon, as opposed to head and neck injuries.

Hartley then asked if "to a reasonable degree of medical probability," Sperry could say whether or

not Ms. Paley was the victim of a homicide. Before
he could answer, Easter objected, saying the proper
standard was "to a degree of medical certainty,"
not probability.

"Well, my concern, frankly, is whether homicide
is a legal opinion," Plaut said, but he overruled
Easter's objection.

"In my opinion, the manner of death in this case
would be properly classified as an accident, because
she died of her head injuries," Sperry said. "That
the head injuries, coupled with the other injuries
on the outside surface of her body, are indicative
that she exited a moving vehicle and struck her
head on the roadway and received those injuries
that then caused her death and, thus, this would
be an accident."

"If there is evidence that Ms. Paley herself voluntarily exited the vehicle, would that change your
opinion?" Hartley asked.

"No," Sperry said. "That would reinforce it."

Hartley took his seat as Easter stood to begin her
cross-examination. This was going to be tough.
Sperry had impressive credentials. It had been a
real coup—and the prosecution was sure the defense would crow about it in their closing arguments—to get a member of the law enforcement
community to agree with their contentions.

Sperry beamed graciously as Easter asked for an
extra moment to gather her notes. He continued
smiling at the jury, though as Easter took her time,
he began to look uncomfortable. At last, the prosecutor began. "Doctor, would you agree with me that

the amount and number of abrasions on the body of a person who has been ejected from a vehicle in some way is going to depend on the amount of clothing they have on to a certain extent?"

"Yes," he replied, turning to the jury. "Factoring in, of course, force and speed and things like that, but clothing will tend to be protective as a general rule, yes."

"When you have gone out to crime scenes where the major injury is a head injury, do you not frequently see large spots of blood in the road?" Easter asked.

"Oh yes," Sperry said affably. "Oh yes. If the person has been there for some period of time, obviously, yes."

"Would you agree with me that the photographs of the autopsy of Anita Paley's face show that her nose is uninjured?" Easter asked.

"Correct, I agree."

Sperry also agreed that there were small abrasions on the left side of Paley's face in a line with her nose and that her ear showed no injuries despite the proximity to the head wound.

"Now, Doctor, you would agree that Dr. Galloway stated in his autopsy report that the laceration of the head had only marginal abrasions surrounding it?"

"That's exactly what it has, marginal abrasions," Sperry replied.

"My recollection of your testimony is that you said there was a huge abrasion around that laceration?"

"Well, you're perhaps not understanding the meaning of what 'marginal abrasion' is," he replied. " 'Marginal abrasion' means that there is abrasion about the margins or the edges of where the laceration is located. That's what that means, not that it's small or tiny."

"If Dr. Galloway had testified that there was a small marginal abrasion, would you agree with that?" Easter asked.

"Not with respect to what the photographs themselves show, no," Sperry replied.

Easter referred to the photograph of the head wound, which was projected on television screens in the courtroom. "The area of abrasion that you see is completely limited around this part of the laceration, is it not?"

"No."

"There is a very round abrasion or contusion, is there not?"

"That is the abrasion, yes."

"Would you agree with me that it's very round?" Easter asked. A small point, she knew, but important—a wound caused by Paley's head hitting the road should have been elongated, as though scraped from one side to the other, not round.

"Yes."

"Would you agree that there are not fractures to any bones, including long bones, except the skull fracture?"

"Yes," Sperry agreed.

"None of her fingers, none of the bones of her hand, not her clavicle, nor arm or leg bones, no rib fractures?"

"No, there were none of that found."

"Would you agree, Doctor, that Ms. Paley has a bruise on her right breast?"

"Yes."

"With no abrasion?"

"Correct."

"And that her elbow shows an area of bruising?"

"Yes."

"Would you agree that the left side of her head, her left elbow, her right breast, are the three injuries which show the most force having been applied?"

"In a relative sense as compared with the other injuries, yes."

"The most perpendicular force?"

"Yes, creating the most disruption of blood vessels and, thus, the most localized bruising, yes."

"And, Doctor, you would agree with me, would you not, that there is a one-quarter-inch contusion just inside Ms. Paley's vaginal orifice?"

"Yes, just before the vagina," Sperry replied.

"Based on that, do you have any reason to believe that Ms. Paley was kicked in her groin area within a day of her death."

At first, Sperry hesitated, realizing that this related directly to at least one of the defense theories as to how the victim received the vaginal injury. Anything was possible, he stammered. When Easter insisted on his opinion, he conceded, "From a forcible kick to this area, I would expect much more bruising."

Easter asked if Sperry was aware of the report of Dr. Harvey Cohen, the OB-GYN specialist. Sperry said he was but claimed he had not been made aware of the specifics of Cohen's testimony.

"Is it fair to say that Dr. Cohen's report indicates

that he did not find any foreign objects in the vagina of Ms. Paley when he operated on her?"

"Correct," Sperry said. "Other than blood, correct, no foreign objects."

"And you are aware, are you not, Doctor, that in addition to the incised wound in the vagina, that Dr. Galloway found a one-and-a-half-inch laceration or abrasion as well?"

"Yes."

"And Dr. Galloway calls the worst vaginal wound an 'incised wound,' does he not?"

"Yes."

"What does 'incised' mean in the medical world?"

"That means that it is an actual cut by an instrument with a sharp edge, such as a knife or razor or glass, something like that."

Easter showed Sperry the photograph of the cut. "Would you agree that's a very straight cut?"

Sperry made a show of adjusting his glasses and examining the photograph. "It is a straight injury, yes, from what I can see here, yes."

Easter asked if Sperry was aware of any debris, such as small rocks or dirt that had been lodged in the head wound or other abrasions.

A nurse may have washed the wounds, Sperry pointed out. "That evidence would have been obliterated."

"Are you aware of any evidence of debris in Ms. Paley's wounds?" Easter repeated her question.

Judge Plaut added, "That's a yes or no question."

Sperry reddened at the judge's admonishment. "Am I aware of any? No, I am not aware of any."

Easter paused. She was about to ask one of the

most important questions of her cross-examination and wanted to get it right. "Now," she began, "is there anything that would lead you to believe that based on her injuries she would have been unconscious for a period of time, and then awakened and had a lucid conversation and then lapsed back into unconsciousness?"

Sperry looked at the defense attorneys who showed no reaction. He wasn't aware of Riggan's claims that Anita Paley had carried on a conversation. "I would not have expected that she would have regained consciousness," Sperry said. "Well, first of all, I think upon impact she was unconscious . . . that would have rendered her unconscious. And then the bleeding would begin to start and the brain would start to swell. . . . I think that she could regain a certain level of consciousness, but I would not expect, given the injuries that she had, that she would be able to maintain a lucid and coherent conversation."

Easter felt Sperry was talking in circles, trying not to damage the defense case. She repeated the point. "You don't really see lucid intervals with these kind of severe contusions and subdural hematomas, do you, Doctor?"

"No," Sperry admitted, "not with the swelling of the brain and the associated skull fractures, no."

"So if the person who is telling you about what had happened to Ms. Paley had included the story that there had been a lucid interval, including a conversation, would you have trouble with that?"

"If it included a meaningful conversation; that is, that she had regained consciousness and was able to converse and exchange in a meaningful fashion, I would find that highly unlikely."

"In fact," Easter said, "would you find it highly unlikely to a reasonable degree of medical certainty?"

"Yes."

The vaginal wound, she pointed out, included a cut artery that would have bled extensively "from the moment it occurred, would it not?"

"Yes."

And if the defendant had sex with the victim, the evidence would have been lost with the blood, Easter contended.

"Oh, well, as far as semen or seminal fluid goes, that would be very radically reduced if the vagina was very thoroughly irrigated like this, and, of course, as we know, there was a lot of blood in the vagina as well, that would tend to obscure and ultimately obliterate such evidence."

Easter put up the photograph of the head wound again. "Do you believe that that head laceration would have bled heavily?"

"Yes."

"Would it have left a lot of blood where it occurred if she laid there for a while?"

"Oh yes."

"And it would have kept bleeding until it clotted off, is that right?"

"Yes."

"So if ambulance personnel who first tended to Ms. Paley at six forty-five on May sixteenth had indicated that her head wound was crusty and dried, you wouldn't have any reason to dispute that, would you?"

"Oh, no, no, no," Sperry said. "If that was their observation, that's fine."

The point for the prosecution team was that the head wound had had time to clot, but Paley was still bleeding from her vaginal wound.

"Doctor, the main and most serious brain injury that Ms. Paley suffered was the contusion on the left side of her brain, was it not?"

"Well, no, it was the swelling of the right side."

"Actually, it was the swelling of both sides, wasn't it?"

"Yes, the whole brain swelled, but the brain was shifting," Sperry replied. "The CAT scan was showing that it was shifting from the right to the left, which is an indicator that the swelling is more severe on the right side."

"Now it is accurate, is it not, to say that the majority of contusion is on the left side of her brain?"

"The contusions, they're related to the fractures themselves, yes, fracture contusions."

"There is a deep contusion, is there not, on the left cerebral hemisphere?"

"Yes, related to the fracture, yes," Sperry agreed.

The smaller contusions on the right side of the brain, Easter asked, were consistent with "gliding contusions" and that anytime there's a blow to the head the shearing forces might cause similar damage.

As Easter tried to make headway against the counter-coup theory, Sperry's arguments grew more and more long-winded and off point. Finally Judge Plaut interrupted him. "Wait a minute. Wait a minute. When Ms. Easter asks you a question, I want you to answer the question and stop and wait for the next question. Do we understand each other?"

Sperry reddened again, but nodded. "Yes, sir."

"Is it fair to say in your line of work that really and truly gliding contusions don't give you any predictive ability about whether an injury is a coup or contra-coup injury?" Easter asked.

Sperry shook his head. "No, not necessarily. . . . I mean, it's a process of looking at all of the pieces of information together."

Easter referred to a medical book that stated again that gliding contusions aren't proof of contra-coup injuries. "Isn't that what the book says, Doctor?" she demanded.

"Well, ma'am, you're asking me a question, and I'm trying to answer the question," Sperry complained. "And I really don't want to argue with you, but pulling an isolated sentence out of there has no meaning out of context with the totality."

"Is it fair to say that the book says that gliding injuries are not good predictors of the location of an injury or whether an injury is coup or contra-coup? I understand the limitations you've placed on it," Easter asked again.

"Well, the limitation is if I choose to ignore everything else that is present and focus solely on gliding contusions, then yes," Sperry said. He was beginning to sweat now, removing his glasses and wiping his brow.

Easter asked if he'd based his opinion on statements made by Riggan. Sperry said he had no idea what Riggan had said.

"But counsel," she said, pointing to the defense

team, "has told you what statements were made and whether or not this or that fit, is that right?"

"Not really, no," Sperry denied, and then looking over at Riggan, added, "I don't really know what this man said in his statements."

"What information did you have that would lead you to the conclusion that Ms. Paley suffered a vaginal wound when she jumped out of a van?" Easter asked, not bothering to disguise her sarcasm.

"As far as . . . well," Sperry stammered, "I don't know that I can answer it in the way that you've asked it."

Easter asked if it would have helped him if he could have seen Paley's body instead of photographs. Sperry shook his head . . . actually, sometimes photographs and reports are more helpful. "It's not a yes or no. Well, I can't answer it yes or no. It depends on the information—"

The prosecutor interjected. "So you wouldn't prefer to see the body—"

Then it was Dennis Hartley who objected angrily. "Please, Your Honor," he complained, "if the witness could finish his answer before being interrupted."

Plaut ordered the attorneys to approach the bench. He was already ticked at the defense for other reasons. The pretty blonde who'd sat at the defense table had made a great show for the jury of leaning on Riggan, chatting with him, and laughing gaily at whatever he said. Out of the jury's hearing, the judge said he found her behavior "outrageous" and ordered her to stop. When she continued later, he had her removed from the defense table and seated back in the spectator gallery.

Now, again out of the hearing of the jury, he blasted Sperry. "I've already cautioned this witness once, and I don't want to do it publicly again, but unless he starts answering the question without all the gratuitous stuff that follows, I'm going to caution him again and it's going to be public. . . . I'm going to take a five-minute recess so counsel can talk to him, but this is not going to be allowed to continue."

Hartley argued with the judge. "Your Honor . . . I really object to having to tell the witness to answer questions that I consider cannot be answered with yes or no answers, are inartful, and probably show a basic lack of knowledge of head injuries, so I object to that. I think it is uncalled for. I think it certainly prejudices the defense in this case and further shows a predisposition on this court toward the prosecution and not the defense."

But Plaut wasn't moved. "The record, of course, will speak for itself as to both the questions asked and the answers given. The court has stated to counsel on the record and out of the presence of the jury and will do so again on the record and out of the presence of the jury that it finds this witness's answers on cross-examination to be significantly nonresponsive.

"This court's only interest in this case is to try it fairly and let the jury reach the result that they want to reach. And, of course, all counsel can make their record on whether they think the court is succeeding in that desire or, as defense counsel seems to suggest, that maybe the court doesn't even have that desire."

Turning to Sperry, who sat red-faced while the

judge lectured his employers, Plaut pointed and said, "But I'll tell the witness right now, because it's very clear to me and will be to anybody reading this transcript who's knowledgeable, that this is a very experienced witness and he knows when he's answering responsively and he knows when he isn't. And if he doesn't answer responsively from here on out, I will caution him in the presence of the jury."

Sperry turned even redder, but Plaut wasn't done. "This court has the very distinct impression that on cross-examination this witness is playing games. And the court specifically finds that the questions are not inartful, and based on the court's own experience with medical-legal issues for nearly forty years, finds them to be competent and appropriate. . . . I have told you, Dr. Sperry, and I hope you understand what I am saying, because the next time I am going to say it more firmly and in the presence of the jury."

Sperry nodded. He again wiped at his brow and took a sip of water as the jury was brought back in.

Easter returned to her questions about the vaginal wound. "What structures protect the vagina?"

"All right," Sperry said. "Okay, well, outside or inside?"

Easter repeated herself. "What structures surrounding the vagina protect it?"

"Oh, surrounding the vagina," he replied, casting a nervous glance at the judge. "I need to understand what you're asking." Muscles and the pelvic bone protect the vagina, he answered.

"It's fair to say, is it not, that the three areas of Ms. Paley's body that show the most direct force are her head on the left side, her right breast, and her left elbow?"

"Yes."

"And that she did not suffer a contusion to her hip or any structures in the lower part of her trunk or upper legs?"

"Okay." Sperry nodded. "No, there were no contusions in those areas particularly, no."

"There are no contusions," Easter repeated. "Were there other signs of any particularly forceful blow that happened to her lower trunk or upper legs?"

"The abrasions on the left flank and hip region going down to the buttock," Sperry pointed out.

"Those are sliding injuries," Easter said. "They are not a direct perpendicular blow."

"They could be."

"They could be?"

"Oh yes."

"They didn't leave a contusion, is that right?"

"Not . . . at least not as . . ." He gave another glance at the judge. "Well, no—"

"Now I want to understand this clearly, and I want to state this correctly. It is your opinion that the vaginal wound is a tear?"

"Yes."

"All right," Easter said, nodding. "And it is your opinion that it was not caused by a knife?"

"Yes."

"And you hold that opinion because you think that there would have been injury to the lower vagina in getting the knife inside, is that right?"

"Yes, that's fair, inside or removing it, yes," Sperry said.

Earlier in his testimony, Dr. Cohen had demonstrated how he believed a knife could be inserted into the vagina without cutting tissue on the outside by holding the lower portion of the opening down with his finger over the point of the knife. Easter demonstrated this for Sperry. "Is it possible?" she asked.

"Yeah, it is possible, yes," Sperry conceded.

"Doctor, do you get significantly different appearing wounds when they are incised as opposed to torn?"

"It's dependent upon where in the body they may or may not be, depending on where these occur."

Easter produced a photograph of a vagina that had been torn and the photograph from Paley's autopsy. "And is it fair to say that they're different, in that one is a nice straight edge and one is really torn and sort of raggedy?"

Sperry would not concede the point.

"So, Doctor, are you saying that you don't believe that a sharp object caused the vaginal wound?"

"No, I have not said that yet, no."

"Have you said that what you think caused that wound is a bluntish object?"

"It could be, yes."

"And a bluntish object would be different from a sharp object, such as a knife?"

"Yes."

"And it is your opinion that Ms. Paley's wound is caused by a bluntish object?"

"I . . . I . . . think I said earlier I can't say to a reasonable degree of medical certainty exactly what it is that caused the injury."

"It could have happened that the vaginal area was cut when Ms. Paley jumped from the van?"

"It could have, yes," Sperry replied.

"And that she was then thereafter placed in the van, is that right?"

"I . . . I don't have a basis to say yes or no."

Easter pointed out that the defense was contending that Paley was placed in the van with her head between the seats after she jumped from the van and therefore, according to that account, after the vaginal injury.

Hartley objected; the prosecutor's scenario was hypothetical, even if it was the defense's hypothesis. Plaut overruled him.

"What sequence of events do you understand happened in this case, Doctor?"

"I . . . I don't have an understanding of the sequence of events to that detail."

"Well, Doctor, you've testified that something happened in the cabin or didn't happen in the cabin, right?" she asked, referring to comments he made in his direct testimony that the blood patterns in the cabin indicated Paley had not received her head wound there.

"Yes."

"Do you have any understanding of what happened between the time that Ms. Paley is supposed to have jumped from the van and the time that she was in the cabin?"

"Not to any detail, no." Sperry shook his head.

"What detail do you have?"

"Well, I don't know," he replied. "The limit that I know is that in some way she was then transported to the cabin upon a sleeping bag."

"All right," Easter acknowledged, "she was transported to the cabin upon a sleeping bag. I am going to have to give you a hypothetical. . . . If Ms. Paley jumped out of the van with an object in her vagina, which broke and lacerated her vagina at that point, she also sustained a laceration to her head, which bled profusely. She was then picked up, carried, and placed in the van where her head was placed between the two front seats, and her vaginal area would have been headed toward the back of the van.

"She was removed from the van and ultimately placed on top of a sleeping bag in the cabin room that you've testified about, and that she was wearing shorts, gray sweat shorts and red panties when she jumped, and a brown or tan shirt—"

Suddenly Riggan, who had been shaking his head throughout much of the cross-examination, blurted out, "That's not true!"

Hartley and Chambers quickly motioned to him to be quiet. At the same time, Hartley objected. "There's no evidence of red panties. . . ."

"Hold it, hold it," Plaut told the defense lawyer. "Let Ms. Easter finish her hypothetical. Before I allow the answer, I will hear any objection."

Easter finished her statement. "And that her shorts were then removed, and she was then dragged, actually on the sleeping bag in the direction of a stream in order that she could be washed off . . . I would ask you—"

"Objection," Hartley said.

" . . . I would ask you to listen to my question," Easter said, turning toward her opponent.

"And I would object to the question, Your

Honor," Hartley replied. "There is no fact that has been established in any form that shows that red panties or gray shorts were on this body at any time in any place for any reason."

Again, Riggan couldn't contain himself. "I guess not," he scoffed, which earned him another warning glance from Hartley and Plaut both. The judge asked Easter to respond to Hartley's objection.

Easter replied that the prosecution was aware that some of this evidence would be brought in by the next defense witness, a man named Milo Beaver. The judge ordered the attorneys to again approach the bench where they could confer out of earshot of the jurors. "Go ahead, Mr. Hartley," he said when they gathered.

Hartley repeated that there was no evidence "there were any gray shorts or any red panties ever on this woman, there is absolutely no evidence of that. . . . There's been nothing that's ever linked it to her."

"Okay," he said, turning to the female prosecutor. "Ms. Easter?"

"Judge, there's plenty of evidence," Easter replied. "First of all, the red panties and gray sweat shorts are found intertwined in the cabin in the room where all the blood loss takes place. In addition, it is the opinion of their expert, Milo Beaver, that she was wearing the items of clothing. . . . That you can see the demarcation line of where the clothing did protect her from the abrasions and where it did not protect her from the abrasions.

"In addition, those clothes have been tied to Mr. Riggan by virtue of Joanne Cordova's testimony."

Plaut noted, however, that Shane Delray had testified that Anita Paley never wore underwear. "You don't agree with that, and you think you're going to have evidence to the contrary?"

"Judge, I think that we already do," Easter replied. "The evidence is that the gray shorts were wound up with the red panties."

Plaut thought for a moment, then said, "All right. I think you may be stepping into dangerous territory, but if that's what you want to do, I'll let you do it."

The attorneys turned to go, but Hartley referenced Riggan's outbursts. "Your Honor, I need to talk to this client." Plaut asked him to caution his client now and then have a longer talk during the next recess.

Everyone returned to their places and Easter went ahead with her questions. She handed Sperry a plastic bag containing a pair of gray sweat shorts with a few drops of blood. "Can you tell me, are those spots on the outside?"

"Yes."

"And do they go all the way through to the inside of the cloth?"

"There is one that nearly does, but the remainder do not seem to," Sperry said, putting the bag and shorts down.

"And that's really out on the leg, is it not?"

"Yes."

"And does there appear to be any blood at all, right in the crotch area?"

"On the inside," Sperry said. "No."

That, Easter said, would not be consistent with Paley wearing the shorts when she received the vaginal wound. "Would it?"

"No," Sperry replied.

She turned his attention to the red panties. "And are you able to see a large amount of blood or anything that would look like old blood on the crotch of those panties?"

"No."

Easter then dragged out the sleeping bag that Paley had been found on, which was now enclosed in a large plastic bag. She pointed out that blood had soaked through in two spots: one near where her head had lain, and the other, much larger spot halfway down the bag.

"If she were wearing those shorts and those panties when she jumped from the van, and if there were only trace amounts of blood found in the cargo area of the van, whereas there was a fair amount of blood found between the seats where her head was, and if there's a large amount of blood in the cabin, and then her head wound was crusted a half an hour later, would you agree that her vaginal wound was not inflicted until after she was taken out of the van?"

The long question confused Sperry, but at last he conceded the point.

"And, in fact, based on the location of her body and based on the blood evidence on the sleeping bag, she bled a lot consistently, did she not, from that wound?"

"Yes."

With that, Easter finished her questioning. Hartley quickly rose to ask a few more questions. He got Sperry to agree that the sleeping bag was absorbent and that the area where blood had spilled over the edge, as opposed to soaking through, was up where Paley's head had been. The inference was that she could have been bleeding from both areas when placed in the van, but only the blood at the top had got on the vehicle.

Hartley turned to the issue of the red panties. "If she wasn't wearing them, there wouldn't be any blood in them, would there?" he asked to the obvious reply of no.

The defense attorney asked if there was any mention in either Dr. Galloway's autopsy report or Dr. Levy's report that "mentioned the words 'gliding contusions'?"

"No."

Hartley ended his questions by asking whether there should have been blood on the blade of a knife used to cut Paley. He wanted to remind the jury that the knife Easter had used for her demonstration had no blood on it . . . nor did the prosecution have such a knife.

"Yes," Sperry replied, "there should have been blood." Looking very relieved, Sperry then got down from the witness stand, left the courtroom, and got on a plane back to Georgia.

Dr. Sperry had been a dangerous witness to the prosecution's case, but Easter had made significant gains, particularly in the areas of Paley's supposed conversations after receiving the head wound, and the lack of any evidence of a significant blow to her pelvic region that could have torn her vagina or broken some sort of device inside of her. It was obvious that the pathologist was working hard to uphold the defense case while stepping around prosecution questions. Now there was one more major defense witness that the prosecution team had to deal with.

The defense next called Milo Beaver, who introduced himself as an engineer and president of Northwest Engineering Consultants in Spokane, Washington.

"What is Northwest Engineering Consultants?" Nathan Chambers asked.

"Currently, it's strictly me," Beaver responded. "I do consulting engineering primarily on the subjects of motor vehicle accidents and injury biomechanics."

"What is 'injury biomechanics'?" Chambers asked.

"Injury biomechanics refers to the study of the effects of forces on the human body," Beaver responded. "In the case of injury biomechanics, which is most of what I do, these forces involve injuries."

Beaver said he was asked to review what had happened to Anita Paley. "And were you asked to determine if those injuries were consistent or inconsistent with her falling or jumping from a moving vehicle?" Chambers inquired.

"Yes, I was."

Beaver said he drew his conclusions from photographs, an examination of Paley's clothing, and statements Riggan made to the police. "And based upon that, you were able to ascertain Mr. Riggan's account of the events?"

"Yes."

"Did that have some effect or some bearing on how you conducted your analysis?"

"Yes, it did. . . . Generally speaking, what I try to do is look at what's being claimed in terms of how the incident took place. And then based on that information, look at such things as the medical records, injury patterns, to see if those injuries are consistent with the account of what took place."

"So you knew that Mr. Riggan, for instance, had said that Ms. Paley jumped or fell from his van?"

"That is correct," Beaver said. He acknowledged that he also was aware of the government theory that she'd been struck in the head and then brought to the cabin, where she was sexually mutilated. Asked if he had an opinion whether the injuries to the left side of her head were consistent with a fall from a moving vehicle, he responded, "It's my opinion that the injury that's depicted here is very consistent with a fall or jump from a moving vehicle."

"Do you have an opinion as to whether it's consistent or inconsistent with being hit with a blunt object?"

"Yes," Beaver replied. "Taken by itself, I would say that this injury is consistent with being hit by a blunt object."

That was not the answer Chambers was looking for, but Beaver quickly pointed out that taking the other injuries into account "this is not consistent with being hit by a blunt object."

"Why?" Chambers asked.

"Primarily, the subdural hematoma on the opposite side of the head," Beaver replied. "That type of injury is associated with a sudden deceleration of the head, which you get from a fall, so the head is in motion, strikes a hard object, whether that's pavement or hard ground. This results in the brain moving within the skull and separating from the skull on the opposite side of the head, which causes forces, primarily stretching of veins and a vacuum within the skull, which causes the subdural hematoma. . . . This is the sort of thing that you don't get being struck by a blunt object. You don't get the deceleration of the head to cause that kind of injury."

Beaver contended that there were not multiple blows to Paley's head. The abrasions on her face, he said, were consistent with a jump or fall from a moving vehicle. In fact, he added, "it appeared to me that this woman slid feetfirst on the roadway, and then after a certain period of time, she decelerated a certain amount, and that she then rolled onto her front side. The injuries to her right hand and right breast occurred when she tumbled and the orientation of her body changed."

"Assuming that Ms. Paley jumped or fell out of that moving vehicle at forty-five miles an hour, do you have an opinion as to how many times she would have rolled?" Chambers asked.

"Yes, I do," Beaver replied. "It's my opinion that she rolled essentially one full revolution before she came to rest in the roadway."

Chambers asked Beaver how far Paley had traveled once she jumped and came to rest.

"The distance is a little under seventy feet," Beaver said.

Chambers moved to enter a "video animation" that Beaver had created showing what he said he believed "is the probable movement of her body on the road."

Before the video could be shown, however, prosecutor Hall asked the engineer, "Suppose that ten Chevrolet Astro vans just like the one bought by the defendant were driven up Highway Six, and suppose that at the same point in the road the vans were going forty-five miles an hour, and suppose at that point a one-hundred-five-pound person fell or jumped out the passenger door. . . . Are you telling us that all those people would receive exactly the same injuries?"

"No. . . . In all probability, they would receive somewhat different injuries."

"Are you telling us that what this videotape shows is a reasonable degree of scientific probability what would happen if a person jumped out of that van on that road at forty-five miles an hour?"

"No," Beaver replied.

"In that case, I object to the exhibit," Hall said.

It being near the end of the day, Judge Plaut dismissed the jurors so that he could listen to the attorneys' arguments for and against the video.

"This witness told the court and the jury that if this happened ten times, it would happen ten different ways and that he cannot say to a reasonable degree of scientific probability that this videotape shows how this incident happened," Hall pointed out.

Chambers countered that this video only tried to point out how the injuries specific to Anita Paley could have occurred. He said the video had three portions. The first time through it showed the incident at about half the speed. The second time it ran about the same speed, but broken up into segments with text to show at what point individual injuries occurred. The third time through, it ran at roughly real time, he said.

After watching the video, Plaut ruled that he would allow it to be shown to the jury. However, he said, he would give the jury an instruction that the video was "just Mr. Beaver's idea of what he believes happened and has no necessary relationship to what did, in fact, happen."

The next morning, October 21, Robert Riggan sat sullenly in his seat, noticeably apart from his defense attorneys, who had their backs to him. Hartley had had his talk with his client about his outbursts in which the ex-marine had warned him in no uncertain terms, "From now on, shut up, or I'll rip your fucking head off."

The day began with Plaut instructing the jury that the video they were about to see was not meant to be an exact re-creation of what happened to Anita Paley, but was being presented to help them understand Beaver's testimony. The video was then played. It showed a cartoon female figure standing on the running board of a cartoon van from the side view. The figure then fell backward, so that her head struck first, followed by her left buttock and hip, causing those abrasions.

"She continues down the pavement," Beaver narrated as the tape ran through the second time, "and rolls onto her front side—and now we have exposure to the face, her right breast, her right hand, and the left knee and lower leg, and the injuries that occur to those parts of her body.

"At this point, she's near a rest and then rolls

again a half a turn onto her back and at that point exposes the lateral upper region on the left side of her back to the point where she comes to rest."

When the video ended, Hall stood to cross-examine the witness. "Would you agree—that all other things being equal—the greater the speed, the greater the abrasion?"

"Yes," Beaver replied.

"Now another factor that would affect the extent of the abrasion to that body would be the downward force applied that pushes the body against the road, right?"

Beaver nodded. "Again, if you held everything else equal, then that's certainly a factor, yes."

Hall then asked if the greatest force had then been to the head. Beaver, aware of the contentions about the vaginal injury, said it might have been the hip, but wasn't as noticeable because the hips were the strongest bones in the body and had a lot of muscle protection.

The animation, Hall said, "is your opinion of what could have happened in this case, right?"

Beaver had not liked the judge's description of his work. "Not what could have happened," he sniffed, "what most probably occurred based on her injury patterns."

Hall nodded. "We'll get to that in a few minutes," he said, "but in the animation, you show that Ms. Paley first hits the pavement with her head, is that right?"

Contradicting his own video, Beaver replied, "No, I don't believe so. In my opinion, she came into contact with the pavement roughly simultaneously with her head, her hip, and her left elbow. I don't know which of those contacted first." He said she may have also hit feetfirst but agreed that there was no evidence of injuries to her feet.

"Mr. Beaver, doesn't the animation show the feet to be up in the air?"

"My recollection is that the feet come into contact with the pavement at about the same time. . . . I would have to look at it again."

"So basically, sir, the animation shows a person standing ten inches above the ground, roughly, and then doing some kind of a partial back flip, is that correct?"

"I wouldn't call it a back flip. She, in my opinion, fell backward out of the van and contacted the pavement."

"She fell backward out of the van?"

"Correct."

Hall looked puzzled. "Now if a person is upright, sir, isn't it true that the head is the part of the body that's farthest from the ground?"

"Yes."

"So if they fall, the head has the farthest distance to go, correct?"

"Yes."

"And ordinarily when they fall, the head is the last thing to hit, isn't that true?"

"Not always."

Hall asked if Beaver was saying that Anita Paley could have struck the pavement with her head and elbow at the same time, with the force of the blow "on one hand sufficient to shatter her skull, but on the other hand not sufficient to shatter her elbow?"

"Yes."

"Would you agree with me, Mr. Beaver, that an opinion is never better than the information on which it is based?"

"That's correct."

"And would you also agree with me that it's one of the jobs of an expert giving an opinion to make sure that he or she has all the relevant information available before he or she reaches his opinion, right?"

"Whenever possible, yes."

Hall apparently dropped that line of questioning to ask if Beaver believed that all of the injuries were caused between the time Anita Paley hit the road and then came to a rest.

"Not specifically, no," Beaver asked.

"Over what other period of time, in your opinion, did she receive these injuries?" Hall asked.

Beaver replied that the head and "other" injuries occurred during the period of time when she fell and slid on the highway. However, he added, "I don't know the origin of the vaginal injury."

Hall nodded. "Let's put the vaginal injury aside for the moment. Is it possible that all these injuries happened at three different times?" The head injury being one. The scrapes and bruises being another. The vaginal injury being the third.

"Anything is possible," Beaver said with a shrug.

"In reaching your opinion in this case, Mr. Beaver, you didn't assume more than one mechanism of injury, did you?" Hall asked.

"My conclusion was that there was . . . well, again, I want to make sure I understand your question," Beaver said. The first two mechanisms of injury could have been contact with the pavement and then sliding along that pavement. "But it's all happening in a very short period of time."

"Talking about the short period of time, sir, is it possible to compute how long this slide would have lasted?" Hall asked.

"Yes . . . a little over two seconds . . . and she would have traveled just under seventy feet."

"Now, Mr. Beaver, if these courtrooms are forty-four feet from that back wall to the door," Hall said, pointing from one to the other with the jury following his hand, "then it's your testimony that Ms. Paley would have traveled on that road roughly one-and-a-half-courtroom lengths, right?"

"Yes."

Hall moved on, leaving it to the jurors to look again at the length of the courtroom and decide in their own minds if someone hitting the pavement at forty-five miles an hour would have turned over only once and, other than the head injury, sustained only small bruises and scrapes even though she was only wearing shorts and a T-shirt.

The prosecutor noted that Dr. Galloway had ended his autopsy report "with his opinion concerning the cause of Ms. Paley's death, is that right?"

"Again, I don't recall," Beaver said. "I would have to review the report."

Hall acted surprised. "Didn't you review the autopsy report before coming in to testify, Mr. Beaver?"

"No, I didn't," he said. "I didn't review the entire report."

Hall handed him a copy of the report, noting that Galloway said Paley died of multiple blows to the head. "So, in reaching your opinion, you've chosen to disregard Dr. Galloway's opinion, have you not?"

"That portion of his opinion I disagree with."

"Now, Mr. Beaver, is it your opinion that you know more about forensic pathology than Dr. Galloway?"

"No."

"In reaching your opinion, did you know that Dr. Galloway has been board certified in all three kinds of pathology for almost twenty-five years?"

"I wasn't aware of that."

"You're not board certified in any kind of pathology, are you?"

"No, I am not."

"In reaching your opinion, sir, were you made aware of the fact that Dr. Galloway has performed about nine thousand autopsies?"

"Did I consider that in forming my opinion? No."

"In fact, you've never attended an autopsy, have you?"

"No."

"You weren't present at the autopsy of Anita Paley, were you?"

"No, no."

"You're not giving us a medical opinion that Dr. Galloway is wrong, are you?"

"I disagree with Dr. Galloway. Whether you want to call that a medical opinion, I certainly do disagree with his conclusion as far as the head injury is concerned."

Hall kept pressing his point. "Now would it be fair to say that you disagree with Dr. Galloway and have relied in large part upon the statements made by the defendant, Mr. Riggan, in reaching your opinions in this case?"

"Only from the standpoint of his descriptions of how these injuries took place, that the injuries are consistent with that description."

"Well, Mr. Beaver, would you agree with me that Mr. Riggan's account of the accident is directly contrary to what Dr. Galloway says happened?"

"Yes."

"Both of those things can't be true?"

"Yes."

"So only one of those two people is right?" Hall wanted the jury to see this as a choice between Ben Galloway and Robert Riggan.

"Correct," Beaver replied.

"The other is either wrong or lying, right?"

"Yes, somehow mistaken."

"And in reaching your opinion in this case, you've chosen to rely upon the statement of Mr. Riggan and to disregard the opinion of Dr. Galloway, right?"

Beaver said he based his opinion on a number of factors, but one of them was not "character."

"I'm not talking about the character, Mr. Beaver," Hall said. "But would it be fair to say that one of the things you look at is whether, say, the defendant's statement is consistent with the other physical evidence in the case?"

"Yes."

Hall then referred to the inmate's statement that Riggan told him that the last person he murdered " 'I beat her fuckin' brains out.' "

"Would that change your opinion?" Hall asked.

"No."

"So you would choose to disregard that statement as well, is that right?"

"It's not consistent with the injury patterns," Beaver replied stubbornly.

Hall pointed out that in his first statements to the police, Riggan said Paley simply "fell out of the car." Beaver replied that falling or jumping could mean the same thing.

"Would it change your opinion, sir, if Mr. Riggan told the booking officer on the night of his arrest, 'She fell out of the car. . . . I was driving down the road and she just fell out of the car.' "

Brooding up to this point, Riggan now exclaimed, "I didn't say that!"

Hartley leaned across the table, looking like he might swat his client. At the same time, Judge Plaut said, "I'll ask counsel to control Mr. Riggan, please."

"Your Honor . . . ," Riggan whined, but quickly shut up under Hartley's glare.

Beaver was told to go ahead and answer the last question. "Would it change my opinion? No. . . . It's my opinion she did fall or jump from the vehicle."

Hall brought up the different accounts Riggan had given for the moments before Paley fell or jumped from his van. He noted one in which Riggan said she held on to the side of the van for several minutes before jumping. "How far would the van have traveled at forty-five miles an hour?"

"A couple of miles."

"Now I know it may depend upon the car, but

can you give me a ballpark of how long it would take to stop a car from forty-five miles an hour?"

"Well, it depends also on how a person stops," Beaver replied. "If one just slammed on the brakes, it would take a few seconds. A gradual slowing to a stop would probably take several seconds."

Hall noted that Riggan said he didn't have time to stop before Paley jumped. "That seems inconsistent with what you've just told us, does it not?"

"Yes," Beaver admitted. "If we take what you're saying about him having several minutes, then certainly that's true."

"That is what he said, isn't it?"

"That's what you're saying," Beaver responded. "I don't recall."

"What I'm after, sir, is the basis of your opinion, not my understanding of the facts," Hall retorted. "Is that one of the things you read in reaching your opinion in this case?"

"I don't recall specifically."

"Would it refresh your recollection about that if I showed you one of the things you relied upon in reaching your opinion?" Hall said, reaching for the papers of Riggan's statements. "Can you read that right there? 'She held on for two or three minutes before jumping.'"

"Yes," Beaver replied.

"And you just explained to us that it would only take a couple of seconds to stop from a speed of forty-five miles an hour."

"Hard braking," Beaver said lamely. "It would take probably three seconds, skidding, so anywhere up from that, of course."

"In reaching your opinion in this case, did you

consider the length of time it would have taken Mr.
Riggan to stop versus the amount of time he
claimed Ms. Paley was standing in the door of his
van?"

"No, I did not."

"Now in those statements, Mr. Riggan also says
something about finding Ms. Paley laying on the
road in a pool of blood, does he not?"

"Yes."

"From your experience in accident reconstruc-
tion, have you become familiar with what happens
when a person is bleeding and ends up lying on
the road for a period of time?"

"In what regard?"

"Well, the blood comes out of their body somewhere and goes onto the road, right?"

"Yes."

"And the blood stays there for a period of time,
does it not?"

"Depending on such things as weather conditions and so forth, yes."

"Suppose that it doesn't rain or snow or anything. The blood stays there for a period of time,
does it not? So if police officers were to go back
and look for this big pool of blood the day after it
was supposedly deposited, you would think they
would be able to find it, wouldn't you?"

Beaver shook his head. "I don't know. I don't
know."

"Did it affect your opinion that the officers did,
in fact, look for this big pool of blood and couldn't
find it?"

"Would that affect my opinion? No, no," Beaver
said. The lack of blood on the roadway was not as

significant as the factors he did take into consideration, he said.

"Now correct me if I'm wrong, but it was his explanation that Ms. Paley was standing in the step-up part of the doorway, right?"

"That was my understanding, yes."

"And she's holding on to the roof of the van, right?"

"My recollection of the information was that it wasn't real clear to me exactly how she was holding on, but basically that she was standing up and had the door partway open and was holding on to something to balance herself."

"So you don't recall whether she was holding on to the door frame or to the roof of the van, is that right?"

"I don't believe he was extremely detailed in exactly how she was holding on."

"In the re-creation, though," Hall noted, "don't you show her holding on to the roof of the van as opposed to holding the door?"

"I show her hands up, holding on."

"In Mr. Riggan's statement, he claimed that Ms. Paley was holding a crack pipe in her left hand, did he not?"

"I believe it was the left hand. I don't recall specifically."

Hall again handed Beaver the transcripts of Riggan's statement to the police. Yes, the engineer admitted, the transcripts said she was holding a crack pipe in her left hand, the same hand that left a palm print on the roof.

The prosecutor returned to the animation. It didn't show Paley wearing socks or shoes though she had both on, he noted. She was wearing a T-shirt and shorts . . . "and that's because it is your understanding, based upon information provided to you, that at the time she supposedly jumped from the van, she was supposedly wearing shorts?"

"That's my understanding, yes," Beaver agreed. Now he remembered that Riggan's own statements said she was wearing shorts. Beaver said he didn't know if she was wearing anything under the shorts.

Hall asked if Beaver had ever been shown the shorts by the defense.

"No."

Hall asked him to look at the shorts now in the plastic bag. "Do you see any abrasions on that item consistent with a scraping along a paved road?"

"No, I don't."

But if Paley had slid some sixty-seven feet "you would expect to see some sort of abrasions on them, would you not?"

"Yes, I would."

Hall noted that in his own report, Beaver saw a "line of demarcation" across the abrasions that indicated Paley was wearing shorts when she was scraped. He then turned back to the vaginal injury. "Suppose that at the time she received the abrasions shown on the photograph she had also received a vaginal injury. Would you expect, sir, to find blood in the clothing that caused those lines of demarcation?"

"I don't know that."

"Sir, based upon your knowledge of medicine, do you know whether the vaginal wound would cause immediate bleeding?"

Chambers objected. Beaver, he said, was not qualified to give a medical opinion.

Hall rephrased his question. "If Dr. Cohen had said the wound would have resulted in immediate bleeding, would you have any reason to dispute that?"

"I could not dispute that."

Hall moved to his original point. If the wound did cause immediate bleeding and Paley was wearing shorts at the time, "would you expect to see blood on the inside of the shorts?"

"I don't know," Beaver replied. This time, even some of the jurors rolled their eyes.

Hall let the matter rest for a minute. He asked if Beaver believed that all the abrasions and bruises "were the result of her scraping along a flat road surface?"

"Yes."

"Well, let's talk abut the facial injuries, then. . . . The road is a fairly large, flat surface, right?"

"Large enough for her whole body to slide along it, yes," Beaver said.

"Would it be fair to say, Mr. Beaver, that a person who rolls and scrapes along a large, flat surface like that would in general receive injuries on things that are called bony prominences?"

"It depends. If those areas come into contact with the pavement, then of course, they're exposed to injury."

Hall produced the photograph of the left side of Paley's face with the three small scrapes. He then brought out a Styrofoam head and asked Beaver to place green plastic stickers on the head in the locations where those injuries were shown.

When Beaver was finished, Hall asked, "Now you noted in the report that there was no injury whatsoever to Ms. Paley's nose, did you not?"

"Yes, that's correct."

"Now, Mr. Beaver, it's your testimony that these three injuries occurred when Ms. Paley's face came into contact with a flat surface, is that right?"

"In my opinion, yes."

Hall gave the head to Beaver and asked him to put the dots on a flat board without also touching the nose to the board. The engineer tried for a couple of minutes but finally admitted, "I can't make them all contact this surface simultaneously."

"Without also contacting the nose, right?"

"Correct."

"And from that, Mr. Beaver, wouldn't one infer that perhaps these three injuries were not caused by a broad, flat surface?"

"I would disagree with that."

"Aren't these injuries, in fact, consistent with being dragged down a rocky slope?"

"In my opinion, they are not, no."

Hall then noted that there was no injury to Paley's left ear.

"There's not apparent injury to the external ear," Beaver agreed.

"And it's your testimony, sir, that it's possible for a flat, broad surface to cause the stellate laceration, but not also involve the ear, is that right?"

"That's my opinion, yes."

One last time, Hall returned to the vaginal wound. "Now, it's my understanding based upon what you've told us so far that you simply have no explanation for that injury?"

"Correct. . . . I can't give a probable cause for that injury."

"Mr. Beaver, does the fact that your scenario or your account of how all of this took place could not explain one of the major injuries cause any concern to you?"

Beaver shook his head. "It's fairly common in this business that we just can't explain everything; that in my final analysis, I have to go with the bulk of the evidence and sometimes there is a piece or two that doesn't quite fit."

Hall smiled. "I have no further questions for this witness."

Fifteen

October 22, 1998

After closing arguments, the jury was sent away to begin deliberations. Against his lawyers' advice, Riggan had insisted that there be no instruction to the jurors that they could consider a lesser verdict, such as second-degree murder. "Make 'em kill me or nothin'," he'd snarled as he was led out of the courtroom in handcuffs and shackles.

The jury's first vote, taken just minutes after they were sent to deliberate, was hardly a victory for either side. Two voted guilty, two innocent, and eight undecided on Count One: first-degree murder after deliberation. Three guilty, three innocent, and six undecided on Count Two: felony murder.

They jumped into the deliberations, reviewing the testimony of both sides and comparing notes. Most believed Dr. Galloway, especially his testimony that it was not possible for some broken container to have caused the cut in Paley's vagina. Dr. Cohen, whose compassion for the victim made a big impact on the jurors, had also convinced them that a fall couldn't have caused the injury.

Milo Beaver—they'd dismissed outright. The defense needed the jury to be convinced that it was possible for Paley to fall from a vehicle at forty-five miles per hour and receive only a few abrasions in addition to the head wound. Hall had remade his point during closing arguments when he pointed out once again that the courtroom was forty-four feet long and then asked, "and yet she rolled over only once?"

Dr. Sperry, however, had made a good case for the theory that Paley had struck her head on the road after jumping from the car. But most of the jurors had noted that Easter had him on the ropes on several occasions.

Hartley, during closing arguments, had tried to make a case that Riggan was a pathological liar who felt he'd needed to elaborate on his story to be believed by the police. The defense was severely damaged by the defendant's claims that he didn't seek medical help for Anita Paley because she told him not to, and that he'd removed her clothing at her request—the possibility of which had been disputed by Sperry.

The defense case was further damaged in the eyes of most of the jurors when Sperry could come up with no viable explanation for the vaginal wound. Hartley had hurt his own cause when he used the imagery of a boxer being struck to explain a coup and contra-coup injury. "That's not a moving head striking an immovable object," the juror said. "That's someone hitting somebody else."

Still, Sperry had his defenders, particularly the blond flight attendant who felt he was more credible than Galloway. As they debated the matter, she kept reiterating Hartley's closing argument statement: Why would a man with Sperry's credentials come all the way to Colorado to testify for the defense if he wasn't sure of the theory that Anita Paley had fallen from the van?

Money, the other jurors said. They openly wondered how many pathologists the defense tried their theory on before finding someone who would agree.

Both sides took hits, though. The jurors felt that the inmate who claimed to have heard Riggan say he beat his last victim's brains out was just another convict looking for a deal. They were unaware, of course, of the other inmate who told authorities that Riggan had confessed to cutting Paley "to the bone" after she refused to have sex with him.

The jurors were evenly split about how they saw Riggan. Several, including the ex-marine who had been elected their foreman, thought they sensed evil in him. The blonde, though, said she thought he looked like he needed someone to mother him.

Certainly, the most intriguing witness had been Joanne Cordova. As they discussed her testimony, they wondered how she had gone from being a police officer to a prostitute. She was as articulate as any of the lawyers in the courtroom. It must have been the drugs, they theorized.

Although the blond juror dismissed Cordova as not being credible, most of the other jurors thought just the opposite. She had come across to them as trying her best to be as honest and forthright as she could under very difficult circumstances. When Chambers hammered away at her and tried to humiliate her, she had gained their sympathy—and he'd lost their patience with his eye rolling and smirks.

Cordova's testimony, most agreed, had been important for several reasons. As the prosecution had hoped, she gave them the knife that could have been used to cut the victim—the knife she'd used to make sandwiches, the knife that wasn't shown at trial because it wasn't in Riggan's van. She had proved Riggan to be a liar several times over. For instance, Riggan had told the authorities that he didn't have sex with Joanne Cordova, and yet, to her obvious embarrassment, she'd testified to how he'd demanded sex and used her violently.

Finally there was the issue of the red panties. Cordova had said she had never worn them or even taken the tags off, yet they had been intertwined with Paley's shorts in the cabin. The fact that there was no blood in either article of clothing proved to most that Anita Paley wasn't wearing them when she received the vaginal wound. The blonde and two of the male jurors who followed her lead, however, argued that the prosecution hadn't proved that Paley was wearing those panties or shorts. This issue would hang up the jury through Friday, after which Judge Plaut sent them home for the weekend.

The waiting affected the attorneys differently. Hall and Easter began to lose hope. It looked like the jury was hung, which would mean a mistrial. They'd given it their best shot and didn't think their chances the second time around would be as good. . . . The defense would have time to plug the holes in their case and come back stronger.

The defense attorneys grew increasingly confident. Every day that passed, they said, was a day closer to a hung jury or even acquittal.

Monday began with a telephone call to the judge from the husband of one of the female jurors. His wife, he said, had been sick since noon Sunday; she didn't feel that she could participate. The judge told the man to appear in court and to bring his wife.

The man and his wife appeared. "She's been vomiting since noon," he told the court. "She and I were up all night." The woman looked pale and ill. Jury deliberations, which like this one could turn acrimonious, had been known to do that to jurors. There was nothing Plaut could do except send the woman home.

The judge then began discussing their options. One would be to bring in one of the alternates. Hartley objected to that—the others had been deliberating for one and a half days; it'd be tough to catch up now. Another option, Plaut said, would be to wait a day and see if the juror recovered. No one was interested in drawing the deliberations out another day. The third option, if the defendant agreed, would be to waive the requirement of twelve jurors and settle for eleven.

Riggan was brought into the courtroom, where he agreed with the third option. His lawyers thought the jury was hung or maybe even moving toward acquittal; he wanted a decision.

"I don't have a good feeling about this," Hall admitted as he left the courtroom to go stew with Easter.

The jury returned to its deliberations, which were growing more heated by the minute. Eight of the eleven now favored convicting Riggan on both counts, but the blonde and her followers wouldn't budge. She seemed to have settled on the mistaken belief that Count One pertained only to the head injury and she couldn't be brought around to believe that Riggan had deliberately struck the victim to kill her. She also mistakenly thought that Count Two pertained only to the vaginal injury. She'd grown more intransigent as the debate got more vehement, and the jurors again went home.

The next day didn't look like it would resolve anything, either. But during a break, the jury foreman was trying to find a way to convince the blonde—figuring the other two would go along with her—and was looking at the evidence when he noticed something about the red panties that neither side had brought up. The panties were frayed on the left side. He looked at the photographs of the abrasions on Paley's left leg. The frayed panty was an exact match for the line of demarcation on one of the abrasions. He pointed his discovery out to the other jurors.

Even the blonde now had to admit that Paley had been wearing the panties—and that meant they'd been removed before she was cut. The blonde and her two cohorts were now ready to vote guilty. But only on Count Two, which contended that Riggan killed Paley as part of a sexual assault. The three holdouts would still not agree to find him guilty on Count One.

That afternoon, the jury returned their verdict. Robert Lee Riggan, Jr. was guilty of felony murder. The jury had hung—eight favoring a verdict of guilty, three against—on the first-degree murder after deliberation charge, which Plaut declared a mistrial. It was a point on which Robert Riggan's life would hang when he faced the death penalty hearing.

Three days after the verdict, Joanne Cordova was sitting in a restaurant disappointed that she would have to go through the weekend without her paycheck from the temporary services agency she was working for part-time. She wanted to go to a movie. She hadn't been to a movie in a long time . . . sitting there with a big box of popcorn. Maybe that would have taken some of the craving for crack away, at least for a couple of hours.

She tried to look on the bright side. At least she had a job, a real milestone as she hadn't worked at a legitimate job for two years. Trying to make a new life had been like waking up from a coma. The trial didn't automatically make everything better. Just like she'd dreamed when she was a rookie cop, she'd testified in a courtroom and put a killer behind bars. But she didn't feel like much of a hero.

There were days since the trial that she was too depressed to get out of bed. She wondered if there was something more she could have done for Anita Paley. Much of what had happened to the younger woman she had learned only after the trial, like the vaginal wound, the thought of which gave her horrors. She had wondered why the defense attorney kept asking her about vaginal containers and why the prosecution seemed so interested in the knife she'd used to make sandwiches.

Jim Burkhalter had called to tell her about the verdict. "We owe you a lot, Joanne," he said. "This guy would still be on the streets if it wasn't for you."

That had made her feel good for a little while. But after that feeling passed, she found herself wishing that somehow she could have stopped Riggan, or at least been there for Paley and taken some of the pain away.

Still, she knew she'd made the right choice and from that believed there'd been a small measure of redemption for all the bad choices she'd made in her life. She was trying to picture herself climbing up a ladder, the same ladder she took to the bottom. If she needed to stop sometimes on a rung and rest for a bit, she figured that was okay. . . . She had a long way to go.

It wasn't easy to look at the world or what she had become without the mask of drugs. It was awfully bright out there, and the brightness illuminated all the mistakes she'd made. Her lost children . . . her lost love . . . her lost career. But most of all, lost time.

Now that she'd testified, her story was known. Her parents and others from her past would know how low she had fallen. She'd had a dream the night following Riggan's conviction. She was living in a glass house. Anybody who walked by could look inside and see what she was doing. She had no clothes, nothing to hide her nakedness behind. She was ashamed and embarrassed. Then in the midst of her humiliation, Anita Paley had appeared, looking as she had when she went out that night, promising to find and return Cordova's clothes.

I'll owe you forever, Cordova had said. But now it seemed that Paley was letting her know that she owed her nothing more. She smiled at her from outside the glass house before turning and walking away. Cordova no longer felt ashamed of her nakedness. There was no reason to hide.

At the restaurant, Cordova finished her coffee and prepared to spend the weekend alone with a book. She wanted to be back in the fold of her family. She wanted her dreams of being somebody again. If someone wanted to throw stones at her, they were welcome to do so, but they'd better watch out. . . . She might throw a few right back.

Sixteen

April 23, 1999

"Briefly . . . in the early morning hours of May 16, 1997, Robert Lee Riggan, Jr. drove his minivan from Denver to Gilpin County, Colorado, accompanied by a twenty-two-year-old woman named Anita Paley."

Judge Frank Plaut began reading the sentencing order as Judge Jack F. Smith, of Arapahoe County, south of Denver, and Judge R. Brooke Jackson, also of Jefferson County, sitting on either side of him, looked solemnly out on the courtroom with no hint of what their decision would be. Smith and Jackson had been selected by a computer to help Plaut with this decision on whether the pale man in the gray jail jumpsuit with the scarred face and the strange, pale blue eyes at the defense table would live or die.

"The prosecution contends that several events followed. First, Riggan parked the van near the Richman Casino in Central City. Either there, or another location, Riggan struck Ms. Paley at least once and probably twice on the head with a blunt object causing a severe and ultimately fatal brain injury.

"Riggan then put the unconscious Ms. Paley in his van, drove her to a deserted cabin, and took her in the cabin, where he inserted a knife into her vagina and cut her internally."

Plaut paused to clear his throat. He was well aware that he was making history as part of the first three-judge panel to rule at a death penalty hearing under a three-year-old change in the Colorado statutes. He'd tried to be careful, but this was uncharted waters. All week preceding the hearing, Denver metro-area defense attorneys and prosecutors had gone back and forth in the press about the new law. The prosecutors argued, as they had before the legislature, that the panels would bring consistency to death penalty hearings and rule according to the law rather than emotions. Defense attorneys, on the other hand, warned that panels of judges would be a rubber stamp for the prosecutors. They foresaw a death row population explosion and executioners running hog-wild.

This first case was a good test. No Colorado jury had ever sentenced a man to die for felony murder—with its lesser burden to prove that he had deliberately or intentionally killed the victim—although that possibility was in the books. Would Robert Riggan, everyone wanted to know, be the first?

Other than the panel in place of jurors, the death penalty proceedings had not changed. They were essentially minitrials in which the prosecution presented its case, trying to prove at least one of two legally defined "aggravators," or justification why the defendant should die as opposed to being sentenced to life without parole. The defense then presented its case, trying to show that there were "mitigating factors" determining that Riggan should not be executed. The judges then had to compare the aggravators to the mitigators, and only if the former outweighed the latter, would they proceed to the ultimate questions: deciding if Riggan deserved to die.

There was one other difference in this particular hearing, and that was the defendant had chosen not to appear.

Shortly before the hearing began a week earlier, Robert Riggan had huddled with his attorneys, Dennis Hartley and Nathan Chambers, in animated conversation. It soon became clear to everyone else in the courtroom what the fuss was about when Chambers announced to the judges that his client was asking that he be allowed to return to his jail cell. "He doesn't want to be here."

When Judge Jackson inquired about the reason, Riggan replied that he had "fifty pounds of shit on my back . . . and I don't want no part of this garbage. Go ahead, kill me and get it over with. . . . I did not kill that girl, but there's nothin' I can do about it."

The prosecution had lied during his trial, he said. His attorneys could have proved it but hadn't tried. When he'd tried to say something to that effect, his lead attorney, Hartley, had told him "that if I didn't stop, he was going to rip my fuckin' head off."

By now, Plaut and the attorneys were used to Riggan's outbursts and scarcely concealed contempt.

At a hearing soon after his trial, Riggan had been brought into the courtroom and seated in the jury box. There was a discussion about whether to seat him at the defense table so that he could confer with his lawyers. That idea was dropped when Riggan threatened to spit on them if he got the chance.

His disposition hadn't improved much in the months since. In fact, at another hearing two weeks before the sentencing hearing was set to begin, Riggan told Plaut that his attorneys weren't communicating with him. Dennis Hartley was not yet present when Riggan complained, "I called his office third-party a week ago. And his legal secretary told me, she says, 'Don't you understand what's going on, Bob?' And I said, 'I know what's going on. You are selling me down the river.' And she said, 'That's right, and there ain't a goddamn thing you can do about it.' "

Plaut, having grown tired of the defendant's belligerence, had instructed him, "Why don't you have a seat, Mr. Riggan."

But Riggan kept talking. "I mean, you are going to kill me for something I didn't do, at least give me my rights. A bunch of neo-Nazi fascist fucks. Real great bunch of motherfuckers."

Nonplussed, Plaut replied, "Well, I can say, Mr. Riggan, that your vocabulary hasn't improved any."

"What do you want, Judge?" Riggan shot back. "You are the most egomaniac motherfucker, but no one has the guts to tell you. I might as well."

Gesturing to the prosecution table, he continued, "These motherfuckers want a death penalty. They want to kill somebody so bad." He pointed to Dennis Hall who was already seated, ". . . including this fuck right now lied to get the death penalty. And every time I tried to corner him, you wouldn't give me that.

"He put it in the motion [that] I threatened him. I never threatened that man. I called him a son of a bitch because he wouldn't release the picture of my kids to me. That is the type of human being this is. These are pictures of my kids. . . . What do they have to do on a murder that happened in Colorado? Fucking human garbage."

At that point, Hartley finally entered the courtroom where the judge apprised him of his client's concerns. "I would like to give you a little time to see if you've got anything you want to pursue with him," the judge said.

But Riggan interjected, pointing at Hartley. "This guy is tampering with one of the district attorney's witnesses," he said, referring to his ex-wife Sandy.

"You need to just keep your mouth shut," Hartley told him.

"Do you want to talk to Mr. Riggan before we proceed, Mr. Hartley?" Plaut inquired.

"I don't need to talk to Mr. Riggan, Your Honor," Hartley replied. "I know what his silly issue is. It is a nonissue." The lawyer had had enough. He told the judge he wanted to be allowed to withdraw from the case. Plaut denied the request.

At the beginning of the death penalty hearing, Riggan had again labeled Plaut a "motherfucking egomaniac." Plaut then found that Riggan "knowingly and voluntarily" had waived his right to be present at the hearing. He directed the court security to remove the defendant. No one was sorry to see him go. Court reporter Lisa Persichitte—a pretty young woman who had grown to fear Riggan, sensing (as so many others had said) that there was something particularly evil about this man who stared at her—looked like the weight of the world had been dropped from her shoulders.

Riggan had been absent the entire hearing, though Plaut asked his attorneys each morning if their client had changed his mind and wanted to return. The answer was always no. He'd been dragged back into the courtroom to hear the verdict, however. Now it fell to Plaut to pronounce Riggan's fate.

"Riggan then placed Ms. Paley, who was bleeding severely, on a sleeping bag and was in the course of dragging the sleeping bag along a path to conceal her when, by chance, a passing motorist saw him doing this," Plaut continued. "Fearing that the motorist would summon the authorities, Riggan abandoned the still-alive but severely injured Ms. Paley, jumped in his van, and left the scene at a high rate of speed. . . . Within another two days, Riggan had been spotted and apprehended walking along a Boulder street.

"Meanwhile, Ms. Paley had been taken by ambulance and Flight for Life to Saint Anthony's Central Hospital, where surgery was performed simultaneously by a gynecological surgeon and neurosurgeon. Despite their best efforts, Ms. Paley died approximately twelve hours later. The cause of death was a severe brain injury. The gynecological surgeon testified that the vaginal injury would have been fatal if not treated. However, due to the surgical intervention, it was not a cause of death.

"While Mr. Riggan elected not to testify at trial, the defense theory of the case essentially paralleled Riggan's statements to the police. He maintained that Ms. Paley, who had a history of depression and who was extremely high on crack cocaine [which he had purchased for her], opened the passenger door of his moving van and jumped out in a suicide attempt.

"He claims that the blow to her head that ultimately proved fatal was caused by her head striking asphalt pavement. Riggan presented no consistent theory as to the cause of the vaginal wounds. One suggestion was that Ms. Paley had been severely kicked by her pimp during an argument the previous evening. Another was that she may have been secreting drugs or money in a container within her vaginal vault, and that the container broke and caused the internal wounds as she bounced and rolled as a result of the fall from the vehicle."

No one spoke as Plaut read. The courtroom was full for only the second time since Riggan went on trial, mostly with lawyers and court personnel. The first occasion was for the jury's verdict back in October. Otherwise, the case could have been a contested traffic ticket for all the attention it got from the public and the press. Neither the defendant nor the victim had any family members in the pews behind the contesting attorneys.

Anita Paley's stepfather and mother had testified during the portion of the prosecution's case known as "victim impact." "All of our family get-togethers have a hole," her mother, Brenda Bibaud, testified. "I miss her every day. And I've found that I can't do things that I used to be able to do. I've been blocking out violence. I don't read the newspaper or watch TV anymore.

"My mind has been under such stress that I can't focus and can't concentrate. . . . I seem to be kind of lost out there and nobody knows what to say to me. . . . I don't have any future plans. I'm going through a divorce because I wanted attention, but yet I don't want anybody near me . . . I'm just taking one day at a time because I'm ready whenever it is my turn to go so I can be with Anita again."

Riggan's first wife, Judy, had begged Dennis Goodwin not to be subpoenaed to testify. She was afraid to even be in the same room with Riggan. The prosecution team had talked it over and felt that they would get enough from their other witnesses, including Pamela Kay Hart who brought some humor to an otherwise somber proceeding with her streetwise tough act and "working girl" clothes, and Riggan's second wife, Sandy, the one, Riggan had shrieked at Hall, who had "everything to do with this case."

Sandy testified about their relationship, the good and the bad . . . how he could pass himself off as a doctor or a lawyer . . . and how he had threatened, abducted, and raped her at knifepoint. Her testimony was a mixed bag.

"When he got out of the, for lack of a better word, the joint, and he came to your house . . . you knew that this was an act of desperation on his part, didn't you?" Hartley asked.

"Yes, it was," she replied quietly. "We were together, you know, for a long time and he wanted to be back with me."

"He loved you, didn't he?"

Sandy nodded. "I believe he did."

"And you had some strong feelings for him?"

"Very strong."

"And still do to some extent?"

Again, she nodded and appeared ready to cry. "Yeah, always will."

Sandy testified that she didn't understand why someone who seemed so self-confident, who could talk his way into and out of any situation, was always pretending to be someone else.

"He was a person that really always appeared to want to be somebody else and not Bob Riggan, isn't that true?"

"Yes."

"Do you think he liked himself?" Hartley asked.

Sandy hesitated a moment before she responded. "He seemed like he had all the confidence in the world to me."

"Well, he couldn't be who he was," Hartley said. "He always wanted to be the doctor or the lawyer or something that was larger than what he was?"

"Yes," she replied.

Sandy testified that Riggan had been trying to reestablish a relationship with his sons. The youngest one "misses him," she said, though the older boy, Bobby, "has kind of mixed feelings because he remembers what happened" on the day of the rape.

"Do you think it would hurt those boys if Bob Riggan was put to death?" Hartley asked.

"Yes."

"We have all kinds of victims in these cases, don't we?"

Sandy wiped at her eyes. "I sure wouldn't be able to explain that to them, at least not for a long time."

At the beginning of the defense case, Chambers had asked that the television cameras be turned off, and after that was done, he called Riggan's sister, Rosie, to the stand.

A tiny woman with mousy-brown hair and glasses that seem too large for her thin face entered the courtroom and was sworn in. Their parents, she said, were Robert and Vernice Riggan, who had married in 1955, a year before her own birth. Her brother, Robert Jr., was born in 1960. Her mother, however, already had two children: George, who was fathered by Vernice's own brother, Bill. And Henrietta.

"And who was Henrietta's father?" Chambers asked.

"I'm not sure, except that he was one of my mother's brothers," she replied.

Rosie recalled the living conditions in the house as "dirty and crowded. . . . My mother never did any housework . . . not that I can recall." There was no place for anybody else to sit in the living room because the laundry was left piled up on the couch until Rosie began doing all the housework— cooking, cleaning, the laundry—at age thirteen.

Chambers asked her about the relationship between her father and mother. "My dad showed love toward her," she responded. "But I didn't see her show love to him."

When her dad was drinking, "he'd knock her around." Her mother was also violent. She recounted the episode when she attacked a neighbor girl who had been "throwing bricks" at the house. The fight ended in the middle of an intersection with her mother "slamming the back of the girl's head into the pavement."

Robert Riggan, Sr. had his own perversions, she testified. He drilled a hole in the ceiling of the bathroom so that he could watch the young women in the house. Even that was nothing compared to those times when George would come by for a visit and sexually assault Theresa and Rose.

Finally, Rosie said, she ran away. "I had to get out of that house."

When she was caught by the authorities, she refused to go back home and was taken to a group home for runaways. "I liked it," she said. "I was at peace. I had friends. . . . At home, we weren't allowed to have friends. It was much cleaner."

Rosie said her only regret when she married to get out of the house was leaving her little brother, Robert, to bear the brunt of the dysfunctional family life. She said he lived with one of his half brothers on the porch of the home with no heat in the winter.

"Did he receive any attention or affection?" Chambers asked.

"None," she responded. "Except when he was getting his butt beat with a leather belt. . . . He never got any affection from my mother."

Throughout Rosie's stark testimony, the courtroom was completely quiet with a lot of head shaking over the horror of such a childhood. Even those sitting on the prosecution side of the aisle—with little compassion for the man Robert Riggan—felt sympathy for the boy with the scarred face and a mutt named Goofy as his only companion.

"Do you want to see Bob executed?" Chambers asked quietly.

"No," Rosie murmured.

"How do you feel about Bob?"

"I love him."

The Reverend Clem Keyes, now retired, had also testified for the defense regarding Riggan's childhood. "It was not a functional family," Keyes said. "There was no structure. . . . The children were starved for love. They would seek out my wife at the church, because she would pay attention to them."

Keyes described Riggan as an "angry kid . . . who thought the world was against him . . . life was not fair . . . it was not a happy home." Nor did the Iowa Department of Social Services do anything to protect the children after he and others made them aware of problems in the home. "They should have intervened," he said, adding that those who could have helped "failed" young Robert particularly.

"What that got to do with why we're here?" Chambers had asked.

"This is a correction for what was not done back in the 1970s," the pastor replied.

As Plaut read the sentencing order, Riggan sat at the defense table from which he had been absent, by choice, throughout the sentencing proceedings. The skin on his face was a yellowish prison pallor beneath the stubble of his hair. He stared straight ahead at the judges when he was brought into the courtroom through the side door and was led to his seat.

At times, as Plaut read, Riggan looked angry and at times on the verge of tears. When defense investigator Ellis Armstead, a former Denver cop, briefly put his arm around the thirty-nine-year-old, Riggan dropped his chin for a moment. He blinked rapidly when he looked back up as Plaut continued to read.

"During the course of the trial, conflicting evidence was presented from experienced forensic pathologists. The physician who performed the autopsy concluded that Ms. Paley's death was caused by one or two blows from a blunt instrument."

At the defense table, Riggan's attorneys sat with their heads bowed and eyes closed as if they were the ones who expected to be punished. There was no love lost between these men and their client. He never wanted them in the first place and had made defending him a miserable experience. Yet it would be hard to imagine a defense team that had fought harder. Hartley and Chambers battled the prosecution at every turn. They challenged and angered Judge Plaut, who respected their efforts enough to thank them and the prosecutors, Dennis Hall and Dana Easter, at the beginning of this day's proceedings for "the best lawyering" he'd ever seen from the bench.

In the trial, the defense attorneys had beat the

most dangerous of the charges—first-degree murder after deliberation. No matter what they thought of Bob Riggan personally, they had done their best during the sentencing hearing to save his life. It had earned them little more than vitriol from their client, but the strain of waiting to hear if they'd succeeded in saving his life was evident on both their faces as Plaut read on. Hartley's hand shook as he reached for a cup of water.

"The physician testifying for the defense concluded from his review of the autopsy findings and photographs that her injuries were consistent with a jump or fall from a moving vehicle."

Hall and Easter seemed more relaxed; though before the judges took their seats that morning, Easter had confessed to "the usual butterflies I get when a verdict is coming." They had acknowledged at the jury's verdict when they lost the first-degree murder charge, that it was going to be difficult, if not impossible, to win at this hearing. . . . If winning was what trying to send a man to death row could be called. . . . For days before he was to deliver the closing arguments, Hall had wrestled with the issue of how he could argue that another man "deserved to die."

But they'd fought just as hard as the defense. Bob Riggan was a remorseless psychopath, Hall argued, who'd intentionally killed Anita Paley and in an *especially cruel, heinous, and depraved manner.*

During the defense case, Chambers had brought in psychiatrist Susan Bograd to testify about Riggan's past psychiatric history, his family life, and her own interviews with the defendant.

"What is the significance of a child not having

his dependency needs met?" Chambers asked, referring to the reports from the Iowa child protection agencies.

"Well, children are dependent on their parents for their basic needs. . . . This speaks to a child who was in need of love, structure, someone to show him the way," Bograd said. "The feeling that the world was a dangerous place, and his concerns about his safety, speaks to some fundamental dependency needs that were not being met.

"To be loved, to be shown affection, to be praised when he does something good . . . to be provided something more than just food and a roof over his head, some structure, some rules, you know, that people can trust each other, that was grossly lacking in the home."

Chambers asked Bograd to explain what was meant by the comment that young Riggan's "interpersonal relationships were disturbed."

"I think he was fearful of life, fearful based on the experiences in the home, not being able to trust that his parents were going to meet his needs and not learning. . . . If you can't trust what is going on in your own home and having your needs met, it is hard to trust other people. How do you learn how to form healthy relationships if you don't have the example of that in your relationship with your own parents, and your parents don't have that relationship with each other? So that the world seemed like a very scary place."

Chambers turned to Bograd's interviews with Riggan between December 1998 and January 1999. "Did he describe his mother to you?"

"He said she was mean. He described her as 'a

tank, German,' said that she was domineering . . . She was sick a fair amount and he said that when she wasn't sick, she was mad. . . . He said she was very violent and described some instances where she was violent."

"Did you talk to Bob about whether his mother loved him?"

"He told me he thought that she did. And I asked him, you know, more about that and why he thought that. And he told me that she never told him she did, but he thought that considering the conditions under which they lived . . . were so awful that she must have loved him because she didn't leave him."

Chambers paused dramatically, then asked, "She loved him because she didn't leave?"

"That is basically what he said." Bograd nodded. "She didn't abandon him, leave him, fly the coop. . . ."

"Did you learn who Bob's closest friend was when he was growing up?"

"Yes." Bograd nodded. "His best friend was his dog, Goofy."

"Are you aware of Bob having a pet while he was in the Jefferson County jail?"

"Yes. I learned from one of the investigators that he had a pet ant."

"A pet ant?" Chambers asked incredulously as jaws dropped throughout the courtroom.

"An ant." Bograd nodded. "Yes."

"And your thoughts on that?"

"I think it is incredibly sad and pitiful," Bograd said. "He has been incarcerated a long time. And I think that there is some part of him that remembered his best friend was his dog growing up. And he wants to connect somehow with something that isn't going to hurt him. I mean, it is a way of kind of reaching out for something, even to an ant." The psychiatrist sighed and shrugged. "It is pretty sad."

"What's the effect of this emotional deprivation that you described?"

"I think he grew up not feeling like he could trust anybody and he really couldn't depend on anybody. And I think that it really wrecked his development as a human being. I mean, the essence of him as a person . . . whatever you want to call that . . . your essence, your being, your soul . . . I think it was crushed, destroyed, even murdered, by all of the emotional deprivation that he grew up with."

"Did he talk to you at all about embarrassment over these proceedings?"

"Yes, he did. He expressed concern that bringing all of this information about his family, his background, out in the open would . . ." Bograd hesitated, looking for the right words. "I don't think he wanted to hear it. He lived it. And he said he found it embarrassing. I think he felt ashamed of it. He made it very clear that it was something that would be very difficult for him."

"Did he talk to you about this case?"

"Not really."

"Did he express to you whether he was guilty or innocent?"

"He told me that he was innocent."

"Did Bob show any emotion during your interviews with him?"

"There were times when he became quite tearful when he spoke about his dog . . . that his dog was his best friend and that she was always there for him and that he got from his dog what he didn't get from anybody else . . . which was some sense of loyalty. And he became tearful on each occasion that he spoke about his dog.

"And he also became tearful when he spoke about the possibility of dying."

Yes, Hall had conceded on cross-examination and then later in his closing, that Riggan had had a rough childhood. But, he pinned the psychiatrist down, that only explained—it didn't excuse—why Riggan behaved as he did.

The prosecutor noted that Riggan had cried about the death of his dog and the possibility that he might die. "But did he ever shed any tears for Anita Paley?" Hall asked.

No, Bograd had to concede, there had been no tears for the victim.

Plaut continued reading. "After three and one-half days of deliberation, the jury was unable to agree unanimously on a verdict on the charge of first-degree murder after deliberation. Accordingly, a mistrial was declared on that count and the district attorney later elected not to retry that count.

"The jury did unanimously find Mr. Riggan guilty of first-degree felony murder, i.e., that in the course or in furtherance of, or immediate flight from, the commission of a Class One, Two, or Three felony (the sexual assault), he caused Ms. Paley's death."

Having finished with the background, Plaut

moved on to the stages he and his colleagues had to consider, beginning with the aggravators. "The people contend that two statutory aggravating factors exist in this case. First, they contend that the defendant committed a Class One, Two, or Three felony and, in the course of, or in furtherance of such, or immediate flight therefrom, the defendant intentionally caused the death of a person other than one of the participants.

"The defense argues that the jury did not make an explicit finding in this case that Mr. Riggan 'intentionally' caused the death of Ms. Paley. The people respond that while the jury deadlocked on the charge of first-degree murder after deliberation, that does not equate to a finding that Mr. Riggan did not intentionally cause the death of Ms. Paley, and that the panel can consider all of the evidence presented at trial and reach its own independent determination on this issue.

"The panel unanimously concludes that this aggravating factor has not been proved beyond a reasonable doubt in this case.

"Second, the people contend that 'the defendant committed the offense in an especially heinous, cruel, or depraved manner.' The people point particularly to the vaginal injury in support of this aggravating factor. The defense, on the other hand, contends that since the vaginal injury was not the cause of death, it cannot be considered. Further, the defense argues, even if the panel were to conclude that Ms. Paley's death was caused by one or more blows to the head by a blunt object, as opposed to the jumping-out-of-the-car theory, it could not conclude that a blow or even two blows can be characterized as *especially* heinous, cruel, or depraved.

"The panel unanimously concludes, beyond a reasonable doubt, that this aggravating factor has been proved. It is inconceivable that the insertion of a knife or other sharp object into a woman's vagina, creating among other wounds what the surgeon described as an almost surgical incision three inches in length, and resulting in massive vaginal bleeding, could be classified as anything other than especially heinous, cruel, or depraved.

"However, were there room in anyone's mind for a reasonable doubt, such doubt would be eliminated by two additional facts that were established by the evidence. The wounds to the vagina were inflicted while Ms. Paley was unconscious because of the severe injury to the brain. And, after inflicting the wound, Mr. Riggan attempted to hide her body and left her to die, lying in a pool of blood resulting both from the vaginal injury and the head injury. This panel finds this conduct to be disgusting and outrageous.

"As for the argument that the vaginal injury was not the cause of death, one need only note that the statute simply states that the defendant committed 'the offense' (of which he stands convicted) in an especially heinous, cruel, or depraved manner. That is precisely what the evidence established to have occurred."

Plaut moved on to the issue of mitigating factors. "The evidence established the existence of one of the mitigating factors expressly listed in the statute. As the prosecution conceded, Mr. Riggan did not have a significant history of prior convictions.

"In addition, in the category of 'any other evidence which in the court's opinion bears on the question of mitigation,' two mitigating factors were established.

"First, it was established through the testimony of family members, a minister, and a psychiatrist that Mr. Riggan was raised in what can only be described as a horribly dysfunctional family. Regrettably, this was a family plagued by incest, sexual abuse, squalor, poverty, and emotional neglect of Mr. Riggan and his siblings.

"By the age of twelve, Mr. Riggan was receiving counseling, though the counseling was short-lived due to the lack of interest and support from his parents. By the age of fourteen, Mr. Riggan was threatening to run away from home, a concept apparently accepted if not endorsed by his parents."

Plaut referred to Bograd's review of the "extensive documentation in the nature of medical and social service records concerning Mr. Riggan's childhood difficulties. She also spent approximately ten hours interviewing Mr. Riggan during December 1998 and January 1999. Dr. Bograd concluded that by the age of fourteen, Riggan was 'almost crippled by overwhelming anxiety and a poor self-concept.' It is hardly surprising, given the evidence of what Mr. Riggan experienced as a child, that he developed feelings of anger, shame, loneliness, and unhappiness.

"Second, in Dr. Bograd's professional opinion, Mr. Riggan suffers from an 'antisocial personality disorder' as described generally in the medical literature in DSM Four. This is a condition properly diagnosed in approximately three percent of all males in the United States but in some fifty to eighty percent of incarcerated males. Persons properly diagnosed with 'ASPD' have a number of unpleasant personality and conduct disorders, including a tendency for repetitive and persistent violations of the basic rights of others, a disregard for the rights and feelings of others, conduct that is frequently deceitful and manipulative, and little remorse for the consequence of one's acts. We note that Dr. Bograd did not specifically find that Mr. Riggan lacked remorse. Rather, based on her overall evaluation of his past and present, she concluded that an ASPD diagnosis was appropriate and that this diagnosis and the background leading to it helps to explain who he is now."

Having found several mitigators, Plaut said, the panel had proceeded on to the third step, weighing them against the aggravators. "The standard for comparison is that only if the panel concludes beyond a reasonable doubt that the mitigating factors do not outweigh the aggravating factors may it move to Step Four. We unanimously conclude that the mitigating factors described above do not outweigh the aggravating factor proved in this case.

"Mr. Riggan's upbringing, and in particular the lack of emotional attention and support from his parents, are nothing short of tragic. By the same token, Mr. Riggan was thirty-seven years of age when he committed this offense. Whether the circumstance of his upbringing might possibly outweigh the heinousness of the crime had the crime been committed in, for example, his teenage years is doubtful, but at least arguable. This history cannot, however, serve to mitigate or excuse his crime against Ms. Paley.

"Likewise, while the diagnosed condition of ASPD and his background may help to explain who Mr. Riggan is today, Dr. Bograd herself acknowledged that ASPD did not cause him not to be responsible for his conduct. On the contrary, the personality and conduct traits of one diagnosed with ASPD reflect an individual who is very capable of violating the rights and feelings of others and engaging in entirely inappropriate conduct, and not because he does not understand what he is doing or its consequences.

"Furthermore, we note that on one earlier occasion, while incarcerated for another offense in Wyoming, Mr. Riggan purportedly attempted to commit suicide in his cell, was hospitalized, and told the evaluating psychiatrist that he was hearing the voice of a soldier involved in the Vietnam War. This resulted in a diagnosis of schizophrenia. Dr. Bograd herself now disagrees with that diagnosis because she has learned that the suicide attempt and claim of hearing voices were feigned by Mr. Riggan as part of a scheme to attempt to escape from incarceration. This history, as well as the trait of deceitfulness that Dr. Bograd testified Mr. Riggan developed as a child and that has carried over into adulthood, necessarily gives us pause as to the good faith of any current claims that a mental disorder was responsible for his hideous offense against Ms. Paley. In any event, that has not been the thrust of the defense's reliance on these mitigating factors.

"The lack of significant prior convictions, even when considered with the other mitigating factors, does not in the panel's view outweigh the heinous nature of the offense."

Accordingly, following the statutory procedure, the panel reached Step Four. The courtroom had been quiet up to this point. If possible, it grew even quieter. Hartley's hand trembled as he picked up a cup of water and took a sip, still with his eyes closed. Riggan sat, blinking up at the judges.

"We unanimously conclude," Plaut said, "beyond a reasonable doubt, that a sentence of death is not appropriate in this case."

At the words *not appropriate,* the tension ran out of Hartley's body like water through a sieve. His hands groped for the cup of water again and this time he drank fully. Chambers tilted his head back and opened his eyes. They might have hated Robert Riggan's guts as much as anyone in the courtroom, but they had just saved his life.

Riggan's response was to turn his head to the side quickly as though slapped. Whether it was a sign of relief or a curse that the judges had not granted his wish to die rather than spend the rest of his life in prison, it was hard to tell.

The prosecution sat unmoving as Plaut continued to read. They'd known what the verdict would be from the start. This panel of judges would not do what no jury had done.

"First and foremost, we note that the jury that convicted Mr. Riggan of felony murder was unable unanimously to agree that Mr. Riggan committed the crime of first-degree murder after deliberation," Plaut read on. "Our system of justice is based upon the jury system. Just as we must have tremendous respect for a jury's verdict of guilt or non-guilt, we must have respect for the fact that the jury that heard the evidence in this case was divided and deadlocked on this enormously critical issue.

"We say enormously critical because we must consider what that deadlock means or at least may mean. At a minimum, it may mean that one or more jurors could not conclude that Ms. Paley died from blows administered by Mr. Riggan. At a minimum, it may mean that one or more jurors concluded that Ms. Paley's brain injury was, as the defense contended, the result of a jump or fall from a moving vehicle, and that Mr. Riggan did not cause the injury that proved fatal.

"In addition, this panel has carefully, thoroughly, and—we think—meticulously examined the evidence produced during the guilt phase of the trial. There was, to be sure, substantial evidence from which the jury could have concluded that Ms. Paley did indeed die as a result of blows from a blunt object struck by Mr. Riggan. There was, however, evidence that could cause a reasonable juror to have a reasonable doubt as to whether this is what happened. We note, for example, physical evidence that Ms. Paley's body as presented at autopsy was scarred by a number of abrasion-type injuries and bruises about her face, elbow, hip, and back that, at least in the opinions of a forensic pathologist and a mechanical engineer, were consistent with jumping or falling from a moving vehicle. A palm print of Ms. Paley's was found on the roof of the vehicle immediately above the passenger door. Her skull fracture was not depressed. There was conflicting evidence as to whether she sustained a 'contra-coup' brain injury; and while such an injury, if incurred, could result from blows from a blunt object, it is also consistent if not more consistent with a moving head striking a stationary object.

"One can imagine scenarios in which Ms. Paley either jumped, fell, or was thrown from a moving vehicle that are not inconsistent with her also having sustained severe and fatal blows to the head administered by Mr. Riggan with a blunt object. In short, even if she did jump or otherwise leave a moving vehicle, that does not necessarily prove that Mr. Riggan did not cause her death in a manner opined by the forensic pathologist who performed the autopsy.

"However, a sentence of death cannot be imposed based upon possibilities or scenarios. If a jury could not unanimously agree that Mr. Riggan did what he was accused of doing in respect to the brain injury, then we conclude it would be inappropriate, and contrary to the careful statutory design of our legislature and the jurisprudence of our Supreme Court in death penalty cases in the past, to impose a death sentence here.

"We note and take comfort in the fact that the only available alternative is a life sentence without the possibility of parole. Mr. Riggan was convicted by the jury of first-degree felony murder. It is, in our view, entirely appropriate that he be removed from society and pay a price that, at least in the view of some, may even be more severe than death itself. But, a civilized society should not and cannot take the life of a human being, even one who commits an especially heinous, cruel, and depraved offense, if a jury could not conclude beyond a reasonable doubt that the individual in fact administered the fatal injury. As much as we are all pained by the loss of Ms. Paley, and the unspeakable affront to her body that was performed by Mr. Riggan, our values must be different than that."

At last, it was nearly over. But before sentencing Robert Riggan to life in prison without parole, Plaut asked the defendant if he wanted to make a statement. Riggan did and began a rambling recounting of his story. . . . Only this time, he said that after Anita Paley jumped from his van, he stopped at a fire station in Black Hawk and banged on the doors, trying to get help.

At the prosecution table, Burkhalter and Lauck rolled their eyes. They would never believe that Anita Paley was Robert Riggan's first and only murder victim. They couldn't prove it . . . not yet, anyway . . . but they knew in their hearts that the man across the way was as evil as they came.

After fifteen minutes of Riggan's speech, Plaut stopped him. There'd been enough lies. This time, Riggan would not be able to talk his way through the cracks of justice.